Living Theology in Asia

EDITED BY JOHN C. ENGLAND

ORBIS BOOKS

Maryknoll, New York 10545

Originally published by SCM Press Ltd., 58 Bloomsbury Street, London WC1, England

Editor's introductions and arrangement copyright © John C. England 1981

U.S. edition 1982 by Orbis Books, Maryknoll, NY 10545

Typeset in Great Britain and printed and bound in the United States of America

Library of Congress Cataloging in Publication Data

Main entry under title:

Living theology in Asia.

   Bibliography: p.
   1. Theology, Doctrinal—Asia—Addresses,
essays, lectures. I. England, John C.
BT30.A8L58 1982   230'.095   82-2288
ISBN 0-88344-298-1 (pbk.)   AACR2

To my fellow staff members of the
East Asia Christian Conference
(now Christian Conference of Asia) 1969–1975,
and our colleagues in struggle and
reflection throughout Asia

Contents

Preface

Theological reflection is an integral part of the lives and struggles of countless Asian Christians and it is their work which makes this book possible. It is in the hope of forwarding that work – in ecumenical mission, human development and social justice – that this reader has been prepared. The content is therefore limited to that Asian theology which is rooted in a national Christian tradition and which arises from the encounter of faith with contemporary historical reality. In any local situation however, even this sampling of contextual theological reflection is seldom available. During more than ten years' work in many different parts of Asia, I have frequently been asked by colleagues for help in obtaining such resources in order to assist their own doing of theology. And although some materials are becoming available through the publications of the Christian Conference of Asia, I have been urged to attempt this introduction to the rice-roots theology of twelve countries in the region for a wider readership. The format therefore is designed so that the readings selected may be seen as part of a living stream of Christian thought and life in a particular country. Full references are provided to allow further exploration and participation.

No one can be more conscious than I am that only a small beginning is made here, and it is only through the encouragement of many colleagues that I have dared to proceed with the task. Since 1972 some thousands of documents have been considered and this is only one of many volumes that could be compiled. Amongst the friends in many countries to whom I am indebted for help and counsel, I wish to thank particularly those whose writing is included here, along with Chung Woong-Sup, Kenneth de Lanerolle, Kayama Hisao, Oosima Koiti, Alfred Simandjuntak, Onesta Capene, Koyama Kosuke and co-workers in the Tao

Fong Shan Ecumenical Centre. Colleagues who shared in the series of national workshops on Theology in Action (1972–75) provided much of the initial impetus for this work and many of them are mentioned in the following pages.

Much of the research necessary was made possible through a fellowship awarded by the World Council of Churches in 1975–77 and through the generous friendship of colleagues in the Selly Oak Colleges, the Chicago Cluster of Theological Schools and the Institute of the Church on Urban Industrial Society. I wish particularly to thank Ian Fraser and Albert Moseley of Selly Oak; Lewis Mudge and Edward Campbell of McCormick Seminary; Richard Poethig and Bobbi Wells-Hargleroad of ICUIS, and Robert Shreiter of the Chicago Theological Union. For additional help in translation I am indebted to Johanna de Fretes, Sumi Michiko, Carmel Budiago, Anita Myung Tennent, Kim Hyun-Kwan and Lucy Loh. John Fleming, David Jenkins, Alister Kee, John Vincent and John Bowden have provided strong encourgement over some years. Particular acknowledgment must go to my wife, Rita, whose faith and practical assistance have made it possible to plod out the vision.

Introduction

It may appear strange in a theological reader to declare immediately that the primary focus of this volume is not upon theology as such; not, that is, upon theology as a body of thought or writing that has its own validity independent of the everyday life of the Christian community in a particular place. Neither the volume itself, nor the individual papers which make it up, have been prepared as contributions to debates with which we are familiar, nor as instalments for a developing Asian theology. And it is not as raw materials for our own (imperialistic?) systematizing that such theological reflections are to be judged. The writers and their communities have their own experience of the Lord's controversy[1], their own receiving of the truth. They speak from within Christian traditions of great vitality and with origins which often long predate the modern missionary era.

I Theological Confession

The selections may of course provide resources for a study of types of contemporary Asian theology (in the period since 1960). They may also meet some of our own criteria for balance and creative theological writing. But if they do so, this will be largely incidental. For to hear what is being said by many Asian Christians is to discover a different motivation and a different role for theological reflection. However competent theologically the writers are, their over-ruling concern is first of all pastoral and missional, in the sense that the present dilemmas facing prophetic and embattled minorities are what determine their response. The purpose of these theologians therefore is not primarily the writing of a theological paper or the construction of a political (or evangelical) theology. It is rather to take the next step in mission, and in the development of people, where they are. However important the theological task is to them, it remains one dimension of their central concern, namely the confessing of the gospel in the concrete life situations of their people.[2]

The present experience and understanding of the gospel, in movements and groups struggling for a just and humane society, is reported and 'storied'. The commitment of a church to the recovery of human rights is affirmed in the face of pervasive repression by a totalitarian government. A declaration of conscience is made by those unjustly imprisoned, in order to forestall the extraction of 'confessions'. The participation of Christians in socialist reconstruction and revolutionary change provides a theological and ideological critique. In these and many other forms, particular situations call forth declarations and reflections.

Such a confession is of course grounded in biblical study. It is sustained by the faith of the larger Christian community. And as it is reflected on and articulated, it forms a living theology. What unites and shapes these elements however, is primarily the act of confessing itself, a wrestling, as Asians Christians, with particular experiences of suffering and deliverance, by which the gospel becomes incarnate in the particular history and culture of a people. Not unexpectedly, such a theology is often more an expression of the dilemmas in which God is now to be found than a finished statement of what he has been like when previously found. Jagged resistant realities in their particular society replace many of the *themes* of Western theology as the genesis of reflection. The *mode* of their response, in theology as in action, is one of contestation in situations of tension and conflict, by which social transformation and authentic spirituality are striven for. Their writings are therefore in a confessing *form*, and approximate the biblical diversity of chronicle and poem, meditation and letter, rather than lecture or treatise.

II Local Theologies

This confessing style is clearly not unique to the Asian region, although many of its expressions will be. There is in Asia, however, a special seriousness of concern for indigenous culture and religion, and a particular apprehension of life in community as it is shaped by these. The vast scale of human suffering in Asian countries and the sharpness of the struggle for human survival has yielded also a vitality of prophetic insight, an immediacy in gospel interpretation, while the unrivalled diversity of peoples, of Christian tradition and of historical experience in the region give a unique character to each of Asia's confessing theologies.

In this sense, these theologies like all others are *local* theologies. They arise at a particular point of history, in the dynamic interaction of gospel, church and culture. They grow out of and serve national or regional Christian traditions and retain the marks of a unique cultural experience. This can be thought to undermine the universality of the Christian gospel only by ignoring the particularity and historicity of God's dealings with Israel and in the life of Jesus himself. Those who would reject the localized character of theological construction are often in fact imposing their own formulations as in some sense normative for all others. And this often veils only thinly the oppressive levelling brought about by cultural (and economic) domination. 'A true universality' writes Robert Schreiter, 'is to be sought not in common denominators, but in radically living out the genius of one's own shared life at the intersection of various life communities'[3]. Theological reflection will be Asian therefore, not because of the characteristics shared with other parts of the region: far less because of the nationality or geographical location of the theologian. Rather it will be Asian, and a witness to the one Lord, in so far as it assists the unique incarnation of the gospel in a local Asian context. The Lord has a personal and particular controversy with the people of the Philippines as with Israel; with the people of China as with Judah. And in each of Asia's peoples, his controversy comes as a different summons. The confession which it provokes like the theology in which it finds reflective form will reveal their different drummers.

The examples given here, only a small sample of the material available, still reflect something of the bewildering complexity of the region. Here is more than half the world's population, in thousands of ethnic and linguistic groupings, every major religion, resurgent in a kaleidoscope of historic cultures. It is possible to distinguish certain major cultural-religious divisions in Asia, according to the dominance of such major influences as the Malay-Islamic, Chinese-Confucian, Sanskritic-Hindu or Sanskritic-Buddhist.[4] But these are subject to so many qualifications that it is more accurate to say that the only major historical experience which all countries of Asia have in common is the destructive impact of colonialism and neo-colonialism. Allied with the policies of feudal or capitalist elites within a nation, this has produced a running fire of violence and domination throughout the region, multiplying the brutal inequalities already present in Asian societies. This is true of every century since the fifteenth, and no less true in the twentieth. Almost every section here chosen reflects this history,[5] but it is especially important for understanding the current theological task in such countries as India, the Philippines, Sri Lanka, and Indonesia.

Within this human community, the Christian community numbers almost 100 millions and reflects every one of these shaping influences. Some churches (e.g. in India) have longer histories than most in Europe; some (e.g. in the Philippines) have founded universities before any in the Americas. They reveal every degree of wealth and poverty, of education and cultural transition, every political and theological position. Their life and work includes every form of congregational life and of community involvement: labour education and organization in Hong Kong or Colombo, lay training centres in Bangalore or Kyoto; 'illegal' prayer movements in South Korea or Taiwan; development motivation in Burma or Java; Christian-Marxist dialogue in the Philippines or in China; colleges and hospitals, lay movements and study centres, peoples' organizations and Christian literature societies. Theological reflection carried out in these Asian churches, as in many others, sometimes, however, remains largely isolated from the particular society and its history within which they are set and from the realities of human suffering which surround them. Of those who do recognize the contextual dimensions of the gospel, many respond only in Western-academic terms, undertaking no critical analysis of cultural situation or historical event. There is then a continuing divergence between theologies of the institution or of professionalized elites and theology being discovered in the engagement of lay movements and team ministries; between theological assumptions transplanted from the West (those of liberation theology sometimes included), unrelated to the harsh conditions of a people's daily life in Asia, and theological reflection where these supply the major issues and insights.[6]

There is also however a growing convergence in theological formulation, at points where context and locality, the concrete life-situation of women and men, are taken seriously, and where the pressure of events is recognized as the locus for a confessing, even 'agonistic' theology. But we already have a surfeit of generalizations (and exhortations) referring to contextual or political theology, and perhaps also in reference to theology which is local and confessing. So it becomes important to unpack some of the situational and co-operative dimensions of the theological process reflected in much of this volume. First some necessary distinctions.

III Theological Process

It will be clear that the different impetus in theological endeavour here characterized is a sharp form of wrestling with daily realities. Some of our Asian colleagues describe it as a struggle for Christian, and human, survival, which is embodied in action as well as words. Such theology is forced from a man or woman, or from a community, as they try to find sense and hope in the anguish and turmoil confronting them. What I have termed the pastoral and missional imperatives of the gospel are here concerned not with how to maintain a Christian tradition but how to sustain an allegiance to biblical justice and love in situations of conflict; not with the elaboration of certain cultural or national characteristics, but with the preservation of a people's selfhood and identity, where this is being threatened.

A confessing theology in Asia is not however merely another version of liberation theology, even though they have in common a radical concern for the poor and powerless and a rejection of ideologies of domination in all their forms. The continuing power of living religions and ancient cultures and the character of the communal life which they have moulded provide both constructive insights and oppressive conditions which shape the Asian theological task. Along with 'superstition and caste, hypocrisy and corruption', there are indigenous traditions of egalitarianism and social justice which offer alternatives to Marxism as models for revolutionary change. Amongst many examples which stand out in recent history are the Dong Hak in Korea, Sarekat Islam in Indonesia, the movements of Gandhi and Vinoba in India, and the Huk Bahalap of the Philippines. Here the elimination of a dehumanizing poverty cannot be separated from a spiritual renewal in which renunciation or non-violence is as important as rural development or political organization.

If we now go further in unpacking some of the processes involved in the emergence of confessing theologies in Asian countries, we find that they often begin in questions of a deceptive simplicity; questions such as: 'What is happening to people . . . what are they suffering and (perhaps) hoping?' 'How are men and women surviving, humanly and Christianly, where many are not?' 'In "a running fire" of domination and violence, how do Christians reflect and find in Bible, prayer and fellowship, strength for the struggle and perspective for larger human purposes?'

The answer to these questions can often be recognized in a particular local community, where people are conscious of being discarded, powerless, or exploited, and the decisive step is taken to choose not despair or fatalism, but hope and mutual support. Actions are taken that point beyond themselves; parents, or neighbours, succour the weakest members; workers show a selfless concern for justice; martyrs die. And in all these there are deeply human aspirations, often expressed in stories told, in songs or declarations, and in the alternative hermeneutic of life in community.[7]

The Christian reflection represented here strives to discern the present activity of God's spirit in this common life and to develop a critical awareness of social reality. In Asian countries it is carried on by a wide range of groups and individuals in situations of tension and conflict. New patterns of mission and ministry lead to growing collaboration for reflection as for action. Political and military repression, and in particular the experience of imprisonment or harassment, provide 'hothouse' conditions for theological confession. Ecumenical coalitions emerge for industrial reform, for the recovery of human rights or for participation in social planning and development, and these prove to be fertile soil for vital theological reflection. Theology therefore now has many other centres, many other sources and agents. To the professional theological educator is added a company of others who contribute no less than he or she to the doing of theology. In theology, as in ministry, the professional is only one of a team, and his or her work depends on the prior struggle and contemplation of those in vastly different occupations and situations.

It cannot be emphasized too strongly that innumerable people, often in the most desperate of circumstances, *are* surviving humanly and Christianly; maintaining through courageous effort, responsibility for each other; discerning and reflecting upon the presence of God's Spirit in their struggle. This is the primary theological task upon which all others depend, and only a co-operative mode for the doing of theology allows it full recognition.

The co-operation is not only inter-confessional and interdisciplinary, but also interclass: labourers and pastors, housewives and students, join with writers and peasants and professors. Some bring historical understanding, some bring hope from their suffering, others contribute their commitment to justice and shalom, their imaginative power or their spiritual integrity. Discernment and perception rather than knowledge or education are the crucial elements in a living, prophetic theology, and to release these a co-operative theologizing is necessary.[8]

A majority of the selections which follow directly reflect the co-operative theologizing of a group or movement, and this is noted in the introductions to each section. Almost all the theologians here represented are acutely conscious of the large body of letters and stories, poems and meditations, which nurture their own reflection.[9] They are conscious too that the particularized and personal character of God's dealings with his people, which is the mandate for all local theologies, brings also this democratization of the theological process, along with a radicalization of its content. For to be serious regarding locality – a central ecumenical and biblical concern – is to attend to, and join with, people in a particular place, and to accept the radical form of their dilemmas and aspirations.

The writings here selected are all in this sense serious about locality; they are people-centred and radical in concern. The theological methodology most frequently implied is one that blends inductive and deductive elements, individual and co-operative reflection, writing and living. Many different combinations and sequences are observable, but the principal elements can be described as:

1. An involvement in, and exposure to, actual life-conditions of suffering and of struggle, what Vivekenanda calls 'feeling from the heart'.[10]

2. A contemplation, and receiving, of this reality, which includes both meditative and analytical processes. The attempt is made to 'see the picture whole', and to relate thought and experience both to each other and to larger, human perspectives.

3. Reflection, which relates the life and teaching of Jesus and of the Hebrew prophets, to concrete incident and local com-

munity. This interprets and clarifies, interconnects and evaluates the 'stories' being told, and the larger affirmations.

4. Engagement, once more, within the situation; in co-operative planning, working, writing. Motivation and understanding are again tested and refined.

The writers here chosen reflect these elements in varying degrees, with the emphasis sometimes more clearly upon contemplation (Bao), sometimes upon engagement (Tsutomu, Saw U). Some pieces are more analytic (de la Torre), some more reflective (Takenaka, Hardowirjono). Within these emphases, some writers have a more critical (Mathew, Wickremasinghe), or methodological (Ting, Claver), concern; a more personal (Katoppo, Kim Chi-Ha), or biblical (Amirtham, Kim Chung-Choon, Caspersz), content. Some are primarily affirmations (Widjaja), or have a constructive purpose (Oracion, Rayan). Others centre more on the shaping situation (Kim Yong-Bok, Srisang), or upon the response of people within this (Fung, Song). And some grow from a searching dialogue with those of other ideologies (Ting, Takao, de la Torre).

But these remain differences of emphasis, for many examples reflect a number of such elements. The more significant distinctions are those arising from cultural identity and locality, from ideological assumption and national history. For a confessing theology, such distinctions are not accidental or peripheral but in fact the flesh by which faith enters history again and again. The selections are grouped by country therefore, and the attempt has been made to present certain key features of each national Christian tradition. If certain themes recur it is because they arise from imperatives within that tradition, regardless of their place in the traditions of Western theology. Amidst all the differences of expression and content, a real unity of purpose, and even of theological approach, remains. In a wrestling with Bible, with people, and with events, the act of confessing joins the Christian communities of Asia with each other and with their Lord, in a living theology, as much as in suffering and in hope.

1 · South Korea

Theology as a living force cannot be summoned or engineered: for the Spirit has his own occasions. But in South Korea in the past two decades it has found its life in streets and factories, restaurants and churches, seminaries and prisons. Although this is closely related to the prophetic witness called forth by particular historical events, Korea's distinctive Christian traditions have played a central role. These have been shaped as much by indigenous religious movements as by Catholicism (since the eighteenth century) and Protestantism (since 1884), and have frequently provided the principal support for nationalist and democratic aspirations.

Although possessing its own dynasty – the Yi – for 500 years until 1910, these centuries were marked by Chinese hegemony, by periodic incursions by Japan, and as often by the feudal excesses of Korea's own rulers. Each of these provoked regular revolts. The revolts of the indigenous sect Dong Hak, in 1864 and 1894, along with Christian movements, came to inspire continuing resistance to the cruelties of Japanese rule (1876–1945) and of more recent dictatorial regimes. The Dong Hak's blend of Buddhist, Christian, Confucian and Shamanist elements with a strong egalitarianism remains also a potent influence in Korean literature as well as in contemporary Christian theology.

The first moves however in the development of indigenous leadership and theology for the Korean churches emerged partly through the exposure of pastors and educators to theological thought in Japan. Groups of capable younger theologians in the 1920s and 1930s, some of them educated in Japan, challenged in their writing and teaching the fundamentalism and missionary domination which they believed were stifling the growth of Korean Christianity. Although some Methodists were active here, it was

a group of Presbyterians who would pursue freedom for theological scholarship and for an ecumenical pattern of mission, until
the founding, on these principles, of the Presbyterian Church,
Republic of Korea (1953). The theologian-educator who has exercised continuing leadership, both in these developments and in
Korean theology as a whole, is Kim Jai-Jun (b. 1901). In theological education (since 1933), in the editing of monthly journals
(since 1936), and in a stream of books and articles, Kim Jai-Jun
has vigorously focused attention upon critical biblical studies,
upon explosive social and political issues, and upon the formation
of a Korean theology. The thrust of all his work was clearly given
in a 1956 issue of his journal 'Soldiers of the Cross': 'We are
called,' he writes, 'to erect the liberating history of Christ within
the history of this nation, so that Korean history itself may be
transformed.'[1] An Old Testament scholar, Kim Jai-Jun is em-
phatic in relating the prophetic vision of a just society and the
holism of Israel's faith to the concrete situations of Korean life,
and one volume of his five-volume collected works is devoted to
his writing on such themes for secular Korean publications. In
recent years his attention has moved from the person of Christ,
whose deeds the Christian must now do in Korean history, to
Christ's suffering servanthood. Suffering is necessary, he affirms,
for any real revolution, spiritual or social. Whatever the cost, evil
must be declared to be evil and resisted, as part of the original
mission of the church.[2]

It is plain in many recent writings that Kim here has in mind
the evils of the Park regime (1962–79): progressively authoritarian, depending upon the brutal methods of a highly developed
central intelligence agency, and imposing a fiercely exploitive pattern of economic development. The human and national cost of
such a dictatorship appals Kim Jai-Jun, as it has a rapidly increasing number of Koreans since 1962. Student, worker and clergy
groups in particular have responded to such conditions and this
has been a major influence in the development of a living theology. The focus for all three groups by the mid-1960s had become
the work of urban-industrial mission, in labour education, trade
union organization and Urban Action training. In association with
two faculties at Yonsei University and the Social Service Development Corps of the YMCA and the Korea Student Christian
Movement, urban mission programmes were by 1971 part of the
wider movement for economic justice and for the restoration of

democracy. But for Christian pastors, community workers and students they were also test models for a biblical and ecumenical theology which reshapes individualist forms of evangelism or social welfare. This is a prophetic understanding of sin and salvation that is not only personal but also corporate. A new tradition was being forged in which it was normal Christian ministry to live in, train for and serve people's movements which are working for social transformation. Those who also fostered theological reflection from within such coalitions included for example Oh Jae-Shik, George Ogle, Cho Sung-Hyuk and Park Hyung-Kyu.[3]

Active and courageous support in this was also provided by pastors and lay people associated with the National Christian Council of Korea, led by Kim Kwan-Suk, and by Roman Catholic leaders like Stephen Cardinal Kim and Bishop Tji Hak-Soun, each of whom has made many contributions to theological writing and reflection.[4] Numerous movements in both urban and rural areas were now involved in a nation-wide struggle for democratic rights, many of them producing a flow of theological documents in letters, statements and meditations. One of the most widely circulated of these is the Theological Declaration of Korean Christians (issued despite government ban on 20 May 1973). Stressing their allegiance to the Lord of History, 'the ultimate vindicator of the oppressed, the weak and the poor', the signatories declare that they 'are compelled by the Spirit to participate in his transformation' of society, history and persons, and proceed bluntly to list their government's 'diabolical acts against humanity'.[5] As in so many other documents from this last decade, the theological basis for such statements is fully outlined. And the theologians at work here include factory workers and pastors, students, political leaders, writers and teachers. Among national leaders personally involved in these campaigns, former President Yun Po-San, Quaker leader Hahn Sok-Han, and the Opposition leader Kim Dae-Jung, gave Christian leadership, despite their frequent imprisonments, in strongly theological affirmations.

As the situation became darker in the early 1970s, arrests, incidents of torture and execution multiplied. To match the situation new ecumenical leagues, like the Seoul Metropolitan Community Organization, were formed, new institutes for Mission and for Theological Study (at Hankuk and Yonsei), and new congregations and communities. These last included the Galilee Church for squatters and evicted pastors, ecumenical prayer fellowships for families of prisoners and the Christian commune, the House of Dawn. From such movements as these comes the most creative theological thinking of recent years, intimately linked with a costly engagement in politics and spirituality.

It is not surprising that the cross of Christ moves steadily to the centre of theological concern in this decade, and one who most vividly embodies this in both writing and life is the poet Kim Chi-Ha.[6] Student leader and rural worker, he stands in the tradition of Korean nationalist literature that voices a sharp social criticism. In his writing, now translated into many languages, he draws on the thought of the Dong Hak and similar movements, but acknowledges the Korean Christian movement for Democratic Rights as the most important single influence in his thought. In poems, dramas, a Declaration of Conscience and lengthy trial statements, Kim Chi-Ha has presented a comprehensive picture of 'the Kingdom of God in the Eastern Sea': the coming of personal salvation and of social revolution in Korea. Central to three ballad-plays is his powerful rewriting of the gospel within Korean experience; the outcast Jesus figure, through a passion for all outcasts and through his conquest of death, brings a salvation which is both concrete food as well as forgiveness for the oppressed people (minjung).

In this Kim speaks out of the agony of 'a few tortured prisoners' – he and his fellow detainees – who together have been enabled to conquer the terror of death. He has himself been often near death during more than six years solitary confinement, but he now exercises a charisma throughout Korea which perhaps only his fellow Catholic Kim Dae-Jung may equal. Many of his images and themes have moreover provided the basis for a developing theology of the Minjung in Korea. Numbers of theologians have experienced, and articulated in writing, something of this theology of a suffering people. Some have themselves been student leaders or pastors, as in the case of Kang Won-Yong, director of the Korea Christian Academy for social education and lay training and vigorous leader in Korean ecumenism.[7] Some, like Park Hyung-Kyu, an editor of the journal *Christian Thought,* have also persisted in urban mission organization, and in a local pastorate, despite frequent imprisonments.

Mun Dong-Whan and his brother Mun Ik-Kwan, professors in Hankuk Seminary, have been most active in the leadership of protest prayer meetings, in leading (with others) the Galilee

Church, and in writing – whether prison meditations, theological papers or public declarations. Mun Dong-Whan's 'Human Liberation and Christian Education'[8] has been widely read outside Korea also, while much of his brother's writing appears in two volumes of poetry.

A theologian who worked closely with Kim Jae-Jun in the 1950s and 1960s is Suh Nam-Dong, former Dean of Yonsei School of Theology. Although showing the strong influence of his earlier studies of Pannenberg, Suh's article 'The Contemporaneous Christ' (1969) depicts a Christ made flesh today in 'the unnamed half-dead man' where the wound and the groan of our neighbour are his word to us. In 'The Korean Church's understanding of the Cross' (1974), he reports a study of current preaching and writing, and finds the deepest understanding to be one which does not merely comprehend the cross through intellect or emotion but which 'realises the meaning of the cross with action and will'.[9] In the present suffering of the Korean people, 'the cross is not a monument', Kim Jae-Jun had written in 1973, 'but nails in my hands and feet'. Suh Nam-Dong will later (1978–9) undertake thorough studies of Kim Chi-Ha's writing and produce two long papers which relate the present experience of exodus and cross to the revolutionary Minjung in Korean history. The central figure remains Kim Chi-Ha's Korean Christ, who is at the same time the suffering Korean people (Minjung) and the means of their salvation.[10]

The image of the minjung has in fact produced its own body of theological reflection, in for example the work of New Testament scholar Ahn Byung-Mu, since 1973 Director of the Korea Theological Institute. In a detailed study of the Gospel of Mark he places discussion of the Korean minjung in the context of recent discussions of the social and cultural characteristics of the people surrounding Jesus. Kim Yong-Bok, now co-director of the Christian Institute for Justice and Development, Seoul, has also highlighted the role of oppressed Korean people as the subjects of their own history. In doctoral studies on the 'People's Revolution in Korean History' and in a series of articles since 1974 Kim has analysed the economic and technocratic forces in Korean society, and the emergence within Korean history of a Christian koinonia in social struggle.[11] By 'koinonia' he means the paradigmatic community which since the March 1st Movement (1919) has worked for the transformation of Korean society through their Christian

witness to the cross and the resurrection of Christ. In the cross
they found the paradox of innocent suffering and the justice of
God, while in the resurrection there is the symbol of transformation in a new koinonia. In other pages of the paper here
excerpted Kim stresses that this koinonia was marked by 'a sense
of the people's history, by the use of Christian Messianic symbols,
and by their commitment to mobilize the resources of Korean
people as a whole.'

There is a clear relationship between Minjung theology and the
thought of Kim Chi-Ha, as well as that of other Christian scholars
like Hahn Bao-Ho ('Power Politics in Korea'), Chung Ha-Eun
('Eighty Year's History of Korean Christian Social Ethics') and
Min Kyung-Bae ('A History of Resistance of Korean Protestantism').[12] Many contributions to the journals *Christian Thought* and
Third Day have dealt with similar themes, while the crucial role
of Shamanist and new religious movements has been clarified by
Ryu Dong-Shik, for some years editor of *Christian Thought*. The
influence of secular writers like Chang Chun-Ha and Pak Tu-Jin
has also been important.[13] Also writing in *Christian Thought* were
a number of university teachers deeply concerned for Christian
mission within the Korean political and social context. These
include Han Wan-Sang, Chang Il-Cho, and Huh Kwan-Son.
Amongst theologians similarly involved are Hyun Yong-Hak,
Park Pong-Nang, and Lee Mun-Young.[14]

Many strands of thought so far outlined find mature expression
in the work of Kim Chung-Choon, President (1961–62, 1969–76)
of Hankuk Seminary (in which many of those mentioned above
have studied). His long term interest in the indigenization of
theological education led to a series of writings 1962–74, and to
the development (from 1972) of parallel courses in Old Testament
theology and Korean history. He has continued to issue scholarly
studies on Old Testament themes – including two widely used
textbooks – but in these too, the present experience of the cross
by a suffering people recurs again and again. Theological reflection on the Crucifixion Day (1973) and on the Afflicted in the
Exodus Event (1977) are followed by 'A Study of Ps. 22' where
the agony of apparent desertion by God remains central (1979).[15]
The extract chosen here brings together a wealth of insights from
Kim Chung-Choon's previous work, and effectively links the work
of his colleague Kim Jae-Jun, and the Third Day group, with
recent writing of Kim Chi-Ha and the Minjung theologians.

Kim Chung-Choon · *God's Suffering in Man's Struggle*

Kim Chung-Choon, 'God's Suffering in Man's Struggle', *Reformed World*, vol. 36, no. 1, 1980, pp. 14–19.

It is true that our God comes to the place where sorrow and sufferings prevail. He comes there not only as the judge or comforter but also as co-sufferer. Man is not left alone, where human dignity is wounded, where human right is violated.

We are accustomed to know and confess our God as One who is Almighty, the Most High, the Infinite, the Omnipotent, who dwells in the Holy of Holies. We think of God in the superlative sense. But God takes human community seriously and suffers in the human history of injustice and violence. God suffers with the sufferer, the poor, the imprisoned, the despised and the rejected. Such an idea of God's self-humiliation is in the picture of the suffering servant. 'He was despised and rejected by men; a man of sorrow, and acquainted with grief.' (Is. 53:3).

We Christians believe that the prediction of the suffering servant of Second Isaiah is historically personified in the life and death of Christ. And the evangelists tell us that Christ identifies himself with the sinners, the tax-collectors, the down-trodden, the imprisoned, the oppressed, the prostitute and the poor. This is the mystery of the Incarnation in which the powerful God becomes the weakest, and the richest, the poorest. In Christ, God identifies himself with the sufferer.

The idea of God's suffering comes clearly to expression in one of our Korean theologians, Professor Suh Nam-Dong, a professor discharged by the Government. In his article 'The Existential Christ',[16] Professor Suh, commenting on the good Samaritan, maintains that the unknown victim, the sufferer, represents Christ, over against the traditional view claiming the good Samaritan as Christ. The unknown victim was stripped, beaten, and left in a half-dead state.

Here we see God's suffering for man. The victim representing Christ challenges those who pass by summoning them 'to share Christ's suffering' (I Pet. 4:13). Professor Suh emphasizes that the Samaritan could have met the 'Secularized Christ' in his daily life. This is always a challenge for the Christians. This means that we are always confronted with the opportunity to follow the good

Samaritan in sharing God's suffering. And this is what Christ said: 'Truly, I say to you, as you did it to one of the least of these my brethren, you did it to me.'

God identified with human plight

Further explanation of 'How God suffers for man?' is required from a different angle. One of the biblical expressions that God is involved in man's sufferings can be understood in a way that God hears the cry of man and sees the suffering of man, and comes down to the sufferer's position. This is clearly demonstrated in the Exodus story: 'I have seen the affliction of my people . . . and have heard their cry . . . I know their sufferings.' (Ex. 3:7). 'And now, behold, the cry of the people of Israel has come to me, and I have seen the oppression with which the Egyptians oppress them' (ibid., v.9).

If we understand the Exodus event as an event of liberation of the oppressed people, it was not originally intended as man's socio-political concern with an ideal society to be achieved through the common effort of men. The liberation event was motivated by God's involvement in the suffering of the people. God's involvement in seeing, hearing and knowing the suffering made Moses see, hear and know the same suffering. Before God summoned Moses for the great work of the deliverance of his people, Moses saw the suffering of his people and in his struggle to solve the problem, he used force and killed one Egyptian. That led him to see the failure of violence. The use of violence to solve human suffering has often been repeated in history. It is also true that violence is not the last word.

God has his own way. He showed this new way when he called Moses at Mt Sinai. God was telling Moses that he himself was involved in people's suffering through his personal concern, as if God himself suffered by seeing the affliction of the people and hearing the cry of the people's suffering and knowing their suffering. The text tells us very clearly that God seems to experience the same suffering in seeing, hearing and knowing (which means, personal fellowship or bodily contact). This means the deliverance out of the land of the Egyptians (= liberation) comes through God's initiative and voluntary participation in the suffering of the people.

We Christians understand the salvation-history of God too easily in terms of the power and mercy of God. In the Exodus story, the liberation of the people was motivated by a divine determination: 'I have come down to deliver them out of that land to a good and broad land . . .' (Ex. 3:8). Prior to that, God was personally involved in the suffering of the people who cried out for help.

Most of the Psalmists who wrote the 'complaint-psalms' seem to believe that their God is the hearer of their cry of groaning, identifying himself with the sufferers. They confess that their God is indeed the helper, protector, comforter and deliverer in time of suffering and mistreatment. Such faith seems to stand on the firm conviction that God could hear the crying or groaning of the Psalmists. 'Out of the depths I cry to thee, O Lord! Lord, hear my voice, let thy ear be attentive to the voice of my supplication!' (Ps. 130:1).

We might suspect the faith of the most tragic psalmist, when he cries out: 'My God, my God, why hast thou forsaken me? Why art thou so far from helping me, from the words of my groaning? O my God, I cry by day, but thou hast no answer; and by night, but find no rest.' It would be wrong, if we understand these lines in terms of the complaint, accusation and hopelessness of the psalmist. On the contrary, these lines are truly the genuine expression of the trusting-faith of the helpless psalmist. All the possibilities of deliverance have been blocked. He was really at the end of his rope. The only way left was to cry out to his God for help, even though God seemed to have forsaken him. It was the only way to cry for help to God, who would hear, see and know the helplessness of the sufferer. So, he cried, 'Eli, Eli lama sabacthani.'

In the time of the Ye Dynasty in the Korean history, there was a big drum, hanging over the gate of the palace. This drum was called 'Shin-mun-go', which means 'the drum for hearing the cry for help of the people'. Whoever was mistreated either by Government officials or by his neighbours could beat the drum, hoping to receive correction from the king. Our suffering humanity is also allowed to beat the drum, hanging over every extremely hopeless situation. Human history is full of such cry or groaning.

In the Bible, we find examples of such a cry. The innocent blood of Abel cried to God. Hearing the voice of the victimized, God put a direct question to the assailant: 'Where is Abel, your brother? . . . The voice of your brother's blood is crying to me

from the ground' (Gen. 4:10). In this question, the writer tries to
express the meaning of community life, which is so easily broken
by the self-centred man. Man must live together with his fellow
man. To deny this principle is contrary to the will of God. The
voice of the victim, the cry of his fellow man reaches God, because
God hears the cry of suffering people. The J writer tries to let his
contemporaries know how innocent blood was shed and cried out
to God, when the ever-increasing political power of Solomon
purged his opponents and surpressed the people with heavy-labour
and taxation.

There is another text, which seems to imply some of the problems of labour and management in modern industrial society:
'Behold, the wages of the labourers who mowed your fields, which
you kept back by fraud, cry out; and the cries of the harvesters
have reached the ears of the Lord of hosts' (James 5:4). God
hears the cry of the labourers who are exploited by the rich
farmers and greedy industrialists. God sees the agony of the farmers who are forced to leave the rural life, and He also knows the
suffering of the labourers struggling for survival.

God hears the human cryings and groanings from the place of
struggle all over the world. The cry of the drowning Boat People
from South Asia; the cry of the rejected and discriminated people
from the lands of racism; the cry of the mistreated and exploited
from the lands of rapidly developing countries under dictatorship;
the cry of the poor and alienated people from the lands of capitalism; and the cry of the imprisoned and rejected people from
the land where one political ideology, like communism is dominant and oppressive.

It is noteworthy that people are struggling for their survival, for
human dignity, for the protection of human rights, for freedom,
social justice, and for the democratic way of life. 'O Lord, my
God, I call for help by day; cry out in the night before thee. Let
my prayer come before thee, incline thy ear to my cry. For my
soul is full of troubles, and my life draws near to Sheol!' (Ps.
88:1–3). Here God is ready to suffer with suffering humanity. The
Psalmist believes that God is the only hope of release from un-
bearable affliction. The cry to God for help is the only hope.

My concluding thesis is this: As long as we believe in God who
is willing to hear our cry or groaning, we have hope to struggle
for. With this conviction, we can sing with St. Paul: 'Now hope
that is seen is not hope, for who hopes for what he sees? But if

we hope for what we do not see, we wait for it with patience.'
(Rom. 8:24, 25).

A Korean concept

I do not believe that 'just waiting' is adequate if we have a hope
that is founded on the living God. God suffers for man not that
we may be mere spectators. How do we share God's sufferings?
This is what we have to struggle for. And thinking of the Korean
tradition, I would like to suggest that we might learn something
from *Shamanism*, which has been rejected as a superstition by
Christians.

The main role of the Shaman in Korean Shamanism is to
appease the grudge of the dead who died with a sense of complaint
or spite or regret or hatred. The spirit of the dead wanders in the
air and is often believed to attack his or her family with illness
and other kinds of misfortune. So, a special ceremony called GUT
is held under the leadership of a Shaman. The purpose of the
GUT is to satisfy the grudge, in Korean, the 'Han' of the dead.
With music and dance, the Shaman, identifying herself with the
dead, spells out all the words that the dead person wishes to say
to his or her family, so that the spirit might leave the house with
satisfaction. This is the ministry of the Shaman to appease the
spirit of the dead.

God's suffering is to be understood in the form of God's ministry for those who cry for help out of the deep human misery,
contradiction and disorder in life. There are cries which reach
God in the political world, where the systems and powers of the
dictator violate human rights; in the economic world, where the
distribution of wealth is unbalanced. There are the groans of
people which rise up to God from the place where freedom of
speech is restricted and controlled; where the voice of conscience
and justice is suppressed, and fraud and fabrication are preferred
to the truth. We Christians are called to hear the cry of the
oppressed, the rejected, the despised, the imprisoned and the
poor. We have to carry out our ministry to appease the grudge of
these fellow brethren. We are told that Christians have to contend
against principalities, powers, and the world rulers of this present
darkness (Eph. 6:12).

It is generally believed that in the consciousness of the Korean
people, a sense of 'Han' (grudge) is so deeply rooted that most of

Korean literature naturally reflects the sense of 'Han' as an indigenous trend of national emotion. Kim Chi Ha, a well-known
poet, defined the idea of 'Han' as follows in his Memo, written in
prison: '"Han" is a feeling, accumulated and formulated through
the sense of suffering and grief of hungry, persecuted and condemned people. In particular, such 'Han' can easily be expressed
in the life-style of the anti-government persons; for them 'Han'
arises as reaction to 'social oppression' and a 'suppressed consciousness"'.[17] According to our poet, our national history is characterized with such 'Han' through repeated 'foreign invasion, war,
riot, rebellion, malignant disease and starvation'.

In this regard, the ministry of the Shaman is desirable for
Korean churches and Christians. God's mission in the life of Jesus
Christ was also to appease the 'Han' of the people of God. They
were suffering under the powers of the Roman Empire. Jesus
seems to be a Shaman when he commanded the sufferer: 'Come
out of the man, you unclean spirit!' Jesus moved around to help
people. Rejected, despised, condemned, exploited, the poor and
sinners. These were the people of 'Han' in those days. They could
only cry out to God and waited for a new life from God.

Our mission today must be the same as Jesus carried out in the
form of the ministry of 'Han'. We Christians should be the Sha-
mans of Christ, full of the Holy Spirit, to carry out the ministry
of 'Han', identifying ourselves with suffering humanity and ap-
peasing the 'Han' of the people. But it should be remembered
that the ministry of 'Han' must not only build an ideal society in
the political, historical and sociological sense but also hasten the
Kingdom of God, promised by the suffering God to a suffering
humanity – the Criminal on the cross.

This ministry of 'Han' should be one of the new subjects of our
theological curriculum and the 'Han' of the people carefully
analysed and studied sociologically, biblically and theologically.
And the ministry of the Church must accent the appeasement of
'Han', so that all the rejected, despised, imprisoned, exploited,
alienated and the poor may have joy and satisfaction.

> 'The Lord makes poor and makes rich;
> he brings low, he also exalts.
> He raises up the poor from the dust;
> he lifts the needy from the ash heap,
> to make them sit with princes

and inherit a seat of honour.' (I Sam. 2:7, 8)

This is the hope for which we struggle, God suffers for our salvation in order to release human reality from human suffering.

Kim Chi-Ha · *The Dream of Revolutionary Religion*

Kim Chi-Ha, 'Declaration of Conscience', in *The Gold-Crowned Jesus and Other Writings*, Orbis Books, Maryknoll, New York 1978, pp. 23–28

Must revolution reject religion and religion be the foe of revolution? I think the answer is No. Perhaps by this reply alone I could not be a Marxist-Leninist. But the Marxist dictum that religion is the opiate of the masses is only a partial truth applicable to one aspect of religion.

When a people has been brutally misruled and exploited for a long time, they lose their passion for justice and their affection for other people. Committed only to self-survival, they lapse into an individualistic materialism. Their near-crazed resentment and rage at social and economic conditions, diverted into frustration and self-hatred, is repeatedly dissipated in fragmented, anomic actions. Our prisons are full of lower-class criminals, thrown there by a ruling elite that spits on the poor and flourishes on social injustice. The prisoners' roster of crimes is diverse: armed robbery, theft, murder, desertion from military service, kidnapping, etc. Yet their wretched tragedy has a common origin in frustration and isolation.

The chief priests and Pharisees defuse the people's bitter resentment and moral indignation with sentimental charity. The people are emasculated by mercy. The god of philanthropy serves the oppressor by turning people into a mob of beggars. That is why I cannot admire Albert Schweitzer.

In similar situations of bondage and deprivation, prophetic religions of love arise in the wilderness and shake the emotions of the oppressed and mistreated people. The slumbering masses awaken like a thunderclap; their human and divine qualities suddenly shine forth. This is the mystery of resurrection – this is revolution. That resurrection fashions people in God's image, opens their eyes to their own dignity and turns their frustration and self-hatred into eschatological hope. This kind of resurrection changes a selfish, individualistic, escapist anomie into a communal, united, realistic commitment to the common good. It becomes a struggle for a humane life and dignity for all the people. This resurrection prevents the people's bitter resentment and moral indignation from evaporating in self-hatred and converts it into a fierce demand for God's universal justice. If necessary, the people's enormous energy may also be directed to a decisive, organized explosion. This is a revolutionary religion. This miraculous conversion which conceived the mystery of revival may also bring a decisive spiritual revival. This conversion is the philosophy of *tan*, the determination to choose the circumstances of one's death, that my hero Chang Il Tam sings about.

Since my college days when I suffered from tuberculosis, I have passionately wanted to understand both my personal situation and my country's. How could I overcome my terror of death and how could South Korea find its way out of the ubiquitous spiritual dehumanization and material poverty? I heard something then about the Tong Hak teaching that 'man is heaven.'[18] At first, it was a low murmuring that made only a slight impression. Later I learned more about the Tong Hak rebellion, and an image took shape in my mind. I could see that awesome band of starving peasants, their proud banner proclaiming 'An end to violence, save the people!' as they marched off to fight. Suddenly that Tong Hak teaching became a loud cry as thunderous as the battle cries of those marching peasants.

I have been grappling with that image for ten years. At some point, I gave it a name: 'The unity of God and revolution.' I also changed the phrase 'man is heaven' into 'rice is heaven' and used it in my poetry.

That vague idea of 'the unity of God and revolution' stayed with me as I continued my long arduous search for personal and political answers, and as I became very interested in contemporary Christian thought and activism. European social reformers, including Ernst Troeltsch, Frederic Ozanam, Karl Marx, and others had been absorbed into the grand edifice of Christian thought. Their ideas were now being re-examined and developed in new directions. I was intrigued by efforts to combine Marxist social reform and Christian beliefs as evinced in the 1972 Santiago Declaration of Christians for Socialism.

The synthesis draws from diverse sources. One example is the adaptation of the teachings of Marx and Jesus. Marx's contribution is his structural epistemology, which maintains that social oppression blocks human salvation. From Jesus' teachings we take his humanism, which advocates love for all people and human dignity, his emphasis on rebirth as the means to salvation, the idea of the God of hope who brings salvation, equality, and liberation on earth, and the activities of Jesus of Nazareth during his life.

The synthesis tries to unify and integrate these concepts. In my view this is not a mechanical process, a rote grafting of bits of Marxism onto Christianity. The union produces something entirely new. (The new synthesis is not finished. Its gestalt cannot be defined; it is still amorphous. Therefore I must decline to use the existing terminology. The Korean people are suffering from the tragic reality of a divided peninsula. This division has become the excuse for brutal repression: Everything is done in the name of 'national security,' the threat from the North. Under this police-state system South Korean society has become rigid, intolerant, frightened; our intellectual life is as airless and barren as the valleys of the moon. The authorities, who are hypersensitive and always suspicious of new and possibly 'dangerous' thoughts, may attempt to label my ideas as a certain ideology; I reject this false labelling of an unfinished 'product'. I stand on my human right to be creative. Original ideas are not mass-produced on an assembly line.)

My image of the unity of God and revolution was clarified by Pope John XXIII's encyclical *Mater et Magistra:* 'The mystery of Jesus and the loaves of bread is a temporal miracle which shows the future heaven.' I also benefitted from the writings of the liberation theologians: Fredrick Herzog, James Cone, Richard Shaull, Paul Lehmann, Jürgen Moltmann, J. B. Metz, Tödt, Hugo Assmann, Reinhold Niebuhr, Dietrich Bonhöffer, and others. Papal statements after Vatican II as well as such encyclicals as *Rerum Novarum* and *Quadragesimo Anno* provided insights. The greatest single influence on my thinking, however, has been my participation since 1971 in the Korean Christian movement for human rights.[19] This experience convinced me that the Korean tradition of resistance and revolution, with its unique vitality under the incredibly negative circumstances prevailing here, are precious materials for a new form of human liberation. This rich lode will be of special value to the Third World. Shaped and polished by the tools of liberation theology, our experience may inspire miraculous new forms of *Missio Dei* in the gritty struggle of the South Korean people.

My ballad *Chang Il Tam* attempts to express these ideas through the teachings and intellectual pilgrimage of one holy man who speaks in the form of gospels. However, the Park regime has seized my notes as proof of a 'conspiracy to publish subversive materials.'

Chang Il Tam is a thief, the son of a prostitute and a *paekchong* [an outcast strata that performs unclean tasks such as slaughtering animals, tanning, etc.]. A failure in life, despondent, Chang suddenly attains enlightenment and becomes a preacher of liberation. Chang emulates Im Kok Chong [Korea's legendary Robin Hood] in believing that the poor should 're-liberate' what the rich have stolen from them and divide it equally among the needy. He begins stealing from the rich and giving to the poor, is arrested and thrown into jail, whereupon he teaches the other prisoners about revolution. One day Chang is unfairly disciplined. Angrily throwing caution to the winds, he shouts 'We must be liberated! Down with the hated bourgeoisie!' (My working notes cover only a portion of his proselytizing in prison; these are his early radical ideas. The government claims they are identical with *my* ideas and therefore constitute irrefutable proof that I am a Communist!)

Chang escapes from prison, is hunted by the police, and finally hides in a filthy back alley where some prostitutes are plying their trade. He calls to the prostitutes, 'Oh, you are all my Mother!' He kisses their feet and declares: 'The soles of your feet are heaven' and 'God is in your decaying wombs' and 'God's place is with the lowest of the low.'

Chang later goes to live on Mt. Kyeryong and preaches about a paradise in the land of the Eastern Sea [Korea]. He teaches a systematic religious discipline in three stages: *Sich'onju,* acceptance of God and service to Him; *Yangch'onju,* cultivation of God in your heart and subordination of everything to God's will; and *Saengch'onju.* Chang preaches 'communal ownership of property,' teaches about revolution, stresses the unity of prayer and action, and advocates 'resistance against the tide.' His major ideas include 'the transformation of the lowest into heaven,' the traveller's path from this world to heaven as revolution, the need to purge the wild beasts that lurk within human hearts, symbolic of the *paek-*

chong's occupation, and the corruption of this world and the paradise of the Eastern Sea in the next.

Chang Il Tam preaches to the workers and farmers. He builds an altar in the wilderness, starts a huge bonfire, and casts everything old into the flames. He teaches the people that although violence is unavoidable, *tan* is desirable. Chang leads the multitude toward the evil palace in the capital, Seoul. The throng all carry beggars' cans. At this point Chang proclaims that paradise is 'to share food with others' and that 'food is heaven.' They reach the capital where food is abundant and continue through the city on the eternal journey toward paradise where food is shared by all.

Kim Yong-Bok · *The Minjung (People) as the Subject of History*

Kim Yong-Bok, *The Minjung (People) as the Subject of History*, World Student Christian Federation Dossier No. 13, September 1977

Today the people of Korea face a very difficult situation ridden with complex historical contradictions. The conflict between the North Korean and South Korean regimes is still interlocked with the worldwide contradiction of the East and West, in spite of the emerging detente. At the same time the people of Korea live in conflict with their own ruling regimes, and with the persisting cultural values of the past Yi dynasty, as well as with international encroachment on technocratic and economic levels.

The democratic opposition movement in Korea faces a number of important questions: what is our concrete vision of liberation? Who is to liberate whom from what? How is this to be done? These questions seem to be the same as those asked in other situations; yet they bear particular characteristics in the Korean situation.

A The Emergence of the Minjung (People) on the Historical Horizon

The most prominent reality of the recent democratic struggle in S. Korea has been the realization that the people *(minjung)* are

the central actors, or subjects of history. There has been an in-
crease of concern on the theme of *minjung* among students,
writers and socially conscious Christian groups such as Korean
Student Christian Federation, Urban Industrial Mission movement, Catholic Young Workers movement and Christian
intellectuals.

This broad concern on the theme of the *minjung* as central
historical subject represents a newly emerging historical consciousness in Korea, both in the society at large and in the church.
Growing awareness of the reality of the people – a process of
historical conscientization – has been brought about through various processes: (1) transformation of social perception through
physical exposure and involvement in the suffering, struggle and
aspirations of the people; (2) critical reflection on social reality;
and (3) actions and movements for social justice and grassroots
democracy (in factories, slums, and rural villages) where the
people live.

In a recent Christian Youth gathering held in a provincial city
of Korea in September 1976, *minjung* became the central theme
of the entire conference. Some of the themes that emerged in this
meeting should be introduced here.

> Who are the minjung and where are they?
> In a word, they are the have-nots. They are farmers, fishermen,
> laborers, unemployed, soldiers, policemen, salarymen, small
> shopkeepers, small producers. They suffer political suppres-
> sion, economic exploitation, social humiliation, and cultural
> alienation.

The minjung's condition of life is described as oppression, exploitation, 'nobodyness', silence, and loss of subjectivity (chuch'e
song).

> The *minjung* have been robbed of their subjectivity not only in
> their expressions and actions, but also in their feelings and
> thoughts. The consciousness of *minjung* is determined by the
> ruling echelon of that particular society at a given time. Thus,
> they cannot handle their own destiny and they become unable
> to discern even their own will and interests; and finally, they
> are consumed by the sense of habitual frustration.

These conditions of the people rise basically due to the unjust
power structures – the structural evil. Thus, the people's life is

understood in terms of power relations or power contradictions.

In recent discussions, the term *minjung* is differentiated from *minjok*, the notion of the people as national entity in a national-istic sense, and also from *inmin*, the notion of the people as proletariat in a classical Marxist sense, although both of these meanings of the term people are implied in the term *minjung*.

> In our history the national people (minjok, in a nationalistic sense) have had reality; yet the minjung people did not have the reality in history. In other words, the real substance (of history) is minjung, whereas minjok is a relational term which is formed to describe the relation to other nations. In fact, minjung has always been exploited in the name of minjok.[20]

Since the modern history of Korea is characterized by the na-tionalistic struggle, the notion of the national people (minjok) against foreign domination has been predominant, but since the end of the Second World War, when the Korean people were 'liberated' from Japanese colonialism, the term minjok has be-come somewhat ambiguous, for it obscures the internal contra-dictions of Korean society, that is, between the dictatorial regimes and the people (minjung). It is clear that the historical motive power of the national independence struggle in Korea is the min-jung. Often, when nationalism is referred to, the national bour-geoisie is regarded as the central force of the nationalist movement. However, in the Korean situation there was no rise of a national bourgeois class during the time of nationalist struggle; the nationalist movements such as March First Movement were sponsored and carried out in the main by the grassroots structures of the Korean people, including Tonghak Religion and Christ-ianity (Protestantism), which may be regarded as religions of the oppressed masses.

The other recent reference to the minjung (people) is found in such writings as those of Kim Chi-ha, a Korean poet. He com-ments about the notion of the people in his statement at the Seoul District Court, as follows:

> Q: In your memoranda, the phrase, 'the minjung' is used fre-quently. What is the minjung?
> A: If we look at Genesis there is a passage where GOD tells man to increase and multiply, developing and occupying the earth. The minjung are those who have increased and occupied the ends of the earth and brought about the establishment of

societies, advanced the course of history by bringing about the universal centrality of man and producing the true worth of humanity. In other words, I think of the minjung as those who made their bread by their own toil, build houses by their own labour, till and cultivate the soil, and then as a society protect, with their own lives, their country and its values. I think of the minjung in these concrete terms.

This was written for the most part as a concept opposed to that of authority (regime). Authority originally comes from the min-jung but there are cases where authority is changed into a tool to oppress the minjung in whom its roots lie. In the course of history it is necessary to revive the general principles whereby the people call back to their own position the authority which is theirs. Authority is opposed to justice, it is unjust to stand on the side which is in opposition to the minjung. It is my conviction that to act on the basis of minjung is just and that they will be victorious.

Kim Chi-ha sharply distinguishes, in this courtroom satement, 'minjung' from 'inmin' (Marxist terminology of North Korea), and insists that 'minjung' is a broadly defined term rather than being defined in terms of productive relations.

Thus minjung has become the governing theme of the Korean Democratic Movement today. This situation has become clear especially since the 1970's, in statements issued by the Korean Democratic Movement, such as *Minjung Minjok Minju*, and Theo-logical Declaration of Korean Christians, 1973.[21]

In all the above references to the people (minjung) there is no precise definition to the term, and yet it is unmistakably clear that it refers to the people who are oppressed and exploited.

The most eloquent descriptions of the concrete suffering of the people (minjung) appear in literary writings such as poems by Kim Chi-ha and novels like *Chang Kil-san* by Whang Sok-young.[22]

The *minjung* are known through their stories: *their social biography*. The stories of the people become the primary means to reveal the total condition of the *minjung*, while social science methodologies are instrumental in the understanding of social conditions and contradictions in which the people live, and thus clarify the structural problems. A typical story of the Korean people in the Yi dynasty is told in the popular (folk) novel, *The Tale of Hong Kil-dong*, which every Korean child knows. This is a story of a traditional Korean rebel, who identifies himself with the oppressed class.

The story that the people bear is the shape of the historical consciousness in a given time. It is through such stories that each new generation mobilizes wisdom from the past traditions throughout human history, and it is through the creation of new stories that the people move into a new future. Therefore, our concern for the story is not merely the question of seeking past wisdom for the present, but it is also the question of creating a new story of the people. In this sense the democratic movement in Korea is the bearer of a new story – still unfolding – of the Korean people, which is connected with the stories of the Tonghak Rebellion and the March First Independence Movement.

B The 'Minjung' As The Chuch'e (Subject) of History

The Korean Democratic Movement regards the minjung as the true subject of historical movement, the true protagonist in their historical drama. This is a total rejection of the notion of the people as the object of rule by Yangban (ruling class of Yi Korea) by colonial powers or by the dictatorial regimes of contemporary Korea. In this sense the *Minjung* is the Chuch'e (subject) of history.

This statement is not a mere abstract proposition, but has positive historical references in the Tonghak (Peasant) Rebellion of 1895 and in the March First Independence Movement (1919). The Korean people recognize these historical events as the paradigm for the liberation of the people, for they represent the story of the people's struggle against the internal and external enemies of *minjung*. These events are a well-spring of Korean national liberation and the revolutionary historical consciousness of the *Minjung*. Through them materialized the assertion of the historical *Chuch'esong* (subjectivity) of the *Minjung*. The present struggle of the people in Korea is an ongoing and ever-emerging realization of the revolutionary *Chuch'esong* of the Korean *Minjung*.

There has been a debate on the idea of Chuch'esong (subjectivity) or Chuch'e (subject) in Korea for the last decade or so. There have been basically two notions. Nationalist historians have advanced ideas such as 'national soul' or 'national spirit', and trace its historical manifestations thoughout the chronicles of Korean history. This notion of Chuch'e emerged during the nationalist struggle formulated by historians in the resistance against Japanese colonial historiography, which incorporates Korean history into Japanese history. This notion of national *Chuch'e* only partially recognizes the people's historical role and places the motive power of history in obscure and abstract notions such as national soul or spirit.

The other idea of *Chuch'e* appeared in a rather recent development in North Korea, particularly after the Sino-Soviet split. The idea of *Chuch'e* of the North Korean regime identifies the proletariat as the *Chuch'e*. But this is no democratic theory in the sense that the people are real subjects, because in fact they are the objects of the regime which governs in their name. Furthermore, this *Chuch'e* does not have any connections with the stories of the Korean people's struggles, such as the Tonghak Rebellion or March First Independence Movement. It is a kind of nationalist ploy to mobilize the people under a nationalist banner and at the same time to solve the problem of international relations between the two Communist states, China and Russia. The international necessity for relative neutrality of the N. Korean regime required a nationalist theme to rationalize their position. What is remarkable about this idea of *Chuch'e* in the North is its closeness to the South's nationalist understanding, because neither regime recognizes the *Minjung* as the concrete historical *Chuch'e*, and thereby to a great extent both obscure the internal contradictions between the ruling regimes and the people (minjung).

Therefore the historical *Chuch'esong* of the *minjung* is revolutionary in both Korean societies insofar as there is no *minjung* democracy in Korea. Such revolutionary Chuch'esong rises as *minjung movements*. Or, through *minjung movements* the 'lost' or suppressed subjectivity of the people is recovered and awakened to an active historical reality. The Korean people witnessed this reality in the Tonghak Rebellion and the March First Independence Movement as well as in the present democratic struggle, in which the *minjung movement* holds the central place.

The main thrust of the minjung movement does not merely lie in a political revolution – an overthrow of the regime – but in comprehensive *historical transformation*, which include transformations of power structures, cultural values, and institutions, and the emergence of a new human community.

Empirically it seems that the minjung movements for such historical transformation have been strongly motivated by the *mes-*

sianic consciousness of the people, which have been catalyzed by the messianic symbols of the religions of the oppressed, such as the Tonghak religion and early Korean Protestantism. In fact there has been an integral and inseparable relationship between the *minjung religions* and *minjung* movements throughout our history.

2 · Japan

The work of a Japanese theology, which is biblical yet socially and culturally involved, has a long history beginning with criticism of the Emperor system in the 1880s by such early writers and teachers as Uemura, Uchimura and Kozaki. In the 1920s and 1930s the Christian principles for social action were first articulated by Kagawa Toyohiko, who wholly lived out his 'consciousness of the cross' and a theology of redemptive love, in selfless service of worker and farmer movements. His colleague Nakajima Shigeru, along with the lawyer Kakehi Mitsuaki and Kan Enkichi, professor of theology at St Paul's University, elaborated a theology of the kingdom of God where salvation was seen as a participation in God's radical reform of society. And this became the emphasis of many in the Student Christian Movement at that time. Their sometimes utopian approach was supplemented by the insistence of Sakaibara Gan, also a lay SCM leader, that work for social justice is the expression of genuinely personal faith in the actions of God.[1]

Although the influence of European and American theologies has been felt in Japan throughout the post-Meiji period, it has always been the specific historical processes within Japan which have proved determinative. This was especially so in the years after 1931 (the Manchurian incident). The rise of militarism, closely related to the growth of an ultra-nationalism, increasing political violence, and the ascendancy of Shintoism as a state religion, encouraged the rise of individualism. Theologies which largely ignored social responsibility (often under the influence of early Barthianism) could offer no effective counter to such policies, nor to the quietism and collaboration which marked much of the church's response up until 1945. An early protest had been raised by Murao (1933), but there would be little resistance on theological grounds apart from a few exceptional people like the Mukyokai (non-church) leader Yanaibara Tadao, the Reformed Pastor Onomura Rinzo, and members of the Holiness and Seventh Day Adventist Churches.

In the political quietism of the majority of Christians during the years 1931–1945 lay the seeds for a large part of both the theological conflict and creativity in the following three decades. The first thorough analysis of New Testament teaching on resistance to the state is found in the writing of Matsuki Jisaburo, of Kansai Gaquin (Religion and Politics in the New Testament – 1948). Abe Kozo, a history professor in Tokyo, accuses Japanese Barthianism of a pessimism which does not recognize the reality of man's economic existence. The result is that 'present day Japanese capitalism is affirmed as an element in God's created order'. The later work of Kuwada Hidenobu also, shows a shift to an understanding of incarnation and cross where social action becomes integral to the proclamation of the word[2] (Theological Understanding of Church and Society 1955).

By now the initial dismantling of military power and of the imperial ideology by the occupation forces was being reversed. A consistent trend during the next quarter of a century would be the reinstatement of the Emperor system, the revival of a compulsory (nationalistic) moral education and the restoration of Shinto as a state religion. Economic growth, accelerated by Korean, and later Vietnam, war contracts would only aggravate the social, political and religious divisions resulting from authoritarian policies in the post-war, and wartime, period. Although churches such as the Kyodan (United Church) now faced the challenge of widespread nihilism and destitution, and were to experience rapid growth in the 1950s in particular, they were unable to resolve their continuing ambivalence toward state and industrial power. Not until 1967 was a Confession of War Guilt possible for the Kyodan, and then largely because of the outstanding leadership of Suzuki Masahisa.[3] A notable preacher, Suzuki emphasized the Christian's call to battle sin in both individuals and society, through concrete experience of the promised forgiveness of God. The Confession, which achieved a significant shift in the Kyodan's social involvement, was for Suzuki one of the actions 'lined with blood' by which such forgiveness was expressed.

There was however much debate both before and after the issuing of the Confession. Avoiding the distortions of 'Japanized'

Christianity in the militarist period, people like Yamaya, Asano and Ishiwara had outlined in the late 1950s a more dynamic relationship between Christian theology and the life situation and culture of the Japanese. Support for this can be found in the work of Hatano (philosophy), Sumiya (social science), Takeda Cho and Doi (in culture and religious studies).[4] A group of 'biblical theologians', the most well-known being Kitamori Kazo, soon came under criticism for furthering as orthodoxy, a form of theology which had provided no foundation for opposition to state tyranny. Kitamori's *Theology of the Pain of God*[5] is seen by many as giving 'the logic but not the feel of the pain of God' with little awareness of the suffering known by many of his fellow Japanese.

This debate would sharply intensify in the late 1960s when alternatives to this approach are taken in contextual Japanese theology. One would arise in the field of urban-industrial mission and lay ministries which have their beginning in the formation of the Kansai Labour Evangelism Fellowship (1956). Amongst its founders, Takenaka Masao stands out as leader, both in organization and theological reflection, for lay and people's movements during the next twenty years. Professor of Social Ethics at Doshisha, and until 1976 Study Director of the Kansai Seminar House, Takenaka has worked with ecumenical and community groups in almost every country of the region to foster Christian lay presence in secular struggles. The extract chosen for inclusion here is part of his John R. Mott Lectures for the East Asia Christian Conference (1961) and states the principles for ecumenical thought and action which his work still expresses. Nothing less than the entire secular world is, for Takenaka, the arena for God's activity, and drawing on the resources of contemporary literature, folk music and Christian art, he pictures theology as a discernment and participation in the creative struggles of the people.[6]

During the 1960s the larger issues of Japan's industrial development, her exploitation of other Asian economies and her involvement in US military policies – notably in Vietnam – were raised more and more insistently by younger pastors and lay-leaders. The US bases, and the return of Okinawa, ravages of pollution, and the exploitation of day-labourers all came under attack. But two events planned for 1970 became the focus of nation-wide criticism especially by university and church groups. These were the renewal of the Mutual Security Pact (of 1960) with the United States and the other was the 'celebration of capitalism' in the lavish Osaka Exposition. Those Christians in particular who were aware of the collusion of the churches in the earlier policies of Imperial Japan could not accept the acquiescence of those same churches in Japan's return to military involvements, to an economic empire, or to feudal (against the Burakumin) and racist (against Korean minorities) domestic policies. Amongst those Christians who had been raising such questions, Iisaka Yoshiaki (in political science), Mushakoji Kinhide (in peace studies) and Shiozuki Kentaro (Asian economic problems) have produced clear critiques. In lengthy debate with Yagi Seichi (Tokyo Technical College), Takizawa Katsumi declares that the 'original fact of Emmanuel' requires theological and political commitments in contemporary issues, a commitment alongside others which he himself made.[7] But it was in New Testament studies that questions arose which would be basic to the political and religious confrontations of the years 1968–1975.

What, asked Arai Sasagu of Aoyama Gaquin, were the social bearers of religious tradition in the early church? And are not similar conflicts between different social and economic interests shaping today's doctrinal debates as they did then? Can theology be independent of class interests? Tagawa Kenzo of International Christian University saw in the rejection by Japanese church leaders of any criticism of a Christian Pavilion for Expo '70, the same kerugmatizing of Jesus that is observable in the Jerusalem church and in St Paul. Instead of the prophetic disturber, friend of the outcast and stern opponent of religious and political leaders in his day, Jesus becomes the transcendent redeemer whose church also transcends and therefore neglects actual instances of injustice and conflict. Arai's later studies of 'Jesus in His Time' (1974) concentrated on the social and historical setting for Jesus' ministry and his particular roles in relationship to oppressed and oppressing groups within Palestine society.[8]

The implications for Japanese churches in 1968–69 were plainly that confessions of faith, and of war responsibility, must be expressed in a prophetic witness to justice and compassion, in both national and international affairs. If biblical theology stresses God's actions in history, said the critics, does this not mean Japanese history also? And is he only acting to buttress the established order? In universities, church assemblies and seminaries, there was sometimes violent debate in which radical societal and theological critiques opposed the often bland orthodoxy which

seemed little different to the quietism of the war years. The debate
in effect still continues, and the divergent interpretations of scripture, and ideology, represented have to some extent polarised the
Kyodan. Amongst the students, professors and pastors who now
work outside the institutional church, Takao Toshikazu (professor
at Kanto Gaquin) is one who, along with Tagawa and Hori Mitsuo
(Tokyo Union Seminary), became deeply involved with students
and citizen's movements.They found in the Zenkyoto movement
in particular, a clear demonstration of love, repentance and justice
– a radical self-negation in marked contrast to the 'Alliance of
Egoists'[9] confronting them in political and religious institutions.
The paper here excerpted reflects Takao's deep concern for the
integrity of the Christian university, now under increasing government control. Those also showing concern for the shape of contemporary Christian mission and the development of Japanese
theology in the last decade, include Ichida Yoshiro (in pastoral
studies), Kumuzawa Yoshinobu (theology in Japan) and S. Takayanagi (studies of Japanese writers).[10] For Koyama Kosuke, the
presence of God in concrete experiences of suffering and broken-
ness is all important. He sees the Christian community becoming
a truly historical fellowship and sharing 'Christ's crucified mind',
only as it shares this presence within all the particularities of a
specific religious-cultural context. Although he now lives outside
Japan, Koyama's writing often closely reflects Japanese Christian
experience.[11] Among contemporary Japanese novelists, Shiina
Rinzo and Endo Shusaku are Christians whose many books have
strongly influenced recent theological work.[12] There still remains
however, a division between theological and biblical studies
centred mainly on the concerns of church or ministry, and those
which are carried on in encounter with the events and movements
of Japanese society and culture.

But a new genre of theological reflection has arisen from the
ministries and involvements of lay people and pastors in local
situations. It continues traditions already outlined but is less
explicit linked to a particular ideology or biblical interpretation.
Theologizing here is a response demanded by participation in
community issues, and is most frequently based on stories of
people's experience of such issues. Nobuhara Tokiyuki and Koyanagi Nobuaki reflect on their own involvement in the dilemmas
of the Korean and Burakumin minorities, and Koyanagi, on the
plight of Kamigasaki day-labourers. Robert Fukada has been con-

cerned with Burakumin issues, and the problems of new-town areas. Hirata Satoshi, like Fukada, a close colleague of Takenaka, writes out of many year's work in labour education, and all three have collected and reported the experience and reflections of many in similar team ministries. [13] The issues constantly arising in relation to the Emperor system have been the focus for theological reflection by, for example, Nakadaira Kenkichi, Nagatoshi Sanpei, and Tsutomu Shoji. It is one of Tsutomu's papers which is reproduced here. Other writings of Tsutomu come from his experience in Japan-Korea relations, Korean and Taiwanese human rights issues, and from the many localized concerns handled by the NCCJ, of which he is General Secretary. He has a deep concern, as do many of those dealing with similar questions, for the development of a living Japanese theology. [14]

Takenaka Masao · *First Fruits of the New Humanity*

Takenaka Masao, 'First fruits of the New Humanity', in J. R. Fleming (ed.), *Christ's Ministry and Ours*, East Asia Christian Conference 1962, pp. 8–9, 15–16, 19–20

Fulfilling the prophecy of Second Isaiah, Jesus Christ stated of his ministry that 'the Son of man also came not to be served but to serve, and to give his life as a ransom of many' (Mk. 10:45). The term 'ministry' derives from the Greek work *diakonia*, which originally was related to *diakonos*, 'waiter', i.e. servant. The meaning of this word is concretely manifested in the world throughout his life from Bethlehem through Gethsemane to Golgotha. We find an astonishing symbolical demonstration of the meaning of the Servant-Lord image in his act of washing the feet of the disciples. Here he, the Lord, became a servant, took the form of a slave, for the redemption of people in the world. Thus the original portrayal of Christ's ministry clearly indicates the serving dimension and intention of his ministry to the world for the redemption of all people. Here we find the irreducible uniqueness of the Christian message, namely, the Lordship of Christ, so concretely manifested through the Servant-Lord in and to the world.

From this original portrayal of Christ's ministry, we can point to several directions in the ministry of the Church.

First of all, in regard to the root of the Church's ministry, it is clear that the task of the Church as the visible body of Christ is to participate in ministry in response to Christ's ministry. Through the organic analogy of the relationship between the head of the Church, namely Christ, and the body of Christ, namely the Church, our ministry is to be obedient to the Ministry of Christ in and to the world.

Secondly, we acknowledge that the Church's ministry has a comprehensive scope that takes in all the body of Christ; not only those who are set apart, but the People of God as a whole are called to take a part in his ministry. It is not that some of those who are especially called to religious office *have* a ministry, but that the Church as a whole *is* ministry in its existence, in its being manifesting and testifying to the ministry of Christ. We reaffirm today the ministry of the laity as the privilege of God's people to share the ministry of Christ. We recognise that every Christian is *diakonos*, a minister called to a ministry. We appreciate the existence of *charismata*, the gifts of grace among God's people. The Church is a charismatic community recognizing the unique and diversified gifts which God has granted in this community, to equip them for service to the world.

Thirdly, the direction of Christ's ministry is always towards the world. To be sure, the Church is certainly called from the world. But at the same time it is sent towards the world. Bishop Gustaf Aulen describes the ministry of the Church by using the image of a 'contending' Church. He writes:

'The Church of Christ is not of this world, but it has its existence in this world. The Church belongs to the new age, but it lives at the same time in the old. This means that the Church is a contending Church, an *ecclesia militans*.'

'The reconciliation demands a ministry. This is not because the atonement needs to be completed or repeated. It has been done once and for all. It remains for all times and generations. But the reconciliation demands a ministry because it addresses itself to every age and every new generation. The victorious act of reconciliation must be carried out in new struggles. The victory of self-giving love does not mean that struggle has ceased. The ministry of reconciliation is a ministry of struggle and conflict. As God's act of reconciliation in Christ was carried out in a struggle against the destructive powers, so the messengers of reconciliation are called upon to participate in this struggle.'

Fourthly, the object of Christ's ministry is the reconciliation of the world unto himself and the bringing of humanity into its right relationship with God. His ministry is not a ministry of condemnation, nor in a narrow sense, of 'spiritualization', but the ministry of reconciliation and restoration of humanity as a whole. Redemption means, as Professor Kraemer states, 'liberation from slavery *(douleia),* the liberation from the slavery of sin'. This means also liberation from those 'powers' which try to suppress God's place of Lordship, the 'powers' by which man in his individual and collective, social, political, economic and cultural life is enslaved. 'The Church being Ministry, being *diakonia* in correlation to Christ's *diakonia,* has the imperative calling to show in her own life signs and evidences of this redemptive divine order which is in Christ an operative fact.'[15]

Thus we are coming more and more to take wordly affairs seriously not because of our sociological interest, nor because we have a ready-made blueprint for the ideal world, but precisely because we believe the redemptive power of God is at work in the concrete social reality of our changing world, for the restoration of true humanity in Jesus Christ . . .

In this sense there is a profound meaning in recognising the Church as the community of the first fruits of the new humanity. Among the various images of the Church described in the New Testament, this concept of the first fruits has a striking significance for the creation of a new Christian style of living in Asia today. It somehow transcends the numerical limitation of Asian Christians and gives a Christocentric representation of the church's existence in the world. In the New Testament Paul states clearly the fact that 'Christ has been raised from the dead, the first fruits of those who have fallen asleep.' (I Cor. 15:20) He is the first fruits of the new creation and the new Adam and the new humanity. A small minority of Christians in Asia are called also the first fruits, representing the new humanity in their particular place of living. It somehow transcends the notion of a majority or minority situation. It gives a real qualitative representation rather than one determined by quantitative number. A Christian layman in industrial society, no matter how insignificant he appears to be, is a first fruit in that particular and concrete place. He is a pledge of the Holy Spirit that the great harvest is to come. I believe this concept of the first fruits gives real strength and support to Christian presence and involvement in a concrete place of work and living in our Asian setting. Formerly, in describing the need of the Church to break its conformity, we sometimes used to say that we must identify ourselves with the world. But the more I have participated in the world, the more I have come to see the meaning of the image of the first fruits, not in terms of Christian identification with the world, but in terms of Christian presence and involvement in the concrete place of work and ordinary life, as a symbolical representation of the new humanity in Jesus Christ. It is a dangerous mistake to think of Christian identification. We believe every Christian, as the first fruits, is placed in a concrete social context as a sign of the new humanity in Jesus Christ.

Having this basic perspective of Christian presence as the first fruits of the new humanity in each place of work and community, I would like to proceed one step further and consider a particular quality of life which is relevant, and should be strengthened at this time in the creation of the Christian style of life today in Asia. We recognize the reality of the Christian as the first fruits of the new humanity which is rooted in the formation of the new man manifested in Jesus Christ. The formation of this new man was not manifested automatically as a natural event in time. It is a concrete form of costly love, taking part in the agony, misery, and anxiety of man in the concrete social context. Through the suffering ministry of Christ in the world, the old man was transformed into the new man, as Christ stated: 'Unless a grain of wheat falls into the earth and dies, it remains alone; but if it dies, it bears much fruit.' (John 12:24) If the task of Christian ministry is to respond to the suffering and victorious ministry of Christ, how will this be reflected more concretely in the Christian style of living today in Asia? In facing the enormous scale of rapid social change and the complex reality of social, political, and economic life in Asia, one is tempted to accept two kinds of easy solution. One is to find a simple or highly idealistic answer. For example, a person may be critical of, or even very negative to the existing social system, but when he comes to the positive constructive alternative, he is very idealistic or even abstract. We find this tendency among some peace movements and student movements in Japan. The other temptation is a much greater one. This is the temptation to retire from worldly affairs and to limit one's concern to one's own sphere of personal interest. This is a life of resignation and withdrawal, and it is very strong in contemporary Asia.

Now in such a situation the image of Christian presence as the first fruits in the concrete place of suffering and conflict, as a signpost for the coming Kingdom, has an immense meaning. It means that the Christian life is always carried with a costly love which is the life of agony, wrestling together with Christ for the restoration of humanity. The outlook of this life of agony is freedom. As we live between the two times, Christ's ascension and his final coming, we constantly experience his judgment and forgiveness at the same time. Professor Jacques Ellul states this point in the following way:

'The heart of this ethic may be expressed thus: it is based upon an "agonistic" way of life; that is to say the Christian life is always an "agony", that is, a final, decisive conflict: thus it means that constant and actual presence in our hearts of the two elements of judgment and of grace. But it is this very fact which ensures our liberty. We are free, because at every moment in our lives we are both judged and pardoned, and are consequently placed in a new situation, free from fatalism, and from the bondage of sinful habits.'[16]

We need today in Asia Christians who have a wrestling participation and presence in the concrete place of work and life as the first fruits, as the new man who is free and contagiously human within the concrete structure and organisation of society, because he is rooted in the humanity of Jesus Christ. Wherever there is injustice in society the Christian has a wrestling presence in the situation to restore justice in preparing the way for the Grace to come. Wherever misery and exploitation of life exist, he has a wrestling participation in the process of the restoration of humanity in the concrete social context . . .

It is certainly not easy to have such 'presence and participation', especially in this organized and complex society. Many of the decisions we make are not absolute decisions in terms of black and white, but are various shades of grey. Many times we must work through the complex organisation of our worldly political machinery in order to protect the rights of man and to assure the grounds of freedom. As salt functions when put into soup, as the first fruits are brought from the field, so the Christian can bear witness through his wrestling presence in the concrete social context. This is his invitation to participate in Christ's costly ministry.

This new man in Christ is not a 'closed' man but an 'open' man. He was a closed man in enslavement to the forces of evil. But Christ himself took the form of a slave and gave his freedom to enslaved man. Man can now open his inner door to Christ, who says, 'Behold I stand at the door and knock; if anyone hears my voice and opens the door, I will come in to him and eat with him, and he with me.' (Revelation 3:20) This means he constantly opens his inner door and listens to what Christ says. We accept the acceptance of Christ who accepted us in spite of our unworthiness for acceptance.

We do not have secular engagement based on our own ability or intention. But we participate in worldly affairs because we open our hearts to the Word of God which directs us to service and witness in the world. In our total ministry of the Body of Christ, there is a rhythmic movement between listening to the Word of God and going out into the concrete place of response in the world. This means that the new image of man in Asia should be rooted in Christ, and rooted in Asian soil at the same time, as the image of the first fruits indicates. Where can you expect to have the first fruits except in the actual soil where the plant is planted and rooted? There has been much talk about the creation of indigenous Christian art, liturgy, music, architecture, and indigenous theology. All this is a good sign in the younger churches. But sometimes it worries me a little, because so much of the indigenous Christian art or architecture is artificial and not very powerful – rather like seeing a Japanese bridge in a garden in California. Real indigenous art should not be a sort of nostalgia for the ancient art form or an object of curiosity for the Western people. Here again we are at the beginning of a whole new development. But I am inclined to think that the starting point of the indigenisation of Christian faith is not so much in the field of architecture or music or art, not even in theology but in the field of the Christian style of living in contemporary Asia. Unless we Asian Christian men and women in our ordinary church life take seriously the responsibility to wrestle with common problems in the ordinary life of Asian society, there will be no spontaneous expression of indigenous Christian faith. If a man is deeply rooted in Christ and deeply rooted in Asian soil, no matter how insignificant and small he be, he magnifies a radiating example of the indigenisation of Christianity, simply by being what he is. Through the searching questions coming out of the struggling experiences

in secular participation, theologians will develop deeper and more
penetrating theological formulations in the Asian situation. From
the struggling of this rhythmic life rooted in Christ and in Asian
soil there will come a spontaneous expression in songs and art
forms expressing joy and thankfulness for his suffering yet victorious ministry. Indigenisation will arise from within, in this sense,
from the process of the wrestling participation of God's people in
the present concrete reality of Asian society.

Takao Toshikazu · *The Impact of the Struggle on Theology*

Takao Toshikazu, 'The Impact of the Struggle on Theology', revised version
of 'The University Struggle in Japan', *Student World*, vol. 62, nos 3 and 4, 1969

Since 1968, in Japan also, 'university struggles' have given a great
impact to all who take 'thinking' seriously. Numerous 'new-left'
students at many universities had formed 'Zenkyoto' (All Campus
United Struggle Committee). Though all of them developed their
movements on their own initiatives and responded in various ways
to their specific problems at their own universities, their movements had shown uniquely common attitudes and approaches that
were radically new in their nature. Though their movements had,
in a sense, ended partly because of their own too impatiently
'politicizing' direction and partly because of suppression by the
state power, leaving the fundamental problems they had raised
unanswered, the issues that their movements had aroused among
us still demand us to grapple with them seriously and carefully. It
is true that many of the practical 'strategies and tactics' they had
often used are to be criticised as 'unrealistic' and not 'timely', but
it is insincere as well as wrong to disregard and discard the very
problems they had raised.

I would like, in the following, to try to 'summarize' the problems
that had confronted us through the Zenkyoto movements. The
characteristically new 'attitudes' that they had demanded of us
could be stated in three ways as follows:

A. Total and radical view-point – Search for the true 'logos'

Through the whole course of the struggles, the students had demanded that we see and grasp any matter in question with a total
and radical view-point, that is to say, to understand or grasp any
matter in its total context in which it is related with other matters,
yet not superficially but deeply digging into its very root (radix).
For instance, Zenkyoto students accused us that we had been
'technical fools' (Senmon baka) who had buried ourselves in 'private' (or self-centred), narrow technical studies that were void of
'wholistic and ultimate' meaning, and therefore not fully responsible for the welfare of humanity as a whole. When a scientist who
majors in nuclear physics does not see the terrible results of his
researches, he is called a 'technical fool'. But, even after his
inevitable role in its total context has been clearly pointed out, if
he sticks to his former research without seeing its role, then he is
mocked at as 'majoring in being a fool' (baka senmon). When the
students had seen so many 'technical fools' who stubbornly refused
to see the criminal roles that their studies were playing, they
began to doubt the 'authoritative' learning at universities. Thus
they began to question such fundamental issues as 'academic freedom', 'self-ruling principle at university (autonomy of university)'
and the 'ultimate meaning of learning'. All these issues had been
taken for granted as if they were self-evident.

Indeed, we have been astray in the labyrinth of our majors and
minors, specialities and differentiations. While we have been taking for granted that our universities are 'ivory towers' where the
truth is being searched, our universities have been woven into the
establishment and nolens volens have been functioning as institutions to support and complement the establishment. Thus the
Zenkyoto students understood Tokyo University as 'Tokyo Imperialistic University' which has been functioning for the past
ninety years as the 'reproductive organ of privileged elites'; and
Nihon University as 'Nichi-Dai Co. Ltd., a reproductive organ of
middle-class labour power' . . .

B. The principle of self-denial – search for the true 'ethos'

The second very characteristic feature of the Zenkyoto students
is that with such a 'radical and total' view-point they had realized
that they were not merely the victims of the establishment but

rather they themselves were 'oppressors' consciously or unconsciously supporting and supplementing the establishment. Thus they developed what they had called the principle of self-denial. To deny oneself here does not mean to lose oneself. Self-denial here means to negate the self that is in reality an 'oppressor' and to criticize one's own self-centred thinking and behaviour in order to grow into a truly 'independent' self. He sees the situation in which he finds himself with truly 'total and radical' view-point and works and struggles with the oppressed searching and creating the true 'solidarity'. This self-denial does not lead into self-hatred, or to an escape from or abandonment of one's own 'setting in life' (Sitz im Leben). One of the leaders of the movements expressed this as follows: 'I must keep denying myself every day so that I could truly become a "man" and work as a physicist'. This same man has to resist becoming an 'armed labour power commodity' in this imperialistic stage of Japanese monopolistic capitalism. This must have been the fundamental reason why the Zenkyoto students at Tokyo University at the early stage of their movements were called 'the least egoistic group'.[17]

When confronted with this kind of 'questioning', all the members of universities, particularly professors, had to question their own 'attitudes'. The problems raised by the students demanded a radical innovation both structurally and individually. Therefore, for any seriously thinking person it was no longer possible to keep himself buried in a 'value-neutral, meaning-devoid, private, reward-expecting technical exercise'. When the students spoke of the need to deny 'Tokyo University *within* themselves', the impact reached to the intelligentia as a whole, for any intellectual living in the present establishment somehow possesses and clings to his own 'Tokyo University *within* themselves' . . .

C. True integrity – search for the true 'pathos'

As described above, the Zenkyoto students have exposed the hypocritical nature of innumerable professors including even those who had been considered 'progressive' and 'intellectual', and we have lost our true 'integrity' begetting an ever deeper 'credibility gap'. Discrepancies between official statements and the real intention or motive behind them, between theories and practices, have been exposed. We were accused of not having real passion for what we had spoken. Theories for revolution and actions for it were comico-tragically disintegrated. We were demanded to identify our words and our deeds. They cried out that historical truth is not merely 'objective', rather it demands our positive 'personal' involvement. They asked us to be 'subjective' in the sense that we take responsibility for what we had spoken. For this kind of attitude we have a word 'shutaiteki'. Though this word is translated as 'subjective', it does not mean 'subjective' in the sense that one wishfully believes in something without any efforts to verify it. For this we say 'shukanteki'. As Kierkegaard said, 'subjectivity' *(shutaiteki* and *shukanteki)* is the truth in history. Some students said that historical truth is not mere 'factum', rather it is, as Germans say, 'Tatsache'. 'Tat' means action. 'Sache' means things. Historical truth is possible only when human actions and things are united. That's why they demanded that we be 'shutaiteki' (integral, responsible and existential), not to be 'shukanteki' (wishful thinking, blind conviction and vain imagination).

What links 'logos' and 'ethos' is 'pathos', passion, 'Leidenschaft'. It is symbolic that both 'passion' and 'Leiden' mean *suffering*. Unless we are keenly sensitive to tears and blood that have been shed and that are being shed in our history we cannot really acquire true 'integrity' or 'identity'. We must always remember that the true witnessing (martureo) somehow ends up with being 'martyrs'.

Theologians and pastors have not realized what role their differentiated studies and church-centred practices are actually playing in the total structure of our society. What do our specifically theological studies have to do with the war in Vietnam? What does the Gospel for the salvation of souls have to do with the new colonialism and the new imperialism? What does the forgiveness of sins have to do with the state monopoly capitalism? What does peace at heart have to do with the new kind of suppression in the 'democratic fascist' structure? Since all these problems were not considered seriously, the Kyodan, though 'subjectively' (shukanteki) opposing any form of suppression, and therefore declaring its war-guilt, objectively supported uncritically Expo '70 in Osaka without recognizing its illusory and deceptive nature . . .

Under these circumstances, many students and young people in the Church began to seriously question what the theologians and pastors had been saying about the gospel. They began to ask what the gospel is, when it is used to justify the theologians and pastors, and what kind of actual role the Church had played throughout history particularly since the 19th century when the European capitalist nations shamelessly tried to exploit peoples in Africa and Asia, what the Church is doing now against the people of Vietnam, and so forth. When they discovered that usually those 'reactionary' theologians and pastors emphasized the 'orthodox' faith, they began to question the relation between the two. In this kind of atmosphere, many critical works that had existed so far were taken up seriously. That's why many 'practical' students who had joined the struggles at universities were at the same time very fervent 'theoretical' seekers studying carefully various representative critical approaches in the Japanese situation today. I have already written an article on 'the representative critical approaches in Japanese Situation today' for the Japan Christian Quarterly,[18] so I will not repeat it here. But we must be sure at this point that in Japan today it is no longer possible to speak about Christianity without somehow referring to all these critical works that have been developed through the course of the 'university struggles' and 'church struggles'.

The 'radicals' doubt the traditional thinking that starts with some kind of 'theological' reflection and from there deductively concludes that certain procedures are right or wrong. Setting of problems should begin with the realities and not from certain theological reflections. The course should be reversed. Our actions should begin with the very need for liberation and our theoretical reflection afterwards should examine our actions whether they have served the liberation of man or not. Therefore our theoretical (not necessarily theological, for we felt that we had to criticize the so called 'theological' approaches) reflections had to ask why and how 'reactionary' behaviour and 'orthodox' thinking are connected and whether there is an inevitable relation between the two. So we had to re-examine the whole course of church history to understand critically how the Christian message was formed and developed and spread, how it was accepted by the Roman empire and later by the ruling class in Europe, how it was used to justify the oppression and exploitation of the ruling class and how it served to justify the European invasion in the 19th century. Thus many 'radicals' have had to conclude that the Christian religion throughout the centuries has played a very powerful role ideologically, supporting and supplementing the establishment, and that the structure of its thinking has had to produce such roles.

That is to say: the Christian *religion* was born out of definitely unconscious effort to solve actual problems and contradictions by means of certain religious 'ideas'. Therefore the 'authentic' Christianity is in itself an idealistic system in which the actual state of oppression is 'sucked up' into a religious sphere and resolved as an unreal problem which can and should be overcome by 'faith'. This sort of thinking we have called 'reversal of realities by means of ideas'. We see this kind of structure already in the theology of Paul and definitely in the later Paulinism.

That is why those who want to 'escape' from 'worldly affairs' into the 'authentic' religious sphere often refer to Paul, emphasizing that the specific and original task of the Church should be the proclamation of the faith in the Saviour Christ and not the social liberation of man. In this way they repeat the age old dualism in which the religious sphere is considered to be of the true reality whereas the 'worldly' spheres are never taken seriously.

However, religion is not alone in reversing realities by means of ideas. All kinds of 'ideologies' function likewise. Unless we have very keen eyes to see the actual function of these ideologies, we are often deceived by their seemingly 'nationalistic' or 'scientific' or 'artistic' appearance. In order to have these keen eyes, critical treatments of religions, particularly of Christianity, are of great significance, because there we can see a typical case of reversing realities by means of ideas. That's why we set before us a common task of deepening our criticism of Christianity and from there a further task of sharpening our criticism of the present 'structure' as a whole.

Tsutomu Shoji · *The Church's Struggle for Freedom of Belief – An Aspect of Christian Mission*

Tsutomu Shoji, 'The Church's Struggle for Freedom of Belief – An Aspect of Christian Mission', in D. Preman Niles and T. K. Thomas (eds), *Witnessing to the Kingdom*, Christian Conference of Asia 1979, pp. 42–48

The Nakaya Case

For those who want to understand the efforts and difficulties of Christian mission in Japan, it will be helpful to know something about the struggle of Mrs Nakaya Yasuko.

On 12 January 1968, Mr Nakaya Takafumi, a soldier in the Japanese National Self-Defense Forces (SDF), was killed in a car accident while on duty. Mrs Nakaya received the news and rushed to his unit; she asked for permission to stay with the body through the night. Permission was refused. The next morning she wanted to bring her husband's body home, but this request also was rejected, and the funeral was conducted by the unit.

Mrs Nakaya returned to her and her late husband's home town, Yamaguchi city. Here now she regularly attends Yamaguchi Shin'ai Church, where her husband's ashes are kept. She found a job in an old-age home in the city and began a self-supporting life together with her son.

Four years later, Mrs Nakaya was visited by an SDF soldier who requested that she permit the enshrining of her late husband in Yamaguchi Gokoku Shinto Shrine (Gokoku means 'defence of the fatherland'). She rejected the request, declaring that she was a Christian and attended a commemorative service every year at her church. But two months after this, a letter came from the Gokoku Shrine notifying her that the Shrine would hold a memorial service for her husband, god Nakaya Takafumi, on January 12 of every year since the needed money for the annual service had been paid.

Mrs Nakaya was very surprised at this and questioned the SDF office in Yamaguchi. The answer given to her: 'It is quite proper for us to enshrine Nakaya Takafumi, for he already belongs to the public after his death. Be thankful for what we did. The enshrining is also necessary in order to raise the sense of pride among soldiers.' When she heard these words, she felt deceived, and was deeply sad. She felt that the Forces had utilized, or exploited, her husband even after his death, and had ignored her religious beliefs completely.

By this time she had recognized clearly the dangers of the SDF. After trying to negotiate with the Forces in vain, she decided to bring the case to Yamaguchi District Court. A trial began on 22 January 1973, in which Mrs Nakaya requested the end of the enshrinement of her husband in Gokoku Shrine. Many people around her, including her father-in-law, reacted against her action; they said, 'Why aren't you thankful? Selfish woman! How scandalous it is to defy the nation!'

But her church minister, Rev Hayashi Kenji, and most members of the church strongly supported her. They organized a 'Support Nakaya Yasuko Society' immediately, and appealed for nationwide support. At present, five lawyers are working on this unprecedented law suit, and more than 3,000 names are listed as members of the Society. Support for her struggle is spreading nationwide, especially among Christians, intellectuals, and labour unions. Nevertheless, Mrs Nakaya has faced and is facing many difficulties in the court case. We cannot make any easy prediction of victory.

People reduced to tools

In Japan, even today people are regarded as tools by those in power. In pre-war Japan, men were coerced into becoming soldiers by the Imperial Rescript for Soldiers: 'Consider that righteousness is heavier than a mountain and dying is lighter than a feather. Do not be branded with infamy by failing to keep your fidelity.' They were compelled to choose death rather than be taken captive. This approach, in which the powerful used the concept of 'righteousness' for their own interests and treated the lives of people as lightly as a feather, brutalised the Japanese Forces. In Mrs Nakaya's case, we discover that such inhuman tendencies are still alive in post-war Japan. Mrs Nakaya was not only denied the right to bury her husband's body; she was even forced to accept his enshrinement. All for the purpose of raising the morale of the Forces . . .

Mrs Nakaya has been blamed further because she is a woman. In her case, her father-in-law represents the social authority by which she is blamed. The idea that a woman is less valuable than a man and should obey him without claiming her own rights is still prevalent in Japan. Perhaps the most popular and harsh way to criticize a woman is to call her a 'selfish woman'. It is assumed that a woman is expected to sacrifice all her rights, even to destroy her human emotions.

Despite these accusations, Mrs Nakaya has continued to resist the worship services in memory of her husband at Gokoku Shrine. She has done so because of her faith, and one may call it a struggle for 'freedom of faith'. However, it is above all a struggle to regain human dignity or human-ness. She has rejected the use of her husband as a tool by the government. In so doing she stands on her own feet, as an independent woman, confronting the government.

Religious Character of the Tenno (Emperor) System

Gokoku shrines have been built in the capitals of each prefecture in Japan, as an important part of an apparatus to encourage people to emulate those who died in the war in loyalty to Tenno, and therefore specially honoured and enshrined as gods. The headquarters of the Gokoku shrines is the Yasukuni Shrine in Tokyo, which could be regarded as the Gokoku shrine for all of Japan. Here, before the war, Tenno presided over an annual ceremony in the capacity of arch-priest and at the same time the god of state Shintoism. Therefore Gokoku Shrines and Yasukuni Shrine provided the spiritual force for bringing and holding together Tenno, state Shintoism, and the military forces.

The character of the Tenno system, including state Shintoism, was radically opposed to the concept of human dignity and human rights. For Tenno was regarded as a 'god incarnate,' ruler 'in the line of emperors unbroken for ages eternal,' and the father of the people, while the people were his children. The duty of the people was to give whole-hearted loyalty to Tenno, if necessary even to die for Tenno and to destroy his enemies. It is quite natural that this kind of religious-nationalist ideology considered people's lives as expendable. It can be easily imagined how the people suffered under this ideology. Men were sent to the battlefield and compelled to render absolute obedience in the name of Tenno, and women were forced to rejoice in becoming 'mothers and wives of military gods.'

However, in stressing that the Tenno system demanded absolute loyalty from the people, we should not neglect another, and perhaps a more important, aspect of the system. In its religious functions, the Tenno system had a means of showing mercy and promising happiness to the people. If we overlook this aspect, we may not understand why the Japanese people could be mobilized as a unit and rushed off to war.

In the Tenno system, Tenno was considered to be the giver of materially and spiritually good things to the people. Since ancient times, emperors presided over a Shinto festival every year which was supposed to bring plenteous harvest to the people. Besides this function, Tenno, since the Meiji era, has acted as the giver of spiritual and moral values forming the norm of people's lives ('The Imperial Rescript on Education,' 1890). The people were educated to find their national identity, mental stability, and moral values through Tenno, the centre of the nation. Moreover, even when they died in the battlefield, Tenno showed mercy to them and delivered them from misery by presiding over the Shinto ceremony which honoured them as military gods.

The people who had been forced to live and die in misery found consolation in this. Therefore people who were destined to live in more tragic situations tried to find honour only through being the children of Tenno.

In June 1945, only two months before the end of the War, the residents of Okinawa resisted vehemently the overwhelming US forces despite their utterly hopeless situation. As a result, one third of the population died. Why did such a thing happen? Because they wanted to show their loyalty to Tenno and thereby prove that they were true Japanese, for they always had been despised and discriminated against as half-Japanese by people in the mainland. Even today, many families of burakumin (outcaste people in Japan) put the picture of Tenno and the Empress on their walls and revere them.

In this way Japanese people were led to cover up their own misery. This was precisely what was required of Nakaya Yasuko, to be thankful for her husband's enshrinement as god. What a distorted happiness! What a miserable salvation it is for people to find happiness through swearing loyalty even more ardently to a man who threw them into misery!

Today we live under the post-war 'Peace Constitution' or 'domestic Constitution' which restricts remilitarization and the recovery of Tenno's political power to some extent. But we cannot consider the misery under the Tenno system described above as a mere nightmare of the past. Many Japanese are satisfied with the article of the Constitution which restrains the role of Tenno within a 'symbol of integration of the people.' But the 'symbol' can be easily used by the national political power to justify and strengthen its reign. The post-war political power has continued to try to return the Tenno system to its pre-war status. The following are some of the critical issues we now face: The Yasukuni Shrine Nationalization Bill which threatens the principle of separation of religion and state; the designation of National Foundation Day based on the myth of Tenno's divine ancestors; the campaign of the Association to Honour the Spirits of the War Dead among the people; increasingly reactionary policies in education; a trend toward return to the authority of the pre-war Imperial Rescript on Education issued in 1890, which based education on loyalty and obedience to the emperor; and a bill to provide a legal basis to the Imperial era name (Gengo) system. These are the means by which the state is attempting to achieve national integrity among the people, and they run parallel with recent policy of strengthening national military power.

Japanese monopoly capitalists are now eager to develop the armaments industry in order to get out of the economic depression and at the same time to defend their economic interests in Asian countries. An 'emergency legislation' for a time of war is now the subject of the most intense political debate in Japan. People are not very conscious of this critical situation for they, on the one hand, are driven to seek better living conditions and, on the other, are in a mood of apathy and irresponsible agreement.

Another problem of the Tenno system is its exclusivist character. State Shintoism, with Tenno at the summit of its structure, had been originally the religion of each village in primitive society, and was integrated politically as the state religion by the Meiji government. The character of state Shintoism was quite different from that of a universal religion such as Buddhism or Christianity, in that people revered and served gods of their own groups. This religion was applied to a large modern nation and thus caused an irrational self-assertion or self-absolutization of his children, i.e. the people of Japan. People of other nations were thought to be less worthy, and could be subjected to defeat, discrimination, and assimilation. Yasukuni Shrine and Gokoku shrines performed a crucial function in nourishing this idea of national self-assertion. Here there is no room for developing a sense of encounter with people of other nations as people, a sense of co-existence based on mutual respect.

This tendency has continued even after state Shintoism was dissolved by law after the war. In the summer of 1978, Yasukuni Shrine publicly announced that it has enshrined 27,800 Taiwanese and 20,000 Koreans who died as Japanese soldiers during the war, and recommended that their families come to the shrine and worship them. Families of victims from Taiwan and Korea have started demanding that the Shrine withdraw their enshrinement, aware that the Japanese not only had compelled their relatives to go and die in battle in the invasion of Asia, but are now using them after their death to romanticise and legitimise the war. Chief Yasukuni priest Mr Ikeda answered by saying, 'Since they joined the war as Japanese willingly, it is proper for us to enshrine them. Most of their families are satisfied and thankful.'

In the circumstances we must ask ourselves whether the Japanese are really able to regard other Asians as persons and therefore truly share with them. We have to ask ourselves if there is any essential difference between our recent commercial expansion, endangering the lives of Asian people, and the past military invasion in which we severely ill-treated our Asian brothers and sisters.

The Churches' Struggle as Part of Christian Mission

The churches in Japan could not organize any effective resistance against the state policies of war and suppression of people. But during the post-war years we became more and more aware of our guilt and our responsibility, and we began to fight against the revival of the Tenno system ideology. As soon as manoeuvres toward the nationalization of the Yasukuni Shrine began in the late 1950s, the churches started resisting. The 'Society for the protection of Freedom of Belief' was organized in the NCC in 1961. This society rallied other religious people, intellectuals, opposition party members, and labour unions, and has no less than five times blocked the Yasukuni Shrine Nationalization Bill. The United Church of Christ in Japan (Kyodan) in its 'Confession of War Responsibility' in 1967 sought forgiveness from the people of Japan and Asia for the fact that the Church did not perform the role of watchman during the war, and affirmed its determination to struggle against the forces of aggression in the future.

Christians were concerned initially to protect the freedom of faith guaranteed in the post-war Constitution, but gradually they realized the implications of the country's economic invasion of Asia, militarization, and the Tenno system with its ideology which supports militarization. With this broadening of their insight, they have now a deepened understanding of the Gospel and of the salvation which Christ offers as the true basis of their struggle.

Christians in Japan have thought of the Tenno system as simply the worship of a pseudo-god or idol, and advocated worship of the true God. But to many in Japan this is tantamount to adding a new deity to the pantheon of many existing gods. Thus it waters down the Christian claim and challenge. Therefore it becomes important for Christians to answer the question: What in fact is an idol? It is an object of human worship which deprives man of *jiritsu* – the ability to stand on his own feet. Man then becomes its tool or slave and with fear and yearning pledges his loyalty to it.

The true God, however, calls man to *Shutaisei* – autonomy – through His revelation; and He liberates persons so that they can stand on their own feet.

Yahweh, when leading the people of Israel from Egypt, where they were slaves, forbade them to worship idols, and demanded that they appropriate the freedom given to them. Jesus proclaimed the Kingdom of God to the poor and the oppressed, and let those suffering from disease and evil spirits stand on their own feet and be themselves.

Today the distortion of faith into idolatry can occur not only in the Tenno system but also in relation to many other things. Our acceptance of dictatorial leadership in a nation, our dependence on the power of big companies and armament, and our reliance on the GNP myth are all varieties of idol worship. In Japan these factors can be more dangerous than in other countries because they can be combined with the Tenno ideology.

This understanding of God and idolatry needs to be realized more thoroughly by seeing it in the context of people's lives.

Tenno is quite similar to Christ in his function in giving grace to people. He has been thought of as being god incarnate, dispensing mercy as a saviour. But Tenno is in truth the one who has benefited by the sacrifice of other people. For example, he and the government leaders around him, though they knew the hopelessness of the war situation, postponed its termination for several months and caused the death of hundreds of thousands of Japanese and other Asians, only in order to obtain a guarantee from the Allied Powers of the maintenance of the Tenno system after the war.

What do the life of Jesus and his death on the cross tell us about the character of the Tenno system? Jesus was the one 'who, though he was in the form of God, did not count equality with God a thing to be grasped, but emptied himself taking the form of a servant, being born in the likeness of men. And being found in human form he humbled himself and became obedient unto death, even death on a cross.'

Christ experienced and tasted the misery of the people as his own, and died on the cross. In so doing he completely became the servant of the people, and therefore became the Lord of all creation.

Perhaps we may say that it is a characteristic of Japanese churches that they have acquired and cherished in a special way an understanding of the suffering of Jesus. One of the examples is K. Kitamori's 'Theology of the Pain of God,' which was written during the difficult years of the post-war period. This theology fits in with the sense of the 'painfulness' of life which the Japanese have embraced through their long history of Samurai rule and militarism. But this sort of understanding of the Christian Gospel was largely confined to the psychological and personal level and did not open the eyes of Christians to the social realities which had brought misery to the people. Therefore the concept of salvation was also confined to that level.

In addition, since the church's struggle to grapple with social realities begins with the modern concept of 'freedom of belief', its role has been largely at the intellectual level, attempting to enlighten people who are again turning to the ideology of national integration, understood in the closed and traditional Japanese sense. It is far more important for the church to be sensitive to the uneasiness and anguish of the people who are caught up in the ideology and policy of national integration. During the last war, too, the churches did not recognise the people's agony which was hidden behind their obedience to state policy. In failing to do so the churches did not minister to the people in their misery. Furthermore, they themselves succumbed to the temptation of national integration.

Rev Hayashi of Yamaguchi-Shin'ai Church once said in an

appeal for support for Mrs Nakaya, 'I ask you to listen sincerely
to the sorrow of Mrs Nakaya. Any theory or action for protecting
human dignity will never be real or effectual if you fail to listen
to the deep sorrow of this one person.' Only when we live with
those who are in sorrow can we see Jesus with them, Jesus who
makes them able to stand on their own. In this sense, activities
on the local church level are very important. Christians in many
areas are struggling for the separation of city authority and Shintoism and have close contact with people in distress. These Christians are the real bearers of the Anti-Yasukuni movement.

Churches in Japan will face more and more difficulties in their
struggle, but only through these difficulties will they know the joy
of following Jesus. For this struggle, we believe, is an integral
aspect of our Christian obedience. Through it we are involved in
mission.

3 · China · Hong Kong · Taiwan

China

The forces which everywhere in Asia have hindered the formulation of an indigenous theology have been especially strong in China. They include the continuing cultural domination (until 1949) by colonial powers, the unquestioned identification of the Christian faith with wholly Western formulations and the progressive destruction of Chinese religious or cultural traditions. This imposition of European or North American tribal theologies may have been inevitable in view of the high proportion of lay missionaries – often with little theological background – working in China, and of the failure of most Christians, whether Chinese or expatriate, to identify with nationalist or revolutionary aspirations after 1911. A small number of missionaries were the exception in their positive response to Chinese culture (James Legge, Timothy Richards and Young J. Allen in the nineteenth century), or in their development of indigenous patterns of ministry and mission (John Nevius, Roland Allen and Vincent Lebbe until the 1930s). The work of these, along with their Chinese colleagues, would be an essential element in preparing for the independence of the Chinese church in the later Three-Self Movement.[1]

The anti-Western movements of the mid-1920s, in part provoked by the 'unequal treaties' which still granted legal privileges to Christians, led some missions and churches to further nationalize their work. And it was in this setting, in a time of acute national disorder, that a genuinely contextual theology arose in China. Advocates for the indigenization of Christianity were in that decade chiefly concerned to show that the church was not just a foreign imposition but was in tune with Chinese culture. Yet central to this concern for indigenization was the encounter with

urgent social issues and the pressing urgency of national reconstruction. The credibility of Christian theology largely depended
in fact on its contribution to national reconstruction, and a number
of creative churchmen devoted themselves to articulating this
contribution.[2]

Hsu Po-Ch'ien (YMCA Secretary, university lecturer and village leader, d. 1944), as much in his life work as in his writings
embodies the unity of knowledge and practice found in both
neo-Confucianism and Christian faith. The unity of 'mind and
hand' of Wang Yang-Ming, and the unity of loving service and
spirituality in Jesus Christ, directly provide the motivation for his
many years of work in rural reconstruction. And his many writings
– on Christian mission, nationalism and reconstruction – reflect
this lived unity of knowledge and practice.

For T.C. Chao (Dean of Religion at Yenching and a president
of the World Council of Churches, d.1979), Christianity was, as
for Hsu, the basis of social reconstruction. Yet reconstruction, he
believed, must follow the transformation of the people through a
purified and indigenized Christianity. In the 1930s he comes to
criticize Western capitalism, but rejects Marxism also, along with
any direct political involvement. In many books and articles however, he provides a full theological basis for such involvement,
concerned for 'the future of the church in social and economic
thought and action'.[3]

A more sharply revolutionary position is that of Wu Lei-Chuan
(who was later President of Yenching, d.1944). In his extensive
writing Wu grapples especially with the conflicts between individualism and collectivism, between reform and revolution. To take
Jesus seriously as a social reformer means for Wu that Jesus'
personal sacrifice for His people becomes ours. National salvation
can therefore only come through participation in a shared struggle.
In 'Christianity and Chinese Culture' (1936) Wu affirms that Jesus'
first concern was social justice, which is now possible in China
only through communist revolution. In less than twenty years Wu
Lei-Chuan along with many other thoughtful Christians felt driven to this conviction, by events, by the gospel and by the demands of their own culture. Others equally active in education or
reconstruction, in ecumenism or church administration during
1930s and 1940s, stopped short of this, however, and voiced in
their writing a vigorous nationalism that included proposals for
the indigenizing of Christianity. Among these were internationally

known ecumenical leaders like Cheng Ching-Yi, Koo Tse-Zung (T. Z), Lui T'ing-Fang (T. T), Wang Cheng-Ting and Yui David Z. T.[4]

It was left for Wu Yao-Tsung (a secretary of the YMCA and the SCM and first General Secretary of the Three-Self Movement, d. 1978), to play a key role in theology and in church leadership, making the theological struggles of the pre-liberation period the foundation for a truly Chinese Christianity. Y. T. Wu never wavered in his conviction that Jesus' way of love provided a principle for Christian action and the form for co-operative social action. But in the face of national evils and the 'contradictions of the capitalist system' mere reform becomes manifestly inadequate. From his conversion in 1918 until the writing of 'Christianity and Politics' (1947), he comes step by step to the affirmation that Christians and Communists can largely agree on goals even though a Marxian revolution is only the first step in the fundamental reconstruction of people and society which Christianity demands. By 1947, he is convinced that a socialist revolution offers the only answer to social and economic needs. Yet he maintains, 'the Gospel of Jesus is an eternal challenge to this world'.[5]

As leader of the emerging Three-Self Movement, Y. T. Wu, along with Premier Chou En-Lai, drafts the Christian Manifesto (1950) which provides the basis on which the Protestant churches are to enjoy comparative religious freedom until 1965. Its two central themes, the elimination of foreign influence, and the role of a self-reliant church in nation-building, had been articulated by Wu many years earlier: they would be important themes in Christian writing for almost three decades. Yet in the period prior to the Cultural Revolution period, many other theological issues were tackled. There may be a noticeable simplification in theological statement along with an acceptance of theological diversity in for example the creed adopted by Nanking Seminary in 1954. But articles in *T'ien-Feng* (the journal of the Three-Self Movement) show at least four major issues upon which, as the Methodist Bishop Kaung said in 1957, God is providing 'new light for new times'.[6]

In place of a widespread attitude of world-denial among Christians, the world is to be loved for the sake of the gospel, and a conference of Christians in Wenchow (1956) affirmed this at the end of their discussions. Regarding church and state relations, Kiang Wen Han (also of the YMCA) accepts the central role of the state, in a biblical study of the issues, but the state, he says, is never free from corruption. Christians can obey a government which serves the people but where this is not so a conflict of loyalties could occur. The distinction between belief and unbelief was often the subject of extended discussion, by for example, Edmond Hsu (1950), Marcus Cheng (1957) and Ting Kuang Hsun. In the fullest treatment we have of the theme, Ting declares that atheism is also an opiate, and that for the believer, sin arises not only from the social system but requires also personal redemption.[7]

In dealing with a fourth issue, the relation of faith and works, it is clear that for some, salvation comes now only through labour. But in Y. T. Wu for example, the Marxist unity of theory and practice recalls Christians to the interdependence of faith and works in the gospel, where both are equally required. In these and many other articles and statements the theological re-orientation of which K. H. Ting speaks below is clearly being forged. *T'ien Feng* was discontinued in 1964, and there is little evidence of extensive theological reflection until interviews and letters again became possible in 1973. One exception reported in a Shanghai Daily[8] throws brief and tantalizing light on the process by which the gospel was raising its own questions in secular socialist society. A group of worker-students in a Shanghai steel-plant publish their studies of European philosophy showing that Christianity was indeed a religion and social philosophy of the poor and oppressed, even though it was quickly distorted for their own purposes by reactionary classes. The emphases here are not far different from those reported by visitors able to talk with Chinese Christians in the 1960s and 1970s – at the centre of both is a Jesus who possessed nothing, a worker among workers, dedicated to and finally dying for, the uplift and liberation of all people without distinction.

Amongst those whose thought first became known outside China since 1976, Chao Fu San (now Deputy Director of the Institute for the Study of World Religions in Peking), produced a historical study of Christian missions in the light of post-1919 movements in China.[9] And Kiang Wen-Han has issued two volumes in his lengthy history of Christianity in China. But Ting Kuang-Hsun's own work provides the fullest source thus far for study of Chinese theology of the last few years. In interviews given as Principal of Nanking Seminary, in 1973 and 1975 for example, he had stressed the new shape of Chinese Christianity

– free of foreign domination, completely self-reliant, identified with the Chinese people, and non-institutional. K. H. Ting had earlier (1957) written that to find strength in weakness is a spiritual task; a 'poor self-supporting church' had discovered that Christ was still Lord of all life. It was to be a prominent note on the series of sermons and lectures given by him during a lengthy visit to Canada and the USA in late 1979.[10]

The lecture, from which a section is here given, highlights some points of theological re-orientation amongst many that are emerging in the work of Ting and his colleagues.

Hong Kong

Despite the pervasive presence in Hong Kong of the People's Republic of China, there is little recognition by the Christian community of Hong Kong of the extent to which they maintain the highly institutionalized and unreflective patterns of mission long rejected by China. In the setting of Hong Kong's highly exploitative society, nineteenth century pietism and moralism, and the role of comprador to colonial overlords (in for example education and welfare) are accepted unquestioningly. On the other hand what has been termed a theology of diakonia does sustain a diverse community involvement for some churches.[11] In Chung Chi College, part of the Chinese University of Hong Kong, staff members like Ng Lee-Ming have made thorough studies of recent Chinese theology. And at Tao Fong Shan Ecumenical Centre a fifty-year tradition of study and religious dialogue in Chinese religion and culture continues in the writing of Peter Lee King-Huan and Deng Zhaoming. The programme and the journal of the Centre provide one of the few forums for continuing work in Chinese contextual theologies and for discussion and co-operation with Christians in China.[12]

But it is from industrial mission that much lively theological reflection has emerged in Hong Kong. In the Hong Kong Christian Council's Christian Industrial Committee a commitment to labour education, negotiation and direct action is linked with Bible study, evangelism and theological reflection. The explicit purpose of Raymond Fung and the committee's workers is to both combat the worst injustices in Hong Kong's largely unregulated industries, and to form worker's congregations in a consciously proletarian church. In meditations, reports and articles, Fung and his colleagues have therefore developed a localized theology of industrial mission, of spirituality, evangelism and of a 'gospel of the poor'. The paper selected here, although first given at a World Council of Churches Consultation, conveys the thrusts in such a theology.[13]

Taiwan

Historically often a part of China, Taiwan has nevertheless ethnic and cultural differences and a unique Christian tradition of its own. The Japanese occupation of 50 years (until 1945), and the rule by Martial Law of the Kuo Min Tang since 1949, have been less significant for this tradition than the identification, over more than a century, of significant sections of the church with the aspirations of native-born Taiwanese. In addition, Christian mission in Taiwan has not been associated with colonial domination (apart perhaps from massive American presence since 1949!), so in theology the necessity to reject Western models has not appeared so sharply as in China.

For Roman Catholics, impetus in the contextualization of theology came from the 'New Voice of Clergy' group (1949–62) and later from the policies of Vatican II.[14] For Presbyterians (the largest Protestant church), and for related churches, Tainan Seminary has played a key role. Concern for tribal groups, for industrial mission, community development and evangelism has been nourished there by vigorous biblical study, as well as by imaginative social and evangelistic programmes such as those initiated by John E. Y. Cheng. Huang Chiong-Hui (Shoki Coe), Principal of the Seminary in the early 1960s, pioneered much of the world-wide discussion of contextual theology itself.[15] Song Choan-Seng, whose report of theological events since 1971 is reproduced here, followed Huang as Principal, and is one of the most prolific and creative of Asian theologians today. In two major books and a score of articles he has elaborated an Asian theology which he terms 'the love of the God-Man in action'. The character of the church's statements in this decade is as Song depicts, that of a biblical confession reluctantly arrived at, yet maintained as integral to the gospel of love and justice and peace.[16] No one embodies the calm faith and resolute prophetic witness of Taiwanese Christians in these years more than Kao Chun-ming, General Secretary of the Presbyterian Church since 1969. In his sermons, Reports to Assembly, and now letters from prison, the central concern is that the 'total fact of Jesus' life' will be known in the physical and mental labours of mankind. Many within and beyond his church share such a theology, and share his work for the Taiwanese homeland in which justice will be known by all.[17] A number of younger pastors and lay leaders are now contributing to creative theological reflection on the present Taiwanese experience. The extract chosen describes this work.

Ting Kuang-Hsun · *Theological Reorientation*

Ting Kuang-Hsun, 'Theological Reorientation in China', *China and Ourselves*, Canadian Council of Churches, Toronto, no. 20, May 1980, pp. 14–18

I think it is quite warranted for me to say that the Chinese Christians constitute that part of the world's Christian population which has entered a new and unique stage of history, the stage of doing away with exploitative systems and of building up socialism in a country which is poor and which has hitherto been semi-colonial and semi-feudalistic. Our response to this transition may be just as momentous and significant as the Reformation during the transition from European feudalism to capitalism. Therefore, to Christians the world over who take to heart seriously the fate of Christianity in the future world, ours may be considered a sort of laboratory whose experiments they cannot afford to miss. This is so not because ours is a big strong church, but simply because history is such that it is we who have been put in that exciting situation.

There are roughly three million Roman Catholics and 700,000 Protestants, Anglicans and Orthodox in China. Before the liberation, there were side by side strong strains of evangelicalism, neo-orthodoxy and the social gospel within Protestantism. It may be helpful to those of you who are younger to know something of the international theological-political orientation of those days, because Chinese theology then was to a very large extent an appendage of that orientation.

When in 1951 I went back to China from Europe, I went there from a theological milieu that had also very much invaded the Chinese scene. I think the following two quotations are very representative of the political-theological thinking of those days.

Here is a statement given by Dr. John C. Bennett in a study pamphlet on the Responsible Society, published by the World Council of Churches Study Department in November 1949. He said (let me add it is not important that he said it, because the statement was reflective of something that was being said by many): 'The conviction most widely held among the member churches of the World Council of Churches is that Communism as a movement which has its base in the Soviet Union and through Communist parties is seeking to extend its power throughout the world, should be resisted both politically and spiritually, and the churches in the countries associated with 'western democracy' should give moral support to their governments in their efforts to check the extension of communist power. . . . The whole ecumenical community, whatsoever differences there may be among its members about policies in particular nations, should recognize that it has a responsibility to do what is possible to prevent the world from coming under Communist domination.'

Another statement was given by Bishop Dibelius of Berlin and published in the Ecumenical Review of July 1956: 'Perhaps the ecumenical movement is the prelude to a general theological or non-theological mobilization of all the Christian churches against the materialistic ideology of the East.'

These two statements probably can give us some idea of the political-theological atmosphere of those days. There was also a lot of talk about the utter depravity of man and the diabolical nature of human collectivities.

Before I left Geneva for China in 1951, I was invited by Dr. Kraemer to go to his study to have a heart-to-heart talk for the last time. I remember very well the last statement he said to me as he held my hand. He said: 'Always put a question mark to whatever a communist says and does.' So I went home to liberated China with this question mark in my mind.

In new China, when Christians were faced with the tremendous political reality of the People's Liberation Movement and of the new People's Republic, I found that all our isms somehow were forced to come out into the open in political terms. Aside from a small number of western missionaries and Chinese church leaders who could see something positive in the people's movement for liberation and wanted to identify themselves somehow with the people's struggle for liberation, I must say all schools of theological thought were found to be on the side of political reaction. Christians were made to pray for Chiang Kai-Shek, the model Methodist, and when the People's Liberation Army was about to cross the Yangtze River, prayers were offered in churches that God would perform a miracle so that the soldiers would drown in the river. Christians were sent to preach on the streets wearing special clothes to make themselves noticeable, warning people of the imminent second coming of Jesus Christ to destroy the world. Within that political set-up, to destroy the world meant really to destroy the People's Liberation Movement. We found that all the strong doses on original sin, on the fallen state of the world, on the meaninglessness and absurdity of history, on the complete separation and antithesis of grace and nature, on the so-called pride in human works and on justification by faith could very easily be turned into a sort of antinomianism which in the name of faith gave blessing to any sort of political stance required by the Kuomintang[18] and U.S. policy. After the liberation of Shanghai, there were Kuomintang bombers that went from the islands near Shanghai to bomb the city. A man supposed to be the leader of a very devout evangelical group organized a band of people to give signals to the bombers from the ground. This man is treated in some circles in North America as a martyr because he was put in jail for this and other crimes. But we in China haven't thought of him as a martyr or someone who had to suffer persecution because of his Christian faith. We have thought of him as a collaborator with the Kuomintang and someone who has committed very serious crimes against the People's State.

The rank-and-file Christians in China are mostly members of the working classes. They didn't have much to lose in the liberation but a lot to gain. They found that the People's Liberation Army was a very disciplined army, entirely different from what they were told. So naturally they were unwilling to follow their reactionary church leaders. The Social Gospellers were not so reactionary politically. Some of them were good exposers of the darkness of the moribund society, but they could advance no programme for change except a few reformist measures which really prettified the Kuomintang status quo and they didn't seem to be able to offer any message that could hold the Christians together.

As to the Roman Catholics, orders came from the Vatican that they should do nothing to support the war effort of the People's Republic in its assistance to North Korea. At a time when there was a very high upsurge of patriotic feelings in our country, the sacrament was denied to those who took part in patriotic activities. Roman Catholic parents were not allowed to let their children wear red scarves, which were a symbol of the popular young people's group, the Pioneers. Even the buying of citizen national bonds was condemned as a sin. So, many Roman Catholic priests who were patriotic felt a strong pressure on their conscience. Many dioceses were being run by western bishops who had to leave under those circumstances. But Rome refused to appoint new bishops for these dioceses. So, in 1958, the Roman Catholic Church in China began to elect and consecrate its own bishops. There are forty or fifty bishops of this kind that have been consecrated without the approval of Rome. I don't know if Rome would take such a stiff attitude today, but I am talking about the 1950s. The conflict was very severe.

So it became very clear to us in those days how political theology really was. I myself began to apply the Kraemer question mark not just to the communists but to many others too.

However, Chinese Christians felt that there is something in Jesus Christ that makes us unwilling to depart from Him. 'Thou hast the word of eternal life, to whom shall we go?' That seems to be the thought that existed in the minds of many Chinese Christians. In spite of all the political reaction that had appeared in the name of Christian faith, we felt there is something in Christian faith that speaks to us about things more ultimate than what the newspapers were talking about, and that speaking we need to hear. We were greatly humbled by the revolutionaries in China, but we felt that the gospel does give us some assurance of things not seen, but real to us nevertheless, no matter how vaguely we could express it. So that's the beginning of our theological struggle, a struggle to keep the Christian faith, but also one against its being used as an obstacle to social change or made a tool of political reaction. It was sort of knitting our theology, or reknitting it in our new environment.

Now to be very brief, there have emerged mainly two theological approaches. The first type still makes theological thinking revolve mostly around the axis of belief and unbelief. The world is still essentially evil and Christ is still somebody extrinsic to this world. Yet, necessary adjustment is made so as to be possible to affirm something of what is happening in new China.

A colleague of ours in the Nanking Theological College was a good representative of this kind of adjustment. He used to talk a lot about the imminent coming of Jesus Christ, denying any value in what was being done by man on this earth. But he began to realize that what the Chinese people were doing in new China was something that he, as a Chinese and as a Christian, wanted to affirm. What could he do about it? He did some *partial* adjustment. He began to tell us a story about a carpenter who was an ardent believer in the immediate second coming of Jesus Christ. Somebody asked this carpenter: 'How can you reconcile your belief in his imminent coming with the fact that you try to do so well in your carpentry? Since Jesus Christ will be coming tomorrow, why do you still have to make strong and durable desks and chairs?' He answered, 'I want to prepare my soul so that I could meet Jesus Christ tonight or tomorrow, but I must work with my two hands as a carpenter to produce furniture that would be good for use for a hundred years or even five hundred years.' This story represented his attempt to arrive at some sort of reconciliation between his pre-millenarian faith in the imminent return of Jesus Christ and his desire to affirm what human beings in China were doing. Later he took a further step by becoming a post-millenarian and taught that Jesus Christ would return to this earth only *after* one thousand years of peace and prosperity. Friends rather welcomed that change because, although it wasn't very satisfactory theologically, he allowed a space of one thousand years for Christians to affirm what is happening in new China. The efforts he made deserve our sympathy but, as you see, this sort of adjustment is necessarily temporary, partial and reformist.

Many other Christians began to engage in more fundamental theological reconstruction. We began to think much more about how large the area of God's concern and God's care is. We shift away from the belief – unbelief antithesis to a greater appreciation of what God is doing in history. God is not an infinite being extrinsic to our human world or apart from human life and history. He is a living, immanent, ever-working God. Creation is not an act completed in the past, in six days or in six thousand years, but a continuing evolution. And the end-purpose of creation is the emergence in the universe of a truly free humanity in the image of God. When we say 'in the image of God', we especially have in mind God himself in his nature of being a community. That is, this new humanity will freely and on its own accord choose to live in community with each other and with God, and then that humanity will be like God; and that is the consummation of history. Creation is an act of God, but it is very much an educative evolutionary process. This world is God's not Satan's. Christ is not an intruder into the world alien to God, but is the first fruit of all creation. He is unique, but also akin to us organically because he himself is the perfection of that which all of us possess as our birthright as human beings, as sons of God. He is unique not because he stands against or stands in contrast with the world process, but as an exemplification of the fullness with which he reveals the nature and the potentiality of the world. Although we say he came down from heaven, we do so with the same kind of mental reservation or lack of it when we talk about the rising or the setting of the sun. And we seem to feel that there is a pre-given engracement of all people through the incarnation of the Son of God. He unites himself to every man and woman in some fashion and, therefore, you will find Chinese Christians not only talking about the Redeemer Christ, but more now about the Cosmic Christ, the Incarnational Christ, Christ as the crown and fulfilment of the whole creative process, the clue to the meaning of creation, the One whom we find very much talked about in the New Testament, especially in the Fourth Gospel, in Colossians and in Ephesians. And in this way we think that many contemporary thoughts and movements are not in contrast with the divine revelation or destructive of divine revelation, but rather means of illuminating that revelation. They are not adversaries but glimpses and foreshadows of the way of Christ. In looking at reality this way, we think we are not diminishing the unique significance of the Christ, but are magnifying his glory and confirming his claims.

We are deeply impressed by the fact that Christ showed very meagre interest in specially sacred doings. We are impressed by His profound interest in the most ordinary doings of secular life. He was interested in lilies and birds, in the sowers and the seeds, in women and children, in a father with two sons, in the fishermen, in baking of bread by the housewife,in the merchant seeking pearls. He didn't aim at turning us away from the natural order and from the world, but used them to enable us to discover in them manifestations of the truth about God.

Now a world which can be used so often to teach us about God cannot be an entirely fallen one. If there is a total disparity between man and Christ, then incarnation would not be possible. We think that to say that man has fallen is really to say that he is not at present in his proper state, the state to which he ought to belong, the state for which he is made. And this verse in Romans Chapter 5 has become very real to us in China: 'For if by the offense of the one man all dies, *much more* did the grace of God and the gracious gift of the one man Jesus Christ abound for us.' We like to emphasize 'much more'. In other words, we are born not only in original sin but in original grace as well. It is inconceivable that the incarnation of the Son of God should make less of an impact on humanity than the fall of Adam. Too often, we have made original sin universal but have particularized or narrowed redemption and divine grace as though Adam had succeeded in carving his name deeper on humanity than had Christ. We surely think that our human solidarity with Christ is more universal, more decisive, and more efficacious than is our solidarity with Adam.

These probably tell you some of the changes that have happened in our minds. We think that what humanity does in history is not going to be simply and totally destroyed or negated at the end of history. Our work will be received, sublimated, transfigured and perfected. In this way we see the worth of what our Chinese people are suffering and striving for.

In this light we see that the dominant pre-liberation Chinese theology was a reflection of our alienation from our own people. Revolving itself around the axis of belief and unbelief it was very useful to bring about enmity between Christians and the revolutionaries who are mostly non-believers. Today, after thirty years, it has shifted to a more appreciative language of practice. We have to abandon certain conceptual frameworks in which we have felt secure for many years. But as Kierkegaard said, 'It is good once in a while to feel oneself in the hands of God and not always and eternally slinking around the familiar nooks and corners of a town where one always knows a way out.' That seems to be the experience of many Chinese Christians as we discover the immanence of the transcendent God in history, in nature, in the people's movements and in the collectivities in which we find ourselves. After all, the God who is worthy of our worship and praise is not so small as to be concerned only with a few million Chinese who profess to believe in him. God's love and care is for the whole of humanity and the whole of the Chinese people. He does not mind terribly much if many, for good reasons, do not recognize his existence. We know that to believe that God is loving and at the same time almighty is difficult anyway, if one is serious about one's belief. But I think liberation in China, with all the material and cultural elevation it has brought to our people, does make it more possible for our people to ponder on such a God. We hope we are able gradually to be an instrument of introducing this God to our people.

Another very important area of re-thinking is in connection with the church. As you know, the Chinese churches were imported from the west and, therefore, it was something western in the eyes of our Chinese people. As far as we Christians ourselves were concerned, we were more or less proud of it. But after the liberation we came to realize that, although many missionaries went to China with the intention of helping and evangelizing China, the missionary movement happened in a stage of history when the west was penetrating China economically, politically and militarily and this movement could not but have a de-nationalizing effect. We want to live down that part of history so that we can be a suitable instrument for bearing the Christian witness. Our movement to promote self-government, self-support and self-nurture is exactly aimed at overcoming that effect and making the churches in China just as Chinese as churches in Canada are Canadian and those in U.S.A. are American.

Another change is that our churches are much more de-institutionalized than yours. I don't mean that we thought about it and decided to de-institutionalize, then proceeded with it. But as we look back, we think that in institutional Christianity, faith is very often replaced by a search for security. Institutional Christianity tends to exist for itself. Perpetuation of itself requires it to unite with the powers that be and become a part of the status quo. It binds men to the dead past. Its investments and bonds are a symbol of the indentification with the social order which it is supposed to question. Institutional Christianity seems to us to sacralize the cultural, social and political structures of domination. Therefore, Christianity in its institutional expressions is often the very denial of the gospel it affirms. It gets in the way of man's vital communication with Jesus of Nazareth and with each other. Prophetic voices do arise in the church here and there, now and then, but only in spite of itself. So de-institutionalization seems to Chinese Christians to be something valuable. It came to many of us as an experience of loss. It was difficult and painful when we had to part company with our universities, colleges, hospitals and orphanages. Something felt to be important to us seemed to die. And yet, through this death, a Christian finds that he is living more intensely, not less so. It is actually an authentic working out of the things that are most important to us as Christians from the very start. And religion as the legitimation of the status quo becomes somehow a catalyst for social change. That is cause for rejoicing.

Now ours is a very small and weak church, of course, and we do feel that international contacts can be a great help to us. We would like to have more of them. But we like to see that international contacts should not mean the undoing of our experiments and the dismantling of the laboratory.

Song Choan-Seng · *God's Politics of Construction*

Song Choan-Seng, *Third-Eye Theology*, Lutterworth Press and Orbis Books, Maryknoll, New York 1979, pp. 219–221

Statements of the Presbyterian Church in Taiwan

We have already made mention of the Christians of South Korea and the Philippines and their struggle for justice and freedom. Another example can be cited to illustrate how God's politics of construction is at work in the midst of the politics of make-believe. This is the case of the Christians of Taiwan. I am here referring to the 'Public Statement on Our National Fate' issued by the Presbyterian Church in Taiwan[19] on December 30, 1971. For a quarter of a century the Nationalist government on Taiwan had been practising the politics of illusion. In 1945 it had emerged from the tragic war of resistance against Japan as a victor, having sustained cruel devastations and an enormous loss of life. But the civil war with the Communists flared up again quickly, giving the Nationalist party no time to recover from the war of resistance against Japan. This time the Communists were victorious. In confusion and chagrin the defeated Nationalists fled to the safety of Taiwan, an island separated from mainland China by the hundred miles of the Taiwan Strait. The tide of history had definitely turned against the Nationalists, but they refused to face the historical reality of their situation. As a result, the international and domestic policies of the Nationalist government were based on two claims: (1) that it was the sole·legitimate government of China, and (2) that its sacred duty was to liberate the mainland from the Communists. In the early days of its exile in Taiwan, these two claims were real and urgent enough to constitute rallying points for the people. But as time went on and nothing came of them, the claims began to lose their impact. They became mere words that had no relationship to reality. And in proportion to the loss of real meaning in these claims, their ideological rigidity was intensified. They became dogmas defying any challenge to their validity or authority. They were elevated to the status of sacred cows that devour anyone who dares to interfere with them. Open alliance to these dogmas became the test of correct thinking and loyalty to the ruling authorities.

Then came the expulsion of the Republic of China – the official name for the Nationalist government – from the United Nations in the winter of 1971. This blow shook the whole island like a hurricane buffeting a small ship at sea. After almost thirty years the people awakened from a bad dream to realize the vulnerability of Taiwan's international situation. There was a great deal of heart searching, especially among university students and teachers. They understood quickly that their national destiny was at stake and that they could no longer entrust their future to a one-party government without a murmur of complaint. But as a Chinese saying goes, misfortune is seldom unrepetitive. Even as a fierce battle was being fought at the United Nations in New York City, United States Secretary of State Henry Kissinger was negotiating in Peking with the rulers of Communist China. An early result of these negotiations was President Richard M. Nixon's visit to China, which the Japanese called the *Nixon shokku*. This put an end to Communist China's isolation from the rest of the world. President Nixon himself later called his visit to China 'a week which changed the world.' The confusion and panic on Taiwan could hardly be suppressed. And in this critical situation the Presbyterian Church in Taiwan, as mentioned, broke its long silence and took the unprecedented action of issuing the 'Public Statement on Our National Fate.'[20] It spoke aloud what the people of Taiwan were thinking and perhaps even what many enlightened Nationalist Chinese officials were thinking too.

The church's statement was, in the first place, an appeal for the unity of all the people on Taiwan regardless of their origin. It affirms the desire of the people of Taiwan to live in peace, freedom, and justice. It rejected an attempt on the part of foreign powers to take over Taiwan. And it claimed in no uncertain terms the right of self-determination for Taiwan. In the words of the statement:

> We oppose any powerful nation disregarding the rights and wishes of fifteen million people and making unilateral decisions to their own advantage, because God has ordained and the United States Charters has affirmed that every people has the right to determine its own destiny.

In this assertion of faith in a specific political situation, God's politics and human politics were joined in the politics of self-determination. The 'self' that here claimed the right to be directly involved in the settlement of Taiwan's political future was not a wilful self-seeking to gratify its own private interests. It was rather the self created in the image of God, and thus it shared the anguish and glory of all humanity. This self was thus inviolable, just as the image of God is inviolable.

The last part of the statement was pointedly directed to 'the leaders of the Republic of China,' that is, the heads of the Nationalist Party. It reminded them that this critical moment had to be grasped as an opportunity to commit themselves to justice and freedom and to a 'thorough internal renewal.' It boldly called for a general election through which a new government might come into existence to charter the future course of Taiwan. It voiced its conviction that the democratization of political power was a true, sure way to a secure, hopeful future for Taiwan.

Once the Presbyterian Church in Taiwan had set out on the course that caused its members' involvement in God's politics, the church became aware of its growing ability to say what had to be said about a political situation that continues to be critical and vulnerable. The immediate question facing the people of Taiwan had to do with the fear that they might be abandoned by the United States, which was beginning to pursue, both openly and covertly, the goal of normalizing its relations with Communist China. And yet there was no sign that the ruling party of Taiwan would take effective steps to ensure the independence and freedom of Taiwan. The only thing the people could hear was the government's hollow claim to be the sole legitimate ruler of mainland China.

On August 16, 1977, the Presbyterian Church in Taiwan published another public statement, 'A Declaration on Human Rights.' Its occasion was the political uncertainty caused by the Nationalist government's stubborn refusal to change its policies in spite of the United States government's new attitude toward Peking. The Declaration, published when Mr. Vance, Secretary of State of the Carter government, was about to make his Peking visit, made it clear that self-determination was a right of the 17 million people of Taiwan which could neither be ignored nor taken away without serious consequences. It expressed the determination to oppose any use of force on Taiwan by Communist China. The Declaration then concluded with words that came right from the heart of the people, even though they could not have been spoken previously without a serious threat to those who proclaimed them.

> In order to achieve our goal of independence and freedom for the people of Taiwan in this critical international situation, we urge our government to face reality and to take effective measures whereby Taiwan may become a new and independent country.[21]

The die was cast. It was now up to the government either to take 'effective measures' by which the independence and freedom of Taiwan could be secured, or to resort to its usual 'repressive measures' once again in order to silence the voice of the great majority of the people on the island state of Taiwan. No wonder the Declaration was drafted and made public only after much prayer.

What we have seen here is God's politics of construction at work through the Presbyterian Church in Taiwan. We must reject as a fallacy the concept that politics must be left in the hands of professional politicians and the ruling authorities. Since policies and the political behaviour of those in power directly affect the well-being of a people and their destiny, each person in a nation should be both the subject and the object of political decisions and actions. There is no question that an involvement in politics is both a right and a duty of responsible citizens. Christians, who are citizens of this world and partners in God's politics of making all things new, have no reason to give up their political rights or to avoid their political duties. For our God is a political God.[22] And above all ours is a God who judges repressive powers, con-

demns tyranny, and puts down the authorities that have become
an instrument of evil rather than of good.

Raymond Fung · *Evangelism Today*

Raymond Fung, 'Evangelism Today', *Change*, Newsletter of the Christian
Industrial Committee, HKCC, October 1979

When Christians talk about evangelism, we think of a person as
a sinner, rebelling against God, needing repentance, and in response, receiving forgiveness. This is as it should be. But I want
to stress that a person is not only a sinner, he is also the sinned
against. I would like to stress that for the purpose of evangelism,
the fundamental reality of a person is that he or she sins and is
sinned against. If evangelism seeks to speak to the very depth of
a person through the proclamation of the Gospel, evangelism
must recognize and deal with the fact that a person is an object
of sin as well as a subject of sin.

When I refer to the 'sinned against', I would leave open the
specificity of the question of 'by whom'. Suffice it to say that it
has to do with the principalities and powers of the world, demonic
forces which cast a bondage over human lives and human institutions, infiltrating their very textures. I am using this rather broad
understanding because I do not wish to exclude in our consideration of evangelism the reality that the poor are sinned against by
economic and political systems; neither do I wish to exclude the
reality that the affluent are sinned against by the same or less
identifiable forces. My emphasis at this point is that people are
not only wilful violators of God's will, they are also the violated.
This realization must have a bearing on our evangelism. To the
sinner in the person, the Gospel says, 'Know your sinfulness. Bow
in humility before God, and receive forgiveness'. To the sinned
against in the same person, the Gospel says, 'Know that you have
value. Stand in defiance against the forces which deprive you of
it, and receive strength.'

I do not think I need to argue that man is sinned against. The
Scriptures are full of references to this effect. And daily experience confirms it. But somehow we have missed taking this fundamental human condition seriously, if at all, into our evangelistic

consideration. In our evangelistic messages, we deal with man the sinner but not man the sinned against. We talk about the bondage of sin, but we only pay lip service to it, believing that individual piety can set our lives and institutions free from the principalities of this world.

This very shallow understanding of sin, in my opinion, is damaging to evangelism. Let me make a few observations out of my experience in Hong Kong in particular, and Asia in general.

1. A Gospel which does not address man as the sinned against poses no problem for those who do not feel that they are the sinned against – mainly people in the upper brackets of society, people who benefit from the social, economic and political system. Sinned-againstness is not part of their experience. And so, looking at themselves, they can honestly say, 'We have become Christians because of hearing the Gospel, and the same has made us prosper. What can be wrong with it?' They do not acknowledge that they are the sinned against, or for that matter, that anyone is the sinned against.

2. A Gospel which does not address man as the sinned against poses a lot of problems for those who are the sinned against – mainly the poor. There are often two kinds of responses from the poor to the Gospel – outright rejection of the Gospel, or, accepting this Gospel, accepting also the sinned against fate as something outside of the bearing of the Gospel. In the first case, no evangelism takes place. In the second, religion serves as an opiate.

Let me illustrate with an experience. As a result of helping out in a labour dispute, I came to know a textile worker in his early forties. He would occasionally come to my office for a chat when he worked night-shift and could afford the time. At one point, we touched on the subject of Christianity, and he tried to provoke me, in a friendly way, by dismissing it as a foreign religion. I asked him if he had ever read the Bible. He admitted that he had not. So I told him to shut up, also in a friendly way, and that until he did, he had no right to criticize my faith. He said 'Okay, I don't want to read the Bible because I don't read books anyway. But I will come to your church for once.' I was caught and couldn't say no. He did, the coming Sunday, at the cost of a day's wages. After the service, he took me to lunch and he said, 'Well, the sermon hit me.' It had been about sin. 'You know, what the preacher said is true of me – laziness, a violent temper and addiction to cheap entertainment. I guess he was talking about me all right.' I held by breath, trying to keep down my excitement. He continued, 'But there is nothing there about my boss – employing child labour, not giving us legally required holidays, putting on false labels, and forcing us to do overtime.' My heart sank. Not simply because this friend of mine is most unlikely to go to church again, but more because there are quite a number of factory owners in the congregation who should benefit from the texile worker's observation.

An evangelistic message which does not speak to the sinned-againstness of man does not speak to those who have been sinned against. Furthermore, my friend the textile worker might agree with the diagnosis of the church, 'You are a sinner,' but he rejects the church which provides the diagnosis.

Given the middle-class character of most churches, at least the middle-class character of those who control the articulation of the evangelistic message, the Gospel which ignores man the sinned against may work among the middle class. (This is happening in some parts of Asia, especially among the ethnic Chinese in urban centres, but not quite – witness the dropout rate of those who fail to go on to universities, the professions or executive-level jobs). But it cannot possibly work among the overwhelming majority in Asia – peasants and workers who are the poor. The evangelistic message which deals with man as the sinner but not the sinned against, coming from a middle-class institution whose members benefit from the status quo, simply conveys too much superiority, condescension, yes, even pity, to make sense, let alone to become credible to those who suffer indignity and injustice every day. The one element necessary in the message and its transmission is absent, namely, *compassion*.

When I look at the Scriptures, I find that compassion is the key element in the Good News of Jesus Christ, and in the way he communicated the Good News. I discover that every time the Gospel talks about Jesus having compassion on the people, he had compassion on the people primarily because they were the sinned against.

Matthew talks about Jesus going ashore and seeing a great throng, 'and he had compassion on them, and healed their sick'. And Jesus told his disciples to feed the people. 'I have compassion on the crowd, because they have been with me now three days, and have nothing to eat and I am unwilling to send them away hungry lest they faint on the way' (Matthew 14:14; 15:32). Luke paints a similar picture. When the Lord saw her, a woman whose son just died, he had compassion on her and said to her, 'Do not weep' (Luke 7:13). And when the Samaritan saw the man beaten and wounded by robbers, 'he had compassion, and went to him and bound up his wounds . . .' (Luke 10:33). The parable of the prodigal son makes the same direct connection between compassion and man as the sinned against. Luke reports, 'But while he (the son) was yet at a distance, his father saw him and had compassion, and ran and embraced him and kissed him' (Luke 15:20). And when Matthew summed up the work of Jesus in the first stage of his ministry in Matthew 9:36, he put it this way, 'When Jesus saw the crowds, he had compassion for them because they were harassed and helpless, like sheep without a shepherd'. In short, Jesus had compassion on people because they were the sinned against. And yet, even more significantly, immediately after this summary, Matthew recorded Jesus' appeal to his disciples for evangelism: 'The harvest is plentiful, but the labourers are few; pray therefore the Lord of the harvest to send out labourers into his harvest.' It is clear that the call to evangelism is a response to the call to having compassion on the sinned against. Mark, in his corresponding passage in Mark 6:34, omitted the 'harassed and helpless' reference, but he made the necessity for compassion in evangelism even more clear. Mark reported, 'Jesus saw a great throng, and he had compassion on them, because they were like sheep without a shepherd; and he began to teach them many things.'

I think I am prepared to make a bold suggestion: that compassion for people is possible only when we perceive people as the sinned against. If we look at people as sinners (as distinct from the sinned against), we may have concern for them, affection or pity, but no compassion, i.e. 'suffering together with another, fellow feeling, sympathy' (Oxford English Dictionary). Many evangelists of today have little perception of people as the sinned against. Most evangelistic activities are devoid of compassion. We must recover compassion in our evangelism. To do that, I think, we need to sharpen our understanding of people as the sinned against, not in a behaviouristic sense, but in a theological sense, in terms of sin, the domination of sin, and of our 'struggle against sin . . . to the point of shedding our blood' (Heb. 12:4).

How do we come to understand people as the sinned against? Again, let us look to Jesus. If we go back on the passages I just quoted, we will find that every single reference to compassion informs us that Jesus saw the people. Jesus saw the people, Jesus saw a great throng. The Lord saw the woman whose only son was about to be buried. Jesus saw the crowd. The good Samaritan saw the half-dead man. The father saw the wayward son and had compassion.

So we must see the people at close range. We must be near them so that we can feel their pulse, and read their sighs. So near that the people become 'you' and not 'they'; they are those right in front of us, whose eyes we must look into, whose voice we cannot but hear, and whose very presence lays claim to our friendship. In short, we must be involved. I would submit that this is the way we can come to understand people as the sinned against, and the way we can begin to be compassionate. I cannot over-emphasize the importance of compassion in our faith and in the communication of our faith. Compassion, not the popular unexamined notion of being sentimental and soft – but in the proper sense – suffering together with, fellow feeling, sympathy. Compassion is important because it is the way to live out the Christian life, and because it works for evangelism.

Compassion is important to the Christian life because there is the element of suffering in it, and suffering is what makes the church authentic. If the church is to be the church, it must have the marks of Jesus Christ upon it – the marks of the beatings, the nails, and the crown of thorns – the signs of the cross. With this, the church is authentic, not only to God, but also to those who suffer, people who are sinned against.

Compassion is important to Christian life and evangelism because there is the element of involvement in it, and the compassion born out of involvement bestows authority on our word and our deeds. When John the Baptist sent his disciples to check on Jesus' messiahship, Jesus answered them, 'Go back and tell John what you hear and see: the blind see again, the lame walk . . . and the good news is proclaimed to the poor.' So Jesus based his authority on his involvement with the poor. He who gave up equality with God and entered into human suffering has a special right to be heard. And Jesus was heard. He spoke as no scribes spoke. It seems all too clear then that if an evangelistic message is to have authority it must be based on experience of involvement. It must come from persons who know what they are talking about when they speak of comfort and of judgement.

Thirdly, compassion is important to evangelism for a strategic reason. Since compassion presupposes fellowship with the sinned against, the sinned against, even before they decide to be Christians, are already inside some kind of a Christian community. So, the communication of the Gospel takes place in a context of trust and solidarity. The non-believer can judge Christianity at work from the inside, and not from outside looking in. Compassion on the part of the Christian enables the non-believer to examine Christianity from within rather than from without. It invites people to look at Jesus as 'you' rather than 'him'. This is how faith in Jesus Christ becomes possible.

Two experiences are illustrative of the above. I was present when an evangelist, having been invited by his factory manager friend, preached to shopfloor workers on the theme: 'Man does not live by bread alone', over a loudspeaker system. It was plain that, without really listening to him, the workers thought he was talking nonsense. Next day, the loudspeaker wire was found cut. Yet, the same scripture, given by an industrial missioner, found positive acceptance. 'Right, poor as we are, money is not everything.'

On a separate occasion, I was invited to a luncheon meeting of a group of prosperous managers. They had some interest in evangelizing their workers. I told them that Jesus had to humble himself and become a human being before he could reach men and women with the Gospel. What made them think they can do the same to workers from their managers' glassed-in offices? (I also told them that their job is to evangelize their fellow managers, and learn how to be a Christian in a manager's role.) This is an extreme case, but I hope it illustrates why compassion for the sinned against is so important to biblical and effective evangelism.

I am aware that without actually announcing it, I have been focusing more and more on the poor whose sinned-againstness is obvious. That is because I happen to know something about the poor in Asia. I'd like to think too that the theological understanding of men and women as the sinned against, the attitude of compassion, and the method of involvement are also applicable in the evangelization of the affluent. Sinned-againstness is part of their reality, too, maybe less obvious to others or to themselves. But it is there. Evangelism must therefore deal with this aspect of their life if the Gospel is to be fully meaningful, if the affluent converts are to see that they share the common destiny of the

sinned against with the world's poor, and if they are to understand
that while they are the sinned against, they are at the same time
sinning against the poor. So I would like to suggest that the
concept of the sinned against is applicable in the evangelization
of both the poor and the affluent. After all, the evangelistic message to the poor and to the affluent is basically the same message.
The call of the Lord that those of low degree be exalted is the
same call that the proud be scattered and the mighty put down
from their thrones. The promise to the hungry that they will be
filled with good things is the same promise to the rich that they
will be sent empty away (Luke 1:47–55). The Lord's command to
the paralyzed man 'Rise, take up your bed and go home' is at the
same time a reminder to the scribes of the evil in their hearts
(Matthew 9:1–8). The parable which tells the unemployed that
the master of the vineyards cares for them is also the parable
which shows those who have already made it, their own selfishness. So the evangelistic message, in compassion, says words of
comfort to the sinned against, and the same becomes words of
judgement, also said in compassion, to the sinning. Conversion
depends, and begins, on their separate response. In this way, the
evangelistic message coincides with the prophetic message. They
are indeed the one and the same message. The evangelist and the
prophet are the same person.

What about the 'sinner' or the 'sinning' aspect of the poor, the
sinned against? Shouldn't evangelism deal with that, too? Yes, of
course, the poor are certainly sinners. Evangelism must help a
person come to a knowledge of his own sinfulness, and of the fact
that he must have a personal relationship to the Lord and Saviour
Jesus Christ. I have not talked about this at length up to now
because the concept of the sinner in evangelism is fairly well
accepted. I have, however, described the abuse of it in practice
as I observe it in Asia. But the question remains: in the case of
the poor, what is the connection between his realization of his
sinned-againstness and of his own sinfulness? In my experience of
ten years working among industrial workers, sharing their struggles and asking them to share my Christian faith, I believe strongly
that there is a relationship, and a direct one. When the Gospel
addresses itself to the sinned-againstness of a person, that person
will also allow the Gospel to deal with his own sinfulness. Or from
the perspective of that person, awareness of his sinned-againstness
comes first, followed by awareness of his sinfulness. I am not

saying that the process will complete itself every time. Much depends on the Gospel's human agent and the person's response. But there is enough evidence in the Urban Rural Mission experience in Asia to support the validity of this evangelistic process.

I am ready to suggest that in evangelism, especially of the poor, we focus primarily on man as the sinned against. This is not to take lightly the fact of sin, this is to take sin seriously, in all of its deadly forms. This is not to absolve a person from personal responsibilities, but on the contrary, this is to make him see how he can be personally responsible.

Finally, what does the Good News do to man the sinned against? The Gospel does not do away with the powers which sin against man. It does not provide ready answers for their destruction. What the Gospel does is to demythologize these powers so that man the sinned against can be clear about them, get hold of them, see himself in relation to them, and see his own sinfulness in the very midst of these powers. In short, evangelism to man the sinned against frees man to deal with the powers which sin against man, and it also frees man to deal with his own sinfulness. In practice, the evangelistic focusing on man the sinned against means a community which identifies with and accepts non-believers on the basis of sinned-againstness, and in the common struggle against the forces which sin against man, confronts all those involved in the struggle of their personal sinfulness, and experiences God's forgiveness and Christian oneness.

4 · Philippines

Major sources for the development of Filipino Christian theology
are found in the nationalist movements arising after 1870, in the
ministries of social diakonia and action of 'mainline' and independent churches alike, and in the lay and religious movements working for societal transformation and the Filipinizing of Christian
life and thought. All can be seen as responses to colonial or
neo-colonial oppression – whether of Spain (1521–1898), the
United States (1903–1941) or Japan (1941–46) – and to the severe
social and economic injustices which have persisted and in many
cases sharpened in recent decades. Along with the active redis-
covery of Filipino culture and national identity, it is this continuing
experience of oppression that shapes all creative theological reflection in the Philippines since 1946. It is therefore this quite
concrete context of suffering which must first be felt if Filipino
theology is to be understood.

Policies of forced labour, which rendered friar and official
odious through more than three centuries are no less vicious
when applied today in the sugar plantations of Negroes. Leaders
of worker and peasant organizations may not be garotted, but
their mutilated bodies are regularly discovered after forays by
land-owners or Philippine constabulary. The vast aggregations of
land by the friars have long been surpassed by the landlords of
today so that by 1972, 60% of national wealth and land was owned
by 0.003% (!) of the population, and the eviction of whole communities is the frequent accompaniment of industrial installations.
The punitive taxes of the Spaniards have their equivalent in the
sales taxes which today supply 75% of government revenue, and
are largely paid by the poor.[1]

Behind such summary descriptions lies a reality that must be
entered into as we read sermon or letter, treatise or liturgy, so

that Filipino theology be allowed to make its own confession within its own history. But for Christians in particular, a further reality must be faced. A version of Christian doctrine is explicitly used, as it had been by Spanish and American overlords alike, to justify such inequities in the name of a supposed 'Christian truth', 'order' and 'development'. And more directly than in other Asian countries, both oppression and revolution have been in Filipino history 'Christian' phenomena. By mid-century it had become even more clear that prophetic social criticism was integral to Filipino theological reflection which in turn was itself one of the first steps in the achievement of socio-economic justice.

Foundations for a contextual theology can therefore be traced to the social apostolate of Catholic orders and the ecumenical and social ministries of major non-Roman churches. From Catholic Action (1925) to the establishment after 1946 of many Social Action Centres, and the nationwide activities of the Federation of Free Farmers (1953), there can be discerned the steady development of a coherent social doctrine. In the 1960s this nourishes serious theological construction – in barrios, as much as in seminaries or lay movements. Impetus also came from the attempts of Hilario Lim and Ambrosio Manaligod to develop indigenous leadership and theology for the Filipino Church.[2] In the case of related Protestant movements, a similar emergence of prophetic thought can be seen in the agencies working for land-reform, co-operatives, and for labour education. Vigorous leadership was provided here by Fidel Galang in the disturbed Pampanga districts, and by Valentino Montes, Richard Poethig and Henry Aguilan in projects of the National Christian Council of the Philippines.

Attempts by President Garcia in 1957 to reduce foreign economic control (represented by the Laurel-Langley agreements of 1954) and by Diosdado Macapagal to radically reform land-ownership (1963) had been largely defeated. Both problems increased during Ferdinand Marcos' first term as president, as did public disorder, government corruption and widespread economic injustice. Echoes of a growing concern for Filipinization and for social justice can be found in statements by the United Church of Christ and the Iglesia Filipino Independiente (the independent Catholic church born in the revolution of 1898–1903). But no consistent policies on such issues emerged either from them or from the many Protestant and Catholic sects which arose as religious and political protest movements.

By the mid-1960s a group of able pastors and educators were articulating a Christian 'responsibility in the streets' (Eliezar D. Mapano), a biblical basis for criticism of the State and the commitment to social justice (Cirilo A. Rigos) and the historical and secular setting for Christian mission (Emerito P. Nacpil). And within a few years a systematic development of field education in four seminaries led to the formulation of an 'Experiential Theology' (Ciriaco Ma. Lagunzad) for everyday life.[3] By the end of the decade a multiplicity of groups and movements were actively promoting Christian reflection, along with community education or social action.[4] A strong stimulus for this was provided by radical traditions in Filipino literature, in politics and in scholarship and by the careful research of social scientists working in urban and barrio areas.[5]

Substantial theological work was also now being done by a number of Jesuit theologians closely identified with lay and ecumenical movements. Notable among these were Horatio de la Costa (d. 1977), a noted church historian and first Filipino Provincial of the Society; Vitaliano R. Gorospe, Professor of Theology and Philosophy at Ateneo de Manila University; and Catalino G. Arevalo, Principal of the Loyola House of Studies. De la Costa's widely-read studies on the Filipino national tradition established this firmly as the context for the church's mission in all human development which allows the people to be agents rather than victims. Action for justice is a constitutive dimension of the gospel, for de la Costa, a process whereby 'the transcendental truths of the evangel are realised in the temporal order'.[6] Gorospe also makes a special study of Filipino culture, and in his work on moral theology stresses the powerful impact of not just individual but collective sin, in a society rent by extremes of wealth and poverty, exploitation and violence. This requires, he believes, a theological renewal, which is, in part, to 'develop a theology of organised violence (against property) on behalf of the poor and oppressed'.[7] Arevelo, who is also a Theological Consultant to the Vatican, has concentrated much of his work on the contemporary form of Christian mission in a secular world. In a key document he develops John XXIII's interpretation of the 'signs of the times' – the aspirations and struggles of ordinary men and women – outlining a theology 'that drives to action' in the promotion of justice. Salvation, he writes elsewhere, only comes through 'the operative practice of charity', and 'the first endeavour of charity is to establish the regime of justice'.[8]

Related emphases can be seen in the writings of Catholics like Bishop Julio S. Labayan, Pedro Salgado OP, Antonio Lambino SJ and Mary John Mananzan OSB, and of younger Protestant theologians like Feliciano Carino and Nael Cortez. It is Carlos H. Abesamis SJ who has most clearly placed biblical studies in the context of contemporary Filipino history and culture. A biblical theologian who teaches in a diversity of seminary and non-formal courses throughout the archipelago, Abesamis maintains that it is 'the mighty questions of human life in the contemporary world which act as the initial catalyst to (biblical) enquiry'. To do theological reflection is to 'describe the present moment in the history of redemption', and requires a commitment to be 'in some real way part of the life and struggle (spiritual, psychological, social)' of the people. So the most important question regarding culture is not 'Am I a European-American or am I Filipino?' but 'Am I putting on the mind and culture of the modern regenerated anawim or not?'[9] Abesamis expounds the biblical and historical basis for this approach with a clarity that owes much to the many lay and religious movements with whom he works.

Growing unrest at the extreme inequalities in Philippine society was met by the declaration of Martial Law in September 1972. Marcos has since ruled entirely by presidential decree, enforced by an array of military and paramilitary agencies against whom numerous charges of torture and brutality have been sustained. After eight years of this 'New Society' a staggering 69% of Filipino families now exist below the poverty line, the official minimum wage being only one quarter of that required by a family with four children. 35% of the work-force is unemployed or underemployed and one in every three children suffers from malnutrition. Yet the national budget allocates only 3.6% to Health, 0.82% to Agrarian Reform and 0.32% to Social Services. This has provoked a growing protest from both Catholic and mainline Protestant bodies. Despite widespread censorship, a stream of literature has come from the Conference of Bishops, the National Secretariat for Social Action, the National Council of Churches, the Wednesday Fellowship and especially from the Association of Major Religious Superiors.[10]

In response to such conditions, what may be termed 'rice roots' theology has emerged also from many people movements in which the seminal influence of the Federation of Free Farmers is apparent. Largely as a result of FFF work, a body of theological reflection by the peasant farmers themselves has been collected by Charles Avila. The long imprisonment of many lay people and priests during the last eight years has led to a flow of letters, poems and stories, now collected in the volume, *Pintig: Life Pulse In Cold Steel*. The numerous masses and acts of worship held by movements for human rights and justice or in protest against Martial Law have also produced countless liturgies and meditations which reflect a continuous theological engagement.[11] Lay leaders such as Jovite Salonga and Jose Diokno have given courageous leadership in movements such as the Civil Liberties Union, and in their addresses and writings.

The extracts which follow are written by three who do much to demonstrate the approach outlined above. Formerly a Professor of Systematic Theology, Edicio de la Torre has been since 1967 closely involved in the formation and leadership of movements dedicated to radical land reform and the establishment of a socialist society. Just prior to the declaration of Martial Law in 1972 he was largely responsible for the formation of the national and ecumenical 'Christians for National Liberation' and its Theological Writing Collective. His addresses and other writings have been issued only in booklet or mimeographed form, but even after his imprisonment (in 1974), these have been widely circulated within and beyond the Philippines. They reveal a skilful blend of biblical and liturgical exposition with detailed social and political analysis.[12] In earlier pages of the lecture from which the first extract is taken, he summarizes the challenges which Maoist thought and practice presents to the Christian.

Francisco Claver has been Bishop in troubled Mindanao since 1969 and deeply concerned with, for example the problems of agrarian reform, Muslim-Christian reconciliation, and with the violent destruction of tribal homelands in the Chico valley. In a number of incisive analyses he has publicly condemned the Martial Law policies of Ferdinand Marcos, and upon the suppression of radio stations and newspapers in his province (1976), began to issue weekly pastoral letters on the life and death issues of 'the little people' who are being daily imprisoned and murdered. The letters are in fact scathing homilies on the continuing Passion of Christ, and advocate a civil disobedience which, says Claver, is 'the violence of the meek'.[13] The extract chosen is from one of a series of lectures relating the gospel to public issues, given during Lent 1976, entitled 'An Offering to the People'.

Levi Oracion is a theological educator who has also participated fully in dialogue with student and youth movements and in such citizen's forums as the Wednesday Fellowship. In his series of Bible studies on the theme 'Jesus Christ Frees and Unites', he discusses current understandings of liberation. This, he affirms, is both a liberation on the level of meaning, when the truth of Jesus on which a man stands comes to expression in him, and on the level of power, in a radical questioning of oppressive powers which favour the rich. For Oracion love is 'a being and becoming where theology is concretely encountered and experienced'. It is through concrete acts of love and care for the poor that we return to the origins of Christian theology.[14] The address reproduced here was first given to the Wednesday Forum, meeting regularly in Manila.

Edicio de la Torre · *The Filipino Christian: Guidelines for a Response to Maoism*

Edicio de la Torre, 'Maoism and the Filipino Christian' in R. J. Bonoan (ed.), *Challenges for the Filipino*, Theology Series no. 2, Ateneo de Manila University Press 1971, pp. 23–31, and *The Passion, Death and Resurrection of the Petty-Bourgeois Christian*, Kilusang Khi Pho Ng Pilipas Readings 1977, pp. 5–8

In line with the spirit of Maoism, I will not discuss Christian response immediately in academic and theoretical terms, basing myself on books and publications about Christian-Marxist dialogue abroad. I will try to present the reflections of Filipino Christians actually engaged in the struggle for national liberation in the Philippines.

What do I mean here by Filipino Christian? I mean somebody who considers himself *Filipino*, who is determined to stick it out in the Philippines and who has responded to the challenge of Philippine reality in one form or another. At the same time, he considers himself a *Christian*, with all the vagueness that accompanies the term, especially in relation to the nationalist struggle (a mixture of traditional belief in God and some philosophical, political and moral concepts).

The people I refer to arrived at their commitment in various

ways. Some initially reacted to an overwhelming experience of
the problem; some reacted initially to a supposedly anti-Christian
danger: Maoism; still others found their commitment as a concrete
direction of the enthusiasm they felt from Christian renewal seminars. Whatever the origins of their initial commitment, they now
share two basic impulses: an impulse to nationalism – to serve
their countrymen, and an impulse to revolution – to serve their
countrymen by instituting radical structural changes in Philippine
society.

The questions they ask are basically two: (1) We are nationalists; what is Christianity's role in nationalism? (2) We are Christians; what is our attitude toward Maoist nationalism?

The Christian attitude toward nationalism

The first question is really the primary one, and it coincides with
what commentators have written about Mao. Revolutionaries feel
first the challenge of the situation as a nationalist challenge. Ideology and theology come later. Again, we need to stress what
should be obvious: all seminars and talks on 'theology of revolution,' 'political theology,' and other current theologies make sense
only to one who has started to act and has started to reflect on his
actions. Theology as such does not breed commitment. At best it
can remove hindrances to commitment.

One of the hindrances is the Filipino Christian's hesitation about
explicit nationalist involvement. He realizes that personal acts of
helping people who are suffering are not enough; that poverty
and suffering are results of structures and systems best labelled as
neo-colonial. Hence revolutionary nationalism (as distinguished
from tradition-bound nationalism) is the concrete expression of
love for promoting his brother's dignity. But 'nationalism', even
as a term, seems to be directly opposed to Christian
'internationalism'.

The 'Christian nationalists' have found enough solid theological
basis for their nationalism, especially the central doctrine of the
Incarnation. 'Christ is God-become-man, in order to save men.
Don't talk therefore of Christianizing the Philippines. Talk first
of Filipinizing Christianity. Christ must become Filipino if Filipi-
nos are to be Christians.' But the very fact that they have to prove
what should be taken for granted reveals the major challenge of
Maoism.

Can a Filipino Christian, as Christian, wholeheartedly and enthusiastically accept nationalism as Mao does[15] instead of considering it reluctantly as a necessary but not desirable involvement? It seems that the colonial origins of Christianity in the Philippines and the continuing predominance of Western sources and writers prevent Christianity from being what it should be – incarnate, not in a Western people but in the Philippines.

The initial demands of such painful birth are parallel to Marxist-Leninism's Sinification: language and peasants (the main bearers of national consciousness).

But these are not enough. Nationalism, if it is to be an effective movement and not just a romantic recollection of an idealized, primitive past, must be mainly concerned with changing inadequate structures, leaders, and concepts – it must be revolutionary. But revolution calls for ideology.

The Christian attitude toward Maoist nationalism

Now, Maoism, or more concretely, the national democratic movement, presents itself as the most vocal and concrete programme and ideology. What posture should the Christian nationalist adopt toward it? Does he have a Christian ideology? Is Christianity itself an ideology? Here, both historical experience and inadequate theological education have caused the Filipino Christian more than normal confusion.

In the past Christianity has been practically identified with certain systems and has become an ideology, a cultural captive and apologist either of feudalism or colonialism. (Perhaps split-level Christianity[16] is but a reflection of our semi-feudal and semi-colonial society.) Nationalist revolution, then, against the rulers of the old order is branded not just subversive but heretical (i.e. unchristian).

As a reaction to such political absolutism, many Christians swing to a-political liberalism. They refuse judgment (modestly claiming incompetence) on any socio-political system and worry mainly about private morality with some excursion into public life when individual or corporate religious privileges are threatened. But such seeming lack of judgment is really consent by silence, as is evident in the rather righteous condemnation of an alternative system whether socialist or not as subversive and unchristian and atheistic.

Reacting against such inadequate presentation of Christian political involvement, Christian nationalists have arrived either formally or implicitly at what might be called a 'political theology'. Again, contrary to petty-bourgeois impressions, political theology does not give a programme or ideology; it simply frees people from false choices and gives guidelines for proper choices. What are its basic outlines?

1. Christianity is faith, not ideology. The Church is not a party. There is no such thing as *the* Christian system, *the* Christian party or programme, *the* Christian ideology or even *the* Christian organization.

2. Hence, the worst error a Christian can commit is to be so satisfied with a system as to identify it with Christianity. This was a 'sin of commission' for many Christians in relation to feudalism. But its reverse – 'sin of omission' (consent by silence) – is the more current fault in relation to liberal democracy.

3. What should be the proper attitude? The basic attitude of a Christian should be to be critical and dissatisfied with any system and to express it (making sure that criticism includes self-criticism because he, too, is part of the system). Here the theme of the pilgrim Church, never established, always on the way to the Kingdom, is very appropriate. This is the the same attitude expressed by the 16 Bishops of the Third World when they wrote:

> Nevertheless, throughout her historical pilgrimage on earth, the Church is in practice always tied to the political, social and economic system that in a given period ensures the common good, or at least an ordered society. So much so that sometimes the Churches may seem to be fused with such a system, united as if in wedlock. But the Church has only one bridegroom, and that is Christ. She is in no way wedded to any system, least of all to the 'international imperialism of money' *(Populorum Progressio)*, any more than she once was to the monarchy and feudalism of the Ancien Régime, any more than she will be in the future to some form of socialism . . . As soon as a system ceases to ensure the common good to the profit of some party involved, the Church must not merely condemn such injustice, but dissociate herself from the system of privilege, ready to collaborate with another that is better adapted to the needs of the time, and more just.[17]

Here, the Filipino Christian faces the Maoist challenge again.

How critical has he been of the present system? How concrete and analytic has been his criticism? How vigorous and passionate has been his indictment of the present injustices? Certainly Maoist nationalists can hardly be accused of consent by silence.

The record of the organized Churches is even more pathetic. We have selective protest which comes a bit late and moderately. Christ's driving the moneylenders from the temple or John the Baptist's protest against Herod would be branded 'imprudent' today.

4. But is criticism enough? No. One must also choose alternatives. Here the question comes again. How should a Christian choose? From among what choices? What would be the basis for his choice?

(a) The Christian must make a political choice. He cannot take refuge in a 'moral' pronouncement that has no political effectivity.

(b) But he must not take the name of God in vain. He cannot simply brand one choice 'unchristian' or promote the other as 'Christian'. This calls for the basic critical posture that I described above. All his choices can only be provisional, not absolute.

The basis of his choice of a programme, party or system, cannot be authority or terminology. 'The Pope says so' or 'Mao said that' cannot be the primary basis for choice. Love seeking to promote the greatest dignity of men should be his main guiding principle.

(c) But to make this principle concrete, he must examine the different proposals of science and ideologies: what economic system, what political system, what methods? Here he must examine all proposals and choose (with the possibility of error) that which the majority would understand and accept as promoting human dignity. Maoism and the national democratic programme is one of such proposals.

We can say therefore that under concrete Philippine conditions a Filipino Christian cannot make a Christian political choice if he does not seriously examine the challenge of Maoism, not just as a stimulus to dedication or as a co-critic of society, but even more, as a concrete proposal for showing effective love to his fellow-Filipinos.

For in the final analysis, to take the challenge of Maoism seriously is to take Incarnation in Philippine society seriously; to

concretely analyze concrete situations and to side with the oppressed people in their struggle for liberation, not as a self-
appointed leader but as a servant of the revolution . . .

Call to Repentance to Petty Bourgeois Sinners

To combat this unchristian superiority complex, we emphasized
the call to repentance, a very basic biblical theme. Christians
should continually be self-critical and should even be ashamed
that others have participated in the struggle for national liberation
much more resolutely and with greater sacrifice. But it did not
seem to be enough. The other youth organizations in the MDP[18]
helped us find the answer. They had also been trying to define
the role of youth as youth, perhaps partly because of that cliche
from Rizal's works: 'Youth is the hope of the fatherland.' Then
they realized that roles are determined principally by class analysis. Hence their decision to engage principally in cultural revolution. Why? Because they are petty-bourgeois.

Suddenly, our feet were on solid ground again. We had started
up in the air with consciousness, rather than social conditions. We
started with the term Christian and got confused, since we could
not even be sure that it meant one and the same for a Christian
landlord, a Christian tenant, a Christian capitalist, a Christian
worker, a Christian Metrocom or a Christian NPA.[19]

We forgot the principal scandal and good news of Christ, 'a
man in everything except sin.' No wonder we were like Pharisees:
'We thank you, God, that we are not like the rest of men. We are
not subject to class analysis. We are not affected by class interests.
We are moved only by theology and ideas. We only need to be
informed about the issues and we will immediately act in favour
of the poor.' This is the meaning of repentance: to admit with the
publicans: 'Have mercy on us, O Lord, we are sinners. We are
petty-bourgeois.' We are both petty and bourgeois.

Why sinners? Because we had unwittingly given proof of the
radicals' complaint that Christians obscure class divisions and
preach class reconciliation (Alinsky: 'Reconciliation means I am
in power and you get reconciled to it'). Of course even the radicals
themselves do not always practice class analysis. They mistrust all
actions of the PBSP and NFSP[20] because their membership is
capitalist and haciendero, yet they would still appeal to Cardinal
Santos and other bishops, not realizing that they are not only

church officials (and presumably acquainted with Vatican II and the encyclicals) but also landlords and capitalists.

Why sinners? Because we had thought of Christianity as a middle class, petty-bourgeois cross. We thought we were witnessing the class struggle between exploiters and exploited from a non-partisan, as yet uncommitted, middle-class ground. Hence we could postpone our optional involvement while we hesitated and carefully weighed the consequences of our decision. Hamlet's soliloquizing, 'To be or not to be'. But we were already partisan, bourgeois, no matter how petty. We were the servant class of the upper class.

Ideologically, we thought that we could find a middle mean between bourgeois capitalism and proletarian socialism and called it Christianity. Yet it was still bourgeois, except for its pettiness. And our middle-class position prevented us from immediately helping the proletariat, because we thought their style of collective action was Maoist while our concern for manageable personal groups was Christian.

Crucifixion, Death and Resurrection

And the mistakes that accompanied their collective acts made us draw back and postpone commitment, while waiting for a pure, sinless revolution. So we crucified ourselves on a cross of our own making, wanting to love, to serve the people, but always holding back because we might be used, because it might violate our principles, and so we loved 'pure and chaste from afar.' Virgins who loved too wisely but not too well, afraid to risk, waiting for immaculate conceptions and virgin births of plans, organizations, movements, societies.

It is terrible to realize how human one is. How painfully cutting the criticism against the petty bourgeois: 'Characteristically subjective, individualist, impetuous or easily cowed . . . careerist, given to anarchist organizing . . . vacillating, opportunist' (Amado Guerrero).[21] Yet, like all revelation, it is liberating. The truth always sets one free, if only from ignorance about one's captivity. Instead of trying hard therefore to lead the struggle for liberation and suffering the numerous vacillations and hesitations and fears that the petty-bourgeois is heir to *(magulo ang isip, mahina ang tuhod)*,[22] he frees himself from impossible dreams and fulfils his historic role of serving the peasants and the workers, the main and leading forces of liberation. The Christian in him is also liberated from the vain task of finding a distinctively, neither bourgeois nor proletarian, Christian path and takes a liberating vow of poverty, of political poverty. There is no distinctively Christian task of mixing capitalist oil and socialist water. His is the freedom to choose the class with whom to cast his future.

This liberating suffering is not the end. There is still some dying to be done. The petty bourgeois is called the transition class. Although it has a distinctive role, it is limited and temporary. As contradictions heighten between capitalists and proletariat, it is bound to die. Does it have no choice then?

It can offer its life voluntarily, defect from the establishment it objectively serves and 'offer the capital it has stolen from the colonial schools and institutions to the revolutionary potential of the people' (Fanon) a la Victor Corpus.

But there is another, more literal meaning to dying: 'It is essential that the revolutionary conviction of each student be so ingrained that he accept it in its totality, even to the ultimate consequences. Poverty and persecution must not be sought after. But, given the present situation, they are the logical consequences of a battle to the end against existing structures. Under the present system, they are the signs which give authenticity to a revolutionary life' (Camilo Torres).

The Christian is faced with an even more frightening death. His God dies. The God who revealed social principles and performed miracles of power is suddenly challenged by the power of people who try to make history. Mao's parable on the *Foolish Old Man Who Removed Two Mountains* poses the problem very explicitly. 'Our God is none other than the masses . . . If they stand up and dig together with us why can't these two mountains be cleared away?'

The God of the fable he quoted, a God who sends angels to clear away the mountains of feudalism and imperialism definitely has to die if people are to achieve liberation. Where does a God come in then? Through a Christ, whose greatest miracle is the miracle of loving unto death.

'He descended into hell.' Chardin interprets this as Christ's touching the very depth of reality, the heart of the matter. Some activists say, *'Talagang sagad kayod, yanig hanggang ugat ang pagka-Kristiyano ko.'*[23] But with them, the paradox remains true: 'One must be willing to lose one's life if one wishes to save it.'

And what about Resurrection? Where is the new petty-bourgeois and the new Christianity? It's too early to say. Besides, the basic resurrection of a new people, of peasants and workers no longer passively accepting oppression but struggling for their dignity, is gathering momentum in many places.

And even now, there is a new people and a new consciousness: with power to take care of their own affairs, without need of the bread and relief goods and cooperatives of Christianity: a proud people that is self-reliant. To them, perhaps, the Gospel of a crucified Christ can be preached without any reactionary or colonial overtones. The 'powerless power' of the Gospel will be real in the face of the freedom of a liberated people. Is it that, or is it the final 'withering away' as some activists predict?

In the meantime, it is Lent and, wandering through the desert, one sometimes looks back wistfully at the secure definitions one has left and remembers with some vacillation the theological, political and economic fleshpots of the Establishment: and grumbles at leaders and each other and thinks of repentance and struggle and hopes that the fight to level the hills and fill the valleys will prepare the way for the coming Kingdom.

Francisco F. Claver · *The Praxis of the Gospel*

Francisco F. Claver, 'The Christian Gospel and Human Rights', *The Stones Will Cry Out – Grassroots Pastorals*, Orbis Books, Maryknoll, New York 1978, pp. 175–79, 182–83

What are some of the elements of this praxis that we are talking of here? Since we are concerned with action, and with action within an existing, concrete socio-political situation of rampant unfreedom and disregard of rights, let me talk freely of what we in Bukidnon are doing as church. It is the church I am most conversant with, and if at times I do sound like the Pharisee Christ reprobated in the gospel, a man blowing his own trumpet to call attention to himself, let me also add that we are enjoined by the same Christ to shout the good message from the housetops. And this, I am afraid, entails a little exhibitionism. So bear with me for these next few minutes. Our 'bragging,' if bragging it is, is not all that self-centred. I will limit myself to these three general areas: speaking out, forming public opinion, and the defence of human rights.

1. *Speaking out.* If the gospel is indeed *Good News*, it must be spoken out. And if the church is the bearer of this Good News, it must speak it out. As St. Paul puts it, *opportune, importune,* 'in season, out of season.' Is this too simplistic a way of looking at the church's primary task of preaching the Word? We in Bukidnon think not. And we have thought so from the very beginning of what is euphemistically called our 'national emergency.' The clergy of Bukidnon are by no means a group of extraordinary men, fault-finding, carping, hypercritical to the nth degree. They can be rumbustious and opinionated at times, true, but by and large they have, like the people they serve, the remarkable quality of knowing how to suffer what needs to be suffered yet not accepting anything as inevitable and beyond the healing influence of personal witness and preaching.

Hence, from the very start of martial law, we as a body have continued to take a critical stance toward acts of government that we judge are undue infringements of people's rights. We have used our pulpits freely for this task as occasion dictates, not by any means to stir the people up to rebellion and violent dissent, but to ask questions that must be asked (and are not being asked for fear), to point to guidelines that must be pointed out (and are not being pointed out because they are deemed 'subversive'), to put the responsibility of action where that responsibility belongs (and where despite claims to the contrary it has not belonged) – the people.

Commentary. If there is anything that our preaching must do, martial law or no martial law, it must be to foster that deeply human right to be intelligent, thinking, critical men and women. And if there is anything that martial law – rule by the gun – does, it is to prevent through induced and excessive fear precisely this right to think as human beings. Hence, when the church speaks out under circumstances in which speaking out is proscribed as a crime, it not only fulfils its task of announcing the Good News. It also effects in a sacramental manner the Good News: It enspirits people; it helps do away with – or at least lessen – the fear that leads to despair or inaction. This form of fear is most dehumanizing and I believe it is a genuinely Christian and human task therefore to destroy it, or, if this is not possible, to help people to face up to it and meet it with something of the courage that

Christ had in going to his passion. Christ conquered his fear. So must we. Only then can we look ahead to the final resurrection.

And if all this is true, I cannot see how the church can remain silent.

2. *Forming Public Opinion.* One of the first rights to be suppressed at the first flush of martial law – and it has remained largely suppressed since then despite claims to the contrary – is the right to information, and consequently, to the truth. The means of mass communication – radio, press, TV – are controlled. The government has relaxed somewhat the tight reins it once held over these media, but purveyors of public news are still benumbed by their fears (I might add their fears are not all of their own lively imagination). I need not waste any further comment on this massive attempt at channelling the thinking of a whole nation along one predetermined direction, and hence toward what is in essence a lie and falsehood, for I believe we all know we are, all of us here, victims of this attempt (including the Metrocom men[24] and other agents of government present in our midst tonight, though most unobtrusively as befits their function as agents of an unknown law).

Thus our problem: If we believe an enlightened public opinion to be basic to the humane conduct of society, how do we, under the heavy strictures imposed by the present system of governance, create it? How do we counteract the deleterious effects of its almost total absence? Even more fundamentally, how do we create the instrumentalities for its formation? The obstacles – the shadow of the gun, the ever-present threat of the stockade and all that it so far has meant, our own fears, imagined and real – are formidable obstacles. But yet they are not by any means insurmountable. We can always begin by taking the government at its word that there is no more censorship, that the media are free. A free media under a dictatorship is a contradiction in terms (and in real life), but it is an idea worth putting to the test in any case.

Commentary. This is where the church can lead the way. We have already discussed its duty and obligation to speak out. But it does not speak out in a vacuum. It speaks to people. And these people are not, should not be, silent, passive spectators as at an oratorical contest. They must respond. Hence the need for creating forums, or, to get at the original meaning of the term, *marketplaces*; marketplaces, that is, of ideas, for ideas, with ideas. This creating of idea marketplaces, this providing of possibilities for the formation of public opinion other than the fear-ridden ones fomented by the state itself, this to my mind is a deeply Christian task and must be part of the praxis that springs from the gospel.

The right to truth is by no means considered a privilege by our people, one which they are willing to shuck off as just so much extra baggage on the long hard trek to progress. This we can firmly say from our own experience. We have a little weekly newsletter in Bukidnon that goes out to practically every nook and cranny of the province every week. It is avidly read, and people in the parishes fight to have copies of it for themselves. The newsletter presents news that does not appear in the papers, and it presents it, we trust, under a Christian perspective. The people's appetite for the truth has been whetted by the premium put on it by martial law. But more than truth, I believe they are most hungry for freedom, and our little newsletter is for them a symbol of that freedom that is otherwise missing in much of their day-to-day life. Freedom too is a concern of gospel praxis: 'The truth will make you free.'

3. *Defence of Human Rights.* So far we have been talking of two major Christian tasks: *speaking out* and *creating public opinion*. These are, we can say, preliminary but essential conditions for Christian praxis with regard to the protection and exercise of human rights in the Philippines today. Here I would like to address myself more specifically to the problematic of rights that have drastically suffered under martial law. And the questions now, similar to those about the creation of public opinion, are: What are the vehicles available to us for the defence of human rights? And if they are not available, how can we create them? What should we create?

The fundamental problem, it seems, is that we do not live under a governing system of law and by law but of men and by men. This *rule of men*, true, tries very hard to cloak itself under the semblance of *rule of law*. I do not think it is succeeding. The very laws (decrees, letters of instructions, etc.) that it cranks out almost every day are quite capricious, to say the least; oftentimes they are contradictory one to another; in some cases, they are known only to the lawmakers themselves.[25] This is a highly immoral situation, however constitutional and legal it may be made out to be by students of the law.

Hence the first alternative that presents itself to Christian praxis is to work for the return to a system of government in which law, not whim, is paramount; a system in which the people who make the laws are responsible to the governed who obey the laws; in short, a system in which the dignity of the citizens is in truth honoured and respected in their right to participate genuinely in the decision-making processes of the state.

Failing this return to more moral and therefore more human modes of governance, the people will have to search their collective imagination and come up with ideas to test in common action. The courts of law are still probably by and large viable; these can be used to right certain wrongs. Military tribunals are harder to take, since accuser and judge are practically the same. Church Military Liaison Committees, where they have been formed, can achieve some measure of good only when the church side is more prophet than diplomat in its witnessing to justice. And the rank and file can always resort to general civil disobedience, as they did in last year's referendum, if all else fails. This disobedience must be nonviolent; it must be peaceful.

Commentary. It is paradoxical, but the best defence of human rights is their very assertion and exercise even while they are being denied or violated. Thus, a person is condemned and punished without due process of law: the very move for due process is itself part of due process. People are deprived of the right of free association: their gathering together for common action is itself an assertion of the very right they want to see restored. And so all the way down the line with other rights such as those to free speech, to participation in government, to responsible media of communication, to security of life and person, etc. These are defended in their actual exercise, their prohibition by edict not withstanding. This paradox, it seems to me, is *the* logic behind the whole concept of civil disobedience to unjust laws. It is also the logic, I might add, from faith: 'He who loses life will find life.' . . .

4. *Fundamental Commitment to the Gospel.* Underlying all we have said above is, or should be, an intense commitment to the Christian's primary task of preaching the gospel. St. Paul states this commitment in no uncertain terms: 'Woe is me if I do not preach the Gospel.' If I read him right, he is saying there can be no compromise where gospel principles are involved: We must preach them whatever the cost.

This is a hard saying. Even harder is the doing. But I am afraid it is a commitment that is basic to Christian praxis. True, this commitment admits of levels and degrees of intensity. But the kind of commitment I speak of here partakes of the nature of what modern moralists call *fundamental options*.

Let me illustrate this with an example, again drawn from real life.

Back in November 1971, prior to the local elections of that year, we read in all our churches in Bukidnon a pastoral letter condemning violence and corruption in the electoral processes. In addition, through the initiative of our Filipino priests, we were able to set up mechanisms for clean elections throughout most of the province through the CNEA. We did achieve more than a modicum of success. In one town, the incumbent mayor lost a closely contested fight for re-election. Within half an hour after the final vote was counted, the parish school went up in flames. Arson. People were prevented from fighting the conflagration by gunshots fired in the vicinity of the burning school. Conclusion: the defeated mayor was the guilty arsonist since, as everyone knew, he blamed his loss on church 'meddling.'

Subsequently I wrote a letter to all my priests on the burning of the school. And I posed this question to them: 'If this [the burning] is the price of our witnessing to justice, are we willing to pay it?' The question really meant: Are we willing to see all our churches, schools, and conventos, the fruits of our sweat and labour for so many years – are we willing to see them go up in flames rather than watering down, out of fear, our preaching of the gospel of Christian justice?

It was not a rhetorical question. Neither was the answer of the clergy. The burning of the school only served to bring them closer together, to clarify their directions in social action, to intensify even more their involvement in justice questions. This involvement continues. And my priests and religious are still of the same mind. They will not compromise. Threats to personal security, the possibility of deportation for foreign missionaries, of the stockade for native priests and religious: before all this, the gospel and its preaching come first. To the clergy, this was a definite 'fundamental option.'

5. Our Definition of the Gospel. To more prudent and perhaps more reasonable people, this stance is folly, out-and-out folly. Perhaps it is. But I am afraid that *is* what the gospel is all about, so is our praxis. If it is folly, please God, it is part of that much more infinitely unintelligible folly: the folly of the cross.

We make no bones about the fact. If the gospel calls for commitment, we give it. If it calls for concern, we give it. And if it calls for service, we try to give this too. Commitment, concern, service; not in the abstract but in the concrete; not in the past but in the present; commitment to people, concern for people, service of people – these spell out for us what the gospel is. Defining the gospel in this fashion may not be intellectually satisfying, granted. But this we know: it has made the gospel for us and our people a living reality – and a reality that forces us to plumb the depths of many a truth we once simply accepted on faith. And as we go on searching and probing we discover that the gospel is not something: not a set of rules and commandments, not a body of truths and dogmas. It is *Someone*, a Person, a God. And the commitment, concern, and service that we speak of are ultimately because of him.

This is our hope. This is our conviction. This also is our actual praxis.

Levi V. Oracion · *A Theological Perspective on Human Rights*

Levi V. Oracion, 'A Theological Perspective on Human Rights', *Wednesday Forum Journal*, August 1979, pp. 2–8 [26]

We should have by now cast off any naiveté about men – and women – who wield or aspire to wield any form of power. They usually tend to think good of themselves and ill of others, and they always believe that their immense power and wealth have liberated themselves from personal and selfish considerations, and are solely motivated by their desire to serve the commonweal. They feel, therefore, that their basic intention for the good of all is beyond reproach and any unjust and untoward event and circumstance in the functioning of government and its agencies can be attributed either to some imperfection in the political process or erring public servants. They believe that they do care for the welfare and good of all, and therefore, those that radically question the foundations and direction of government must by all means be silenced. Radical critics are the death virus of any society led by men and women of good will; they must, therefore, either be isolated or simply eliminated.

The repressive nature of modern societies seems to be erected also on a misunderstanding of the nature of modern technology in its application to human affairs. We are, as any perceptive observer of government operations would see, ruled by technocrats. A technocrat is one who can effectively interrelate separate technologies into a vast organic system and apply it towards the analysis and solution of problems encountered in various branches of government. Simply put, it is the scientific method applied to human affairs, particularly in the realms of economics and politics. Technocrats can make correct analyses of problems, and have the know-how to propose and implement the right solutions. The obvious implication of this state of affairs, that is, of the sovereignty of technocracy in the sphere of politics, is the death of democracy. If, for instance, we are on a ship in the midst of a vast ocean, and for some reason or other our directional mechanism breaks down, I do not think you'd expect the captain to take a vote among his passengers to find out which is south or north; you would rather trust that he would use his knowledge of the positioning of celestial bodies to determine the right course of your journey. Technocratic rulers, therefore, feel very much superior to those who voice their criticisms of government on their sense of justice and right. They have determined truth scientifically and therefore their decisions can brook neither dissent nor opposition. Protesters are at best misguided cranks who pose a real danger to society, and the most rational way of dealing with them is by elimination.

The next point I would like to make in trying to understand the repressive atmosphere of our times is the political judgment that the mass vote usually swayed by demagoguery and partisan politics can no longer adequately deal with the very complex nature of modern societies with their very difficult and complex problems. Democracy to be effective must rest on the informed, intelligent vote; but it is a fact that people simply vote with their idiosyncrasies, prejudices and subjective feelings. Such a political mechanism cannot cope with the bewildering array of contemporary economic problems that are intimately interconnected with practically every activity of modern Man – from what fascinates teenagers to the long standing hatred of the oil rich Arabs against

Western economics which exploited their natural wealth for so long. People must, therefore, be the object of socio-political planning of those who have the knowledge and the power to do what is right. People must therefore be made tractable to the designs of government so that the latter can pursue what is good for all without any dissent or opposition. Viewed in this light, man is a much more manageable being if he were stripped of his freedom and dignity!

It may now sound to you that I am providing rational justifications for a repressive socio-political order. Far from it, I am stating these things in order to let you know that I am quite aware of some of the good justifications for a repressive order so that no one would say I am spinning my theology out of a context of ignorance of obtaining realities. These realities cannot simply be swept away by a huge resentment over the new barbarism perpetrated by those in power against their radical critics. In fact, I think it is noteworthy that we in the 20th century would rather speak of 'human rights,' than use the more classic term, 'the rights of man.' The latter term connotes a more positive and aggressive dimension to man's claim to his inherent, inalienable rights as a human being than our contemporary term of 'human rights.' When Rousseau and Paine, the former the principal theoretician of the French Revolution and the latter its avid defender, both championed the 'rights of man,' they were speaking of man's claim to shape the content and give direction to his historical destiny vis-a-vis that of the State. Both Rousseau and Paine were so deeply convinced of the 'sacredness of the human person' that they considered him the primary and indissoluble unit of human society whose rights and interests must be protected at all costs. Both of them raised the right of man to revolt and overthrow a government which does not hesitate to transgress the rights of man.

Both Rousseau and Paine shared a basic naiveté about man; both of them had a very optimistic view of natural man which was a fundamental characteristic of democratic liberalism. We are much less sure, or even quite dubious of the positive virtues of individual man, so we satisfy ourselves by simply making a claim for the rights of a person as a human being, and thus speak of 'human rights'. We are, in other words, speaking of illegal detention, of torture as an instrument of forcing confessions and ferreting out information, of the freedom of movement and speech, of the right to live a decent human life according to the present requirements of modern society. We seem to have accepted the rights of technocrats to provide the shape and content of our present as well as our future and wish to preserve only a nuclear human space where our rights as human persons will not be violated by those who rule us. I hope that this is not true of people in the Wednesday Forum, but by and large, this is a characteristic of men everywhere.

Rousseau and Paine overstated their claims for the rights of man and over-looked man's huge capacity for hypocrisy and self-deception, and thereby spawned a socio-political system that spoke glowingly of human freedom and dignity even as it allowed such freedom to debase and dehumanize the greater number of its citizens. Our generation may be guilty of understanding our claims for man in its failure to see new possibilities in the human reality and thus condemn future generations to a mechanistic order of life bereft of the humanizing element of imagination and spirit. I think it is within this context that we should raise the issue of human rights theologically. How does our theological understanding of human rights help locate the creative, meaningful, fulfilling interaction between the citizens and the State? It is a very difficult problem and I am quite sure that I cannot offer any clear solution to it. I can only raise it here and discuss some theological realities that bear on human rights and hopefully start an intelligent and meaningful discussion of the problem within the Philippine context.

Man as Created in the Image of God

The Christian faith grounds the reality of man on the highest reality it knows, in the reality of God. Man did not occur as an accident in some meaningless movement of things; he is rather a purposeful and deliberate creation of God who is understood as the sovereign power in all reality by whose will and act the things that are have come to be. God holds the totality of things in His hands and is sovereign in his freedom which He exercises in consonance with His nature as love. Man, therefore, has a purposeful existence and destiny in God whose own self-realization is consistent with God's ultimate purpose in creation. And man does not merely have a divine providence which he shares with all things for he alone in all creation has been *created in the image of God.* What does this awesome symbolic figure mean – to be created in God's image?

To be an image is to share something with the Original without being quite exactly the Original itself, but what is shared can be the basis of a creative and fulfilling relationship. Dialogue is one aspect of this religious symbol that immediately comes to mind. Man is the only creature to whom God has bestowed the privilege of entering into a dialogical relationship with Him. It means that man has been elevated from the rank of creation, ruled by necessity and spontaneity to the level of reason, understanding, freedom and love. The image of God in man forbids us to treat him as a mere means or instrument of anything as it would violate something quite essential about him which is grounded in the very heart of Ultimate Reality itself. Reason and love are the processes of dealing with him that may lure out the *image* in him and the dialogical relationship that may build up may provide a context for the fulfilment of man and of nature that supports him.

Man, as the bearer of God's image in creation, is also the space in and through which God's care for His creation may find expression and His will in history may find speech and action. In other words, man is God's light in nature and in history in whose act and being creation becomes self-conscious of its reason for existence and destiny. In the Genesis story of creation man has been entrusted with the lordship of all creation so vividly symbolized by his act of naming 'all the birds and all the animals'. Man's responsibility is not only to care for and rule over creation but to bear on nature and history his own unique self-understanding that God is present in both of them, and it is man's vocation to be their shepherd in leading them to a fulfillment of God's will. Deeply imbedded in man's nature is the care and concern for everything that God has made, and the desire to help others along in directing their processes and to realize their highest creative possibilities. Man is the only entity in creation who responds to God's call and care for God's creation. He must therefore be treated as a willing and active participant in the processes of human life and not a mere pawn in a game played by despots pushed from square to square without knowing the whence and whither of his existence.

We cannot pass judgment on the way man is manipulated and barbarously treated in repressive societies simply on the theological affirmation that man was created in the image of God. Such an affirmation is merely that first movement in the Christian dialectic in articulating its theological bases for human rights. It must also be said that man has by a strange combination of fate and freedom placed himself in radical opposition to the God whose image he bears. Only he who has been granted the high privilege of dialoguing with God runs the risk of being utterly opposed to Him. And as we have come to know the human story, such an ignominy has actually become the fate of man. God's image – the very possibility of man's high privilege and glory – by man's fall, has been transmogrified into a demonic power that propels man to regard the whole of creation as mere materials for his own willing, and creates a world that would insure his own security against all possible threats to his power and being. This is the demonic logic that has given rise to men with a consuming passion to lord it over other men and treat them as mere instruments of their will and power in their bid to establish a permanent and absolute dictatorship. The fall of man has plunged the world of men into a dreadful power game where those who gain the upperhand would so readily destroy their enemies, crush the poor and powerless, seduce and cajole the many or actually terrorize them to maintain and intensify their power over men. It is the nature of the powerful to arrogate high moral virtues to themselves and attribute a base nature to their enemies which arms them with a moral justification to deal with their enemies as if they were not human beings. So, the Nazis believed that they were purifying the German race by completely eliminating the Jews! The game continues and now the world has divided itself into oppressors and oppressed. A Christian should not at all be surprised at man's barbaric acts upon his fellowman for he is only following the demonic logic of his fallen nature. There is no horrifying human crime against his fellowman that cannot be comprehended by the horror man has inflicted upon God himself on the cross.

We have inherited from St. Augustine a strange doctrine which says that unbelieving man, or man in his natural condition, is not free not to sin. Man's entire being is infected by *peccatum originalis,* original sin, and therefore, the entire expression of his being is sinful. In more slightly modern language we say that man is under the domination and oppressive power of some evil force, and he in turn seeks to dominate and oppress others. This theological judgment can be verified in practically all realms of human existence such as economics, politics, culture, and even in very intimate personal relationships. Man, in setting himself up as an independent entity that now seeks to provide the rationale and basis for his own existence has alienated himself from God, and has fallen under the power of evil which has brought about distortions in all dimensions of his being, giving rise thereby to a world of agony and conflict. So man now perceives his fellow human being as a threat to his own power and security which provokes in him a reaction that wills to reduce the other to something less than human. Such human evil gets articulated in the structure and process of our world, and therefore those who control them are given powerful and deadly instruments for the dehumanization of their fellowmen.

The heart of the Christian Gospel is that God, out of his radical opposition to evil and his deep love for man, has denied himself the power and privilege of divinity and completely identified himself with man. Within the fate and limits of human finitude he makes a radical opposition to man's injustice, pride and hypocrisy out of his great love of the poor, the powerless and the oppressed, and thereby suffered the full wrath of man's hate. But he maintained his opposition to man's evil and love for him to the very end, and succeeds in conquering man's evil and hate even within the limits of our historical world. God's action in Jesus Christ is good news in that man who has delivered himself over helplessly and hopelessly to the power of evil is now offered full liberation in God's grace in Christ, where the only thing man has to do to gain liberation is to acknowledge the reality of his liberation.

Jesus was a particular historical person who lived in a particular time and place; but what God has done in and through him was revelatory of the fundamental truth of the human condition and of the universal presence of the power that alone can truly liberate man. God said something new in Jesus: that man no matter how corrupt and depraved he is can be acknowledging the reality of grace, can be a new man. *Human rights, as seen by the Gospel, is based on divine grace. Anyone, therefore, who violates, tampers with, denigrates, enslaves and oppresses any human person sets himself in opposition to God!* This is the reality of the human situation and the ministry of the Church is to make this reality known and effective and supreme in the life of the world.

The mind of man delights in universalization. All men have come short of the glory of God; all of us, therefore, are sinners and stand in need of grace – rich and poor alike. The Gospel is for the poor as well as for the rich. It comes as a shock to us, therefore, to read in the Gospel, particularly in the Gospel of Luke, that Jesus offered the Gospel primarily to the poor and the oppressed. In fact, the poor in the preaching of Jesus occupied the centerpiece of the Kingdom of God, and almost always Jesus made a radical reversal of the status of the rich and the poor in the life beyond. Even in the New Testament, the rich man is invariably the oppressor and the poor man, the oppressed. And it is principally for the latter that Jesus has come.

To be poor is to have little or no food, no dwelling place, no education, no influence, no power, no future. To be poor is to be nothing! One has lost his 'human rights' if he is nothing. In such a condition, man can no longer depend on his resources to be human because he has no resources to speak of. He cannot create his own world for he does not even have dreams, dreams that really matter, with which to build his world. His life and his world are things that are mockingly and brutally given by those who have robbed him of his humanity in their efforts to establish their own security in their own world; an act that strikes at the very heart of God. The poor, therefore, symbolize God's own body in the world – that body against which all economic and political injustice, all acts of torture and cruelty to man, all forms of human oppression are directed. Jesus was not using a mere figure of speech when he said, 'if you have done it to one of my little friends, you have done it to me.'

Jesus was put to death because his word, act and being introduced a profoundly subversive element within his own socio-political order. The leaders of Jewish society, the Scribes and the Pharisees, the wielders of wealth and power, believed that their meticulous observance of the Law and intimacy with the rite and ritual of the faith made them the principal citizens of the coming Kingdom, and the outcasts of society would not even make it to the gate of the Kingdom. *But Jesus, in his proclamation and entire manner of being, made it painfully clear to them that the outcasts of society have been granted the privilege of being the first citizens of God's Kingdom, and the high and the mighty may enter the Kingdom only if they give themselves in service to the poor.* The threat that Jesus' message posed to the socio-political system of Jewish society was obvious. Jesus had to go. He must be eliminated. Jesus died for those whose human rights had been denied.

It is only after we have spoken of the centrality of the poor and the oppressed in the proclamation of Jesus do we gain the right to make universal and general statements about the Gospel. Jesus has revealed to us the structure and dynamics of the human reality and how one might grapple with it to liberate what is human in us and give it its most authentic expression. God's act of becoming man, his radical opposition against those who enslave and oppress their fellowmen, his infinite compassion to the victims of man's hate and greed, and his resoluteness with which he pursued these passions to the point of death constitute the ground on which we base our commitment to human rights. The Incarnation speaks of God's total investment of his own self to give worth and dignity to man; it is in man that God can find a meaningful realization of His nature as love, so no matter how much man has distorted the *imago* in him, God made a total effort to win him back by sharing his fate and taking up his cause. Jesus, the righteous and holy one, died to liberate the poor from the clutches of religious hypocrisy and political injustice. So the crucifixion reveals the depravity and moral bankruptcy of those who oppress and enslave the poor and powerless even as it reveals the boundlessness of God's love to those who have nothing but Him. The crucifixion means it took nothing less than the death of God to make it possible for man to maintain and give full expression to his possibilities as a human being, and thus those who are committed in the struggle for human rights may have to go through the same fate as Jesus' to allow the right of man to his humanity to shine like the brilliance of a million suns. And death no longer holds any terror for those engaged in the struggle for human rights for they, like Jesus, have already known and conquered death and are given assurance to declare that God is with us!

5 · Mainland South East Asia

Despite their ethnic and social complexity, countries of the South East Asia mainland share a similar cultural and religious heritage in Theravada Buddhism and in Sanscritic and Chinese cultures. And if Burma, Thailand and Vietnam differ markedly in their social and political history, they each share a similar experience of the destructive impact of Western imperial powers, even though in the case of Thailand the domination would be economic and cultural rather than military or political. It is this impact which has ensured that each of the three countries, like the Philippines, Malaysia, and Indonesia, have experienced continuing civil war since 1945. The national Christian traditions of each country nevertheless stand out as unique.

Vietnam

Following a thousand years of Chinese depredations, the French conquest of Vietnam (1883) after forty years' warfare, led to seven further decades of repression and resistance. Despite severe repression, a national literature emerged in the 1920s, using the vernacular kept alive by the Roman Catholic Church, and in 1925 the Young Revolutionaries Association of Ho Chi Minh was formed. After 1941, the Vietnamese suffered, and finally defeated, repeated foreign invasions, by Japan, France, Britain and the United States of America and their allies. The third and final nationalist liberation would come only after thirty years of most hideous warfare.

The favoured status of Catholics, under French colonial rule, and the rejection of any indigenizing influences, ensured that the majority of Catholics would remain politically and culturally alienated from their people throughout much of this period. The conservative theology of almost all Protestant missions (in Vietnam since 1911), brought a similar result in the south and allowed the Christian community widely to accept the anti-Communist policies of Diem, Thieu and their allies. The Tin Lauh Evangelical Church in North Vietnam, in contrast, with forty congregations and thirty pastors, was identified with the socialist cause thoughout the war.

From the 1950s small groups of nationalist Roman Catholics had developed from the work of such priests as Ho Thanh Bien (d. 1976), later the President of the National Committee for Catholic Unity and a member of the Hanoi Assembly. From 1960, groups of Catholics, Buddhists and French Reformed worked together for peace under the leadership of Buddhists like Thich Nhat Hanh and Thich Thien Minh. During the following decade, the growing unity of Christians and Buddhists who opposed the Saigon government was to make possible the steady growth of a militant 'Third Force' for peace. In 1963 the Buddhists initiated dialogue between Marxists and anti-Marxists and in 1966 called for a total cease-fire. They were soon joined by groups of Catholic priests led by Tran Viet Tho and Hoang Quynh.[1]

In this period, the Catholic hierarchy in South Vietnam issued a number of Collective Pastoral Letters, which called for fuller political participation and personal dedication to the good of 'the collective whole'.[2] Christian Churches in South Vietnam now received every encourgement from the United States authorities and from related aid agencies, despite the criticism by some Catholic groups of the political corruption involved.

One of three aid agencies which assisted community development in both North and South Vietnam was the Asian Christian Service of the East Asia Christian Conference. It encouraged the fullest participation by Vietnamese in community programmes and also fostered theological reflection upon the 'necessary commitment to peace, justice and forgiveness'.[3] Many groups of priests and lay people were now involved in the peace movement, opposing both police repression and government corruption. But few examples of biblical or theological reflection appear in the extensive protest literature.

At the fall of Saigon (April '75) there was no such exodus as that from the North in 1954, but the mood of Catholic leaders was one of resignation, even to possible death. It was therefore remarkable that within two weeks of liberation the Archbishop of

Hue applauded the liberties accorded by the Provisional Revolutionary Government to the faithful of all confessions, and Archbishop Nguyen Van Binh of Saigon declared 'we rejoice in the peace and participate in the common life of the people under the direction of the People's Revolutionary Government'.[4] Archbishop Van Binh in particular has from that time led fellow Christians in such a participation and the reorientation it demands. Catechetics must speak clearly to a Marxist milieu he asserts, yet face differences honestly. Seminary training is modified to include the formation of work co-operatives, and whole communities of religious move to the countryside to join in the work of communes there in response to the Archbishop's invitation. His pastoral letter of 2 September 1975 is a clear theological statement concerning incarnation and the kingdom of God, which, he says, allow Christians to 'accept all the values of the Revolution with joy'. And he goes on to describe an open church which accepts righteousness wherever it is found, as the sign of the Lord's presence in the world. 'We Vietnamese Catholics', he writes, 'encounter God in the life of our people'.[5]

But there is no underestimating the reorientation of life and belief this involves – nothing less than a painful cultural revolution for the church, which includes also a return to the revolutionary values of the gospel.

The letter of Fr Bao reveals the experience of those who come to welcome the new society on theological grounds, and it is one of many such letters and documents now available. It is clear that despite ambiguities and hardship, large numbers of Christians are in fact able, as Ho Thanh Bien urged in his last letter, to express their love for Vietnam in service to society and as part of their obedience to the teachings of Jesus Christ.

Thailand

From 1932–1973 Thailand was ruled, except for two years, by a military oligarchy claiming to follow a Western-style democratic ideology. Power remained, however, in the hands of the sakdina class – royalty and high government officials – as it had done in previous centuries, although now in alliance with foreign capital and Thai military leaders. Legitimation was provided by Buddhism, the state religion, which is headed by the King and which has long been identified with the sakdina classes in, for example, land ownership. Nationalist feeling developed during the Japanese occupation, despite the collaboration of government and army with Japan, and along with left-wing groups contributed to the forming of a post-war socialist government. But this was quickly overthrown by military coup, which in effect restored a feudal structure of power. Nationalist and socialist traditions continued however in Thai literature – in the work of such writers as Kulap Saipradit, Seni Saowaphong and Chit Phumisak – until the fierce repression by the Sarit government (1958–63) and that of Thanom-Praphat (1963–73).

In the same period, the Student Christian Centre, established by the United Church of Christ in Thailand, has played a leading role in fostering both study and social involvement. Under the direction of Kosong Srisang the centre pioneered, in the 1960s, joint programmes in which the church, the university and community groups worked closely. In the same years the Catholic Young Christian Workers, led by Snan Vongsuthee, contributed to the revival of the labour movement, and from 1962 dates the church and labour programme of the united church. Samrit Wong-sang has, since 1964, extended this work into the largest slum and industrial areas of Bangkok and in regular reports articulated a Thai Christian response to the desperate issues facing Thailand's poorest communities.[6]

The Thailand Theological Seminary at Chiangmai has prepared many for such ministries as well as for those in rural development and adult education. And in association with the Student Christian Centre, the Seminary was instrumental in forming in 1968 a Religion and Society programme for inter-religious co-operation on community issues. Amongst faculty members who have related the task of theology to Thai issues are Samran Kwangwaena, (Ms) Prakai Nontawasee, and Maen Pongudon (see below). Catholics involved in both theological reflection and social action in the 1970s included Paul Chamniern, Joachim Pranom Sion of the Social Action Centre, Bangkok, and Fr Bunluen Mansap (later secretary for human development of the Federation of Asian Bishops' Conferences). In a speech given in 1973, Bunluen Man-sap stresses the interdependence of action and reflection in the creation of a 'down-to-earth' theology, but for this the church must be buried in the life of the people.[7]

Deepening political and economic divisions however were now evident, especially between Bangkok and Thailand's rural majority. The policies of the military Junta of Thanom – Praphat, and the military and economic presence of the United States, had by 1970 led to widespread corruption, greater extremes of wealth and poverty and a sharp polarization on ideological lines. When a broad coalition from liberal and socialist parties and from the universities succeeded in restoring democracy in October 1973, a gradual liberalizing of government followed with a wide expression of democratic aspirations.

But there would be only three years before forces of reaction – in industry, government and especially the army – would bring a traumatic reversal in the violent coup of October 1976. It was three years of mounting assassinations, of farmers and worker leaders, students and politicians. In this period of precarious democracy, a small number of writings appear articulating a Christian theology which is clearly Thai, rooted in contemporary events and open to dialogue with all religious and community groups. Koson Srisang, whose article on 'the power to be human' is reproduced here, became General Secretary of the Church of Christ in Thailand in 1974. His writings at that time stress the role of a Christian community wholly reoriented to serve the welfare of all Thai people. By March 1976 he was amongst the leaders of 'People Concerned about the Political Situation' and largely responsible for the inter-religious centre for Religion and Society both of which now issued statements of concern. In 1975, the Thai Catholic Bishops' Conference issued their Pastoral letter in which they called for the renewal of the church. This 'changing situation means that we must push on with Vatican II reforms' they declared. And in anticipation of the National Election in April 1976, a symposium on 'Christians and Politics' was published, including articles by Chuwit Wutikane, Maen Pongudon and Pong Dananon. The last two also issued a collection of meditations entitled 'Stop and Think Two Minutes'.[8]

Burma

In Burma also, contextual Christian thought has grown in the encounter with nationalist and socialist movements and with a resurgent Buddhism. Nationalist groups, in which Buddhists played an important role, were active in Burma by the year 1920. Because one outcome of British rule (since 1885) was a decline in the practice of Buddhism, it was easy for the Pongyis (Buddhist monks) to see in the rise of nationalism the revival of Buddhism. Few Christians however were then involved, for the largely ethnic churches were closely identified with the British colonial presence and were suspicious of Burmese nationalism. Not until the mid-1930s were religious and ethnic minorities given fuller recognition by the Thakin (nationalist) groups led by Aung San, as in part a counter to a narrowly Buddhist nationalism. It was at this time also that Christian associations again gave support to nationalist causes and there were early moves towards self-reliance by the largest Protestant church, the Baptist. Theological concern in the pre-war period was mainly concentrated on the intelligent communication of the gospel in a Buddhist milieu and on a theology of mission for a church which was ethnically divided and pro-British yet desiring selfhood as the Burmese Christian community.[9]

Following the war and the granting of independence, the socialist government of U Nu survived the violent civil war of 1948–52 but quickly moved from a Marxist to a Buddhist form of socialism. The contribution of minority groups was recognized by U Nu despite their involvement in the earlier insurrections and Christians in particular worked to dissipate distrust of their 'foreignness' or 'anti-nationalism'. By the time of the 1960 election however, the establishment of Buddhism as the State religion became the primary reason for U Nu's decisive victory.

Christian theology since 1945 had stressed in apologetics the concerns common to both Christians and Buddhists and many articles appeared, such as those by Pe Maung Tin (first Burmese Rector of Rangoon University) and U Hla Bu (Professor of Philosophy at Rangoon), interpreting Christian witness amid social and religious change.[10] There was also a strong ecumenical concern developed by the well-established Student Christian Movement and from the work of, for example, U Hla Bu, Archbishop Ah Mya, U Ba Myin (who preached the opening sermon at the New Delhi Assembly of the World Council of Churches), and the young U Kyaw Than.

After 1962 the government of Ne Win brought strongly secularizing influences in the implementation of a democratic, rather than Buddhist, socialism. Along with major industries the educational and medical institutions of the churches were now nationalized, and all but a handful of missionaries left the country. But many churches, especially the Baptist, had already achieved a high level of indigenous leadership, amongst whom were a number of lay theologians including U Hla Thwin (Chairman of the Burma Christian Council), U Pe Thwin (of the Christian Literature Society and a prolific writer), and U Khin Maung Din (Lecturer in Philosophy, Rangoon).

Burma's most widely known ecumenist, and theologian, U Kyaw Than, has made his major contributions in the theology of mission. His many writings and lectures (as for example, visiting Professor of Mission at Yale), reflect deep concern that the Ecumenical Movement in Asia reflect both the wholeness (in concern for social justice) and the incisiveness (in concern for Christian identity) of the gospel. The focus for such a mission Kyaw Than sees in the apostolate of a laity theologically and socially alert in every secular situation. For him it is the cosmic implications of Christ's work which enable us to discern his suffering in the economic and political struggles of our people.[11]

Similar conclusions appear in a radical study of the encounter of Christianity with Buddhism in Burma in which U Khin Maung Din outlines the consonance of Buddhist and Ying-Yang categories with a christology that stresses function and process in the historical present. Palestinian images are therefore seen in the light of the continuing Christ-event in Burma; we 'listen and see how he dwells among us' in our common problems suffering and hopes. Here the present test for both Buddhism and Christianity does not concern their knowledge of God, but 'their concrete love for man'; with Marxist and non-Marxist they 'meet their common neighbour in need'.[12]

Despite widespread Christian involvement in ecumenical and social service programmes, led for example by the Burma Christian Council, these emphases are not usual. The majority of Burmese Christians, like many others in Asian countries, have accepted quietism, diakonia or revolution as models of Christian witness, without attempting to relate these to Christian social witness in a Socialist society. The paper of Alan Saw U is one of the few attempts made so far and arises from the developing urban-industrial ministries of the Burma Council of Churches. Preparation for this can be seen in the lay training programmes beginning in the late 1960s, which included studies of the Christian faith in relation to secular life and to socialism. William Lay of the YMCA and Arthur Kc Lay of the SCM were among those providing leadership along with faculty members of the Burman

Theological Seminary. After 1971, regular Urban Industrial Mission programmes commenced with the assistance of U Aung Khin, General Secretary of the Burma Christian Council and have now found a particularly Burmese character in motivating churches to participate in local social action programmes. Saw U's paper gives the basis for this.

Bao · *Letter from Ho Chi Minh City*

Bao, 'Letter from Ho Chi Minh City', mimeographed December 1978

Christianity has never wanted to be an 'ism', but in fact it is one (in French christianisme). Socialism never wanted to be one either, in the profound expectation of its leaders and adherents, but in fact it is also one. In Vietnam we are a whole people in the process of creating a Vietnamese society which wants to be a community and not an 'ism'. Whether we shall succeed or not depends above all on how we act. Today, as conscientised Christians, men who have rediscovered the deep meaning of what it is to be human, we would like to do all we can for Vietnam to become truly and fully a 'community of brothers' and do it through the dynamism of our christian faith, not with the ambition of holding the helm but with the deep conviction that we are 'subjects of history', truly responsible for our own destiny both individual and national. For us Christians, Socialism does not have everything. But it has some fundamental elements that fit in absolutely with our authentically Christian way of considering and defining the human being in the light of Christ himself: to be men as brothers with the others, or 'for others before being for oneself'. The greatest commandment of Vietnamese socialism is 'let each one live for all and let all take charge of each one'. With regard to that rule, we must admit that christianity with its gospel has nothing more as 'human value' to offer in heritage to mankind. What christianity offers us that is original is not this or that additional human value but rather a completely new dimension to each human value. And that goes beyond any ideology. Our Christianity, as full meaning of human life, is of quite a different order from ideology; we have to give witness to the full scope of it by our existence of love in the midst of others who are also living their life of love of mankind.

So, our good fortune in being christians in socialist Vietnam today is that we can rediscover our own christian identity, beginning by learning to grasp what it is to be a man: to be together among equals. In this fundamental equality there are always dialectical relationships between individuality and collectivity, with actual priority given to collectivity: nobody is born alone, nobody learns anything alone, nobody develops all alone. Alone, man does not exist and can do absolutely nothing, not only on the sociological but also on the metaphysical and spiritual level. So the meaning of our existence, true human happiness, can never be found except in community; that is why in the search for and the construction of the happiness of mankind we must particularly insist today on the collective meaning of our action as the most urgent need, instead of giving too much emphasis to individual notes such as 'the rights of the person' according to a 'capitalist' conception which has led christianity itself into the impasse where it is today and where it has lost too much of its credibility . . .

For us communism is not everything, it will never take the place of christian life. But in this land where we are living our christian faith amid communist atheists we can affirm without any complex, without fear of error, that christian salvation, the Redemption that Jesus Christ willed to bring to the whole of mankind, is basically nothing other than this human society constructing together on the basis of that communist golden rule: 'Let each one live for all and all look after each one'. We who are christian believers should carry it out right to the end because of God, because of Jesus Christ and his Gospel. Of course there is also the influence of differences in the methods of concrete realisation, there is the influence of various ideologies (let us at least be honest about it like our communist brothers!) in the organisation of society, as in the organisation of christianity itself. But here again there are dialectic relations to create existentially, through our human commitments, in fraternal complementarity and not with antagonistic powers, because the dynamism of the spirit cannot be fitted into the system of our 'power relationships'. The 'Violence of the Agape' is something quite different. What is at stake here is the question of knowing whether we christians will dare to live as true christians, as true believers in the spirit rather than as neutron bombs . . .

Where is your brother? That is the question that God is still ceaselessly asking us in face of the duty to construct a humanity-community, in which we have failed and which has been taken up by the marxist non-believers. We keep on calling out for the rights of the person, wishing the East to have a 'socialism with a human face', and at the same time, with pious hypocrisy, we continue to give full and formal support to the ever more refined atrocities committed by those fascist regimes directed by the christians themselves. Let us go round the world and see clearly whether christian personalism can do anything effective for the immense mass of 'human-animals' in the Third World.

What is happening in socialist Vietnam today? On the national level we are in the pains of beginning. But what is it that causes us christians to make a clear option for socialism, without any fear for the faith? The cause is the true sign that in the construction of the regime itself there is an efficacious concern for humanity; in concrete, the policy towards people of the former regime both soldiers and civilian officials. If a Catholic president did not hesitate to sign the death sentence for more than a thousand 'collaborators' with the former regime in a 'Catholic' country, the Vietnamese atheist communist leaders have not yet signed a single death sentence against someone of the former regime because he was of that regime. And against Catholics, including some priests who had been anti-communist out and out, there have been no measures of repression or discrimination, no imprisonment, except for new serious faults committed since the Liberation of Saigon. Priests in charge of the Refugee Movement of 1954–55,[13] those in charge of christian settlements in strategic regions and places in the South, priests who had been condemned to death in the North before 1954, including the former curate of my parish, who led me to the monastery . . . they are still there, engaged in pastoral activity. The victorious revolutionaries of Vietnam are not blind to this, nor are we blind to it: those are realities that have became so ordinary that many people no longer think about them. The policy of political re-education of people of the former regime involves austerities that are inevitable in our situation, where even the innocent and the most deserving still don't get enough to eat normally . . . But this policy is quite consistent with the spirit of national reconciliation, which is authentic and effective. Of course, the Western capitalists will never believe it, because that would constitute a condemnation of their 'personalist regime' itself. But from our actual observation here, seeing with the sincere light of faith, we must admit that it is something unique in the history of wars, and so it is for christians a 'shameful' challenge, because of the counter-testimonies we gave in earlier times.

But on the other hand you may rest assured that we Vietnamese christians would not content ourselves with just following communism and constructing socialism. Driven by the dynamism of christian faith we plan to go right to the end of the road with the communists and keep on going further, following the christian dimension of our life of faith. We shall go further because of God, because of Christ and of his Gospel. There is no contradictory opposition between the fundamental aim of marxist humanism and christianity; it is for us to make our contribution so that the journey forward may be accomplished in the conditions that are best according to our christian anthropology. Western christians are always afraid that the success of socialism may lead to the end of religious beliefs; it is rare for someone to have understood the full scope and significance of true Christianity in the work of humanisation of society. In other words we think it is the particular original contributions of effective christians which should assure for socialism true and full success, success which will bring to every man the happiness of being truly and fully human, equal to all and brother to all. On the ideological level one can continue to disagree and continue arguing right through our whole existence. Each one on his side should behave in such a way that opposing ideas do not become oppositions between adversaries wiping each other out; as has unfortunately happened in the history of churches as of peoples and governments.

The word became flesh to make us 'truly human'. Now capitalism, constructed on a basis of individualism which is in our eyes the original sin of mankind, is in fundamental contradiction with the biblical, and thus with the christian concept of man. Are we going too far when we have in Vietnam drawn the conclusion that a lucid christian can never opt for the capitalist way, and that a consistent capitalist can never be a true christian? But capitalism has been for many of us like 'something inborn', and the metanoia can only be carried out as a grace. This is said in order to show you that what we are experiencing on the socialist path in Vietnam we want to live as grace from the Lord, even our fits of anger against imperialism.

This letter is already very long. But as the distance does not allow us to correspond frequently I permit myself to add something more about the way in which we brothers of the Virgin of the Poor are trying to integrate our religious life in the common work of construction of the country in which each one of us sees himself obliged to contribute positively and actively as a formal duty. What we said above should be sufficiently enlightening as to our fundamental attitude. In practical life we try to organise our life in such a way that our commitments for the service of the fatherland can be effective and that the religious aspect of existence may be seen to be well-looked after; living. Our discussions have led us to see that in order to live in a christian manner the socialist maxim 'each for all and all for each', it is indispensable that we live as real poor people and also as real contemplatives. Poverty and contemplation are two poles forming dialectically the central axis of our whole religious life, a project of evangelical life.

To live like the poor, that is very difficult, if not contradictory with the profound nature of the human being, that is always trying to be more and have more. Traditionally christianity has made a virtue of it, following after Christ. But very rare are those who do not see a pejorative note in it, a certain loss, an evil, to say the right word. It is because at the moment when we see a 'virtue' in it we are only considering poverty as a 'sacrifice', a diminishing of oneself, an impoverishment: the truly poor are very rare for this reason, it seems.

Now, in socialist Vietnam we have the occasion to reflect about it a great deal. Here every form of poverty is condemned and according to the socialist point of view, which is trying to be really human, no evangelical poverty is possible because Christ himself all his life was a judgement, an unrelenting condemnation of every form of poverty. He made himself poor so that not one of the sons of men should ever again be impoverished, diminished, dehumanised. And then I remember the way the Taizé brothers understand poverty a little differently from the way we Catholic religious conceive of the vow of poverty: they do not say that through the vow of poverty one no longer possesses anything, but that all possess those goods in common. It is an almost imperceptible nuance, but it reflects two different spirits: on one side the Catholic emphasizes renunciation, on the other the Taizé monk practises the positive aspect of the vow of poverty, no longer seen as a diminution, but as a true human and spiritual enrichment. And then one goes on to think of our fervent monks who, in order to be 'poor', make holes in their new clothes and then mend them up again! That really makes one think, not to laugh at our brothers, but to reflect on our traditional concept of the 'the virtue of poverty', to make it comprehensible to the people of today, and do so through our commitments to the service of humanity.

To be true, it is impossible for us to live as 'poor' in the bitter struggle against every form of poverty that our whole people is engaged in now. Attempts are sometimes made to escape from this contradiction by insisting on the spirit of poverty, but man is not pure spirit. So it is for us to find the way to carry out the demands of the gospel in this respect while at the same time participating actively in the common struggle against poverty in all its forms, including in ourselves. It is impossible to cultivate 'diminution', renunciation, loss; Christ lost enough for us. In the socialist situation in Vietnam the 'communal' meaning of the human being makes us turn the gospel demand in the positive direction: man cannot live as man except in community; the community, by delivering man from his solitude, saves man from all forms of poverty, and on the contrary enriches him immeasurably, makes him fully human. On this basis, to live the demands of the gospel in the relationship that we should have with earthly realities together and amongst others, we ought no longer to cultivate our personal poverty, but rather contribute with all our strength to the enriching of the whole community including ourselves individually.

According to a certain traditional theological concept it is necessary for man to feel weakness, powerlessness, so that Divine power and glory may be manifested, and this idea is said to be supported by the Pauline doctrine: 'It is when I feel weak that I am strong'. But the theology of christian hope is just the opposite of such a march backwards. So let us get on with the battle against poverty for the enrichment of the whole human community so that each one may be able to reflect in a worthy manner the face of God, Master of the universe. It is not a question now of making sacrifices in material or spiritual goods to enrich others. Nor is it a matter of seeking to share with people who are poorer than we are. Every sacrifice (many are necessary), all sharing (much of that is necessary too), is now lived not on the axis of renunciation but on the axis of construction in common of the common welfare.

Giving away your second habit to someone who is naked is not practising evangelical charity, it is elementary justice if you want to be merely human.

So in practice for us in the fraternity, there is no longer any question of trying to arrange a style of living close to that of the really poor, to be poor with the poor. Fundamentally it is a matter of entering fully into the carrying out of social programmes aimed above all at the common good of all, following the maxim 'each for all and all for each one'. In a society that is applying distributive justice in a systematic way our efforts to live an evangelical life should now consist not so much in acts of sharing and renunciation as in effective contributions to the task being shared by all. The non-believers do it simply because of their this-world humanity, we believers do it because of Christ and his gospel. Renunciation of self and of individual goods is thus carried out within the struggle to enrich the community in which we are with others and for others.

How can that be lived in a christian way without a constant relationship not with the gospel but rather with Christ himself? We must then cultivate that relationship, get to the point where we can state with Paul that for us to live is Christ. In our last letter to you we said something about the contemplativity of our religious life in our concrete situation in Vietnam.

We cannot or rather we do not wish to make the contemplativity of our life into a 'specialisation', a separate aspect of existence. There must be acts of the formal exercises of contemplation, but these practices are not considered by us here as essential, because of our way of considering the contemplativity of religious life in the context of a socialist society. Nor do we want to seek leisure time for that, although each one should be trained to practise daily contemplative prayer as a vital requirement of authenticity.

If we contented ourselves with a certain kind of idea about the Incarnation of the Word then contemplative worship as a specialisation would be essential to the occupation of religious. The monastic tradition, disparaging active life, explains the matter its own way. If on the contrary we see the Incarnation of the Word as a reality that keeps marching on, like God's creative act which is always continuing as a beginning, then we should take the whole field of our 'earthly' existence as place of contemplation, as place of love being exercised, as place of the incarnation of God by means of us. So we are learning to make the whole day our

programme of contemplation, of practical life in the loving presence of Christ present everywhere and in all. It is difficult and
almost impossible. It is even illusory. Yes, it would be, if we
didn't have Christ with us right from the start; if to begin with we
were not already living in the grace of his friendship. The initiation
is indispensable, as in every science and practical skill.

How should we get to see and love Christ in the communists?
Certainly not by contemplative prayers in the oratory, nor by
secret resolutions made in the shadow of our cell. Here it is a
practical apprenticeship in encounters, in active collaboration, in
interpersonal relations, with faith that the Spirit of Christ is constantly at work there, even in situations where atheists shout out
insults against the 'impostor Christ' of the christians. That should
create in us a true passion for Christ, precisely because of the
provocation from nonbelieving brothers who have rightfully been
disgusted by the 'impostures' of a false Christianity. As we told
you in our last letter, the Incarnation of the Word and so of
Christianity itself is lived today by means of socialist expressions
laden with materiality, just the opposite of a platonising conception, which in order to establish contemplation takes man out of
the material world. As testimony of the contemplative aspect of
our life, i.e. its transcendental dimension, we must each day learn
to understand more deeply and develop in ourselves the free
giving of one's life to others because of Christ, through concrete
acts done clearly for the common good of society.

Because we are convinced of this we shall always to the end of
our lives try to make eternity bloom in this world, where in fact
are the seeds of blessedness, by drawing the logic of the Incarnation out to its end.

Koson Srisang · *Recovering the Power of Life*

Koson Srisang, 'Recovering the Power of Life', *Ecumenical Review*, vol. 32,
no. 1, January 1980, pp. 66–74

What is it, then, that we are searching for? Naturally, we are
searching for what we need but do not now have. Or perhaps we
had it once but have somehow lost it. We are searching to be who
we are not yet – a fully human people – as God intended. More

specifically, in the context of contemporary Asia, from the perspective of the overwhelming majority (which includes the ethnic and cultural minorities) who are poor and oppressed, what is desperately needed now is the power of life. That is to say, the power not only to survive the present oppression and exploitation but also to actualize their full humanity, the power not only to produce and enjoy material life sustenance but also to live in freedom and community, justice and dignity, friendship and celebration. In short, the power to love God and to be in union with him . . . the power to be truly human.

I The Human Condition in Asia Today

Mountains of documents are available and millions of eye-witnesses are there to testify that the people of Asia are crying and dying in pain today. The pain in Kampuchea is but an example, a consequence or a result of a much deeper pain:

— the costly struggle of Koreans against the oppressive *Yushin* system;
— the popular unrest in China;
— the atrocities against the scheduled castes and the scheduled tribes in India;
— the plight of tea plantation workers in Sri Lanka and the Tamil minority there;
— the systematic oppression of the Koreans in Japan along with the Buraku minority in that country;
— the land-rights struggles of the Aborigines in Australia and the Maoris in New Zealand;
— the sense of meaninglessness and alienation of the relatively well-paid workers in Singapore;
— the increasing poverty of the Thai peasants and the systematic assassinations of their leaders . . .

All these, and thousands more, are other examples of this same pain. Truly, if we have anything in common in Asia today, it is certainly this pain of our people.

The painful destruction of life, culture and nature by international and systematic human actions is by no means limited to the above examples. Nor is it decreasing. As a matter of fact, the ugly threats of more death and destruction seem imminent, especially in Southeast Asia. Only a few years after the most destructive war in human history, the people in Kampuchea have suffered another war. Whether this war is called 'Vietnamese invasions' or 'national salvation' supported by the Vietnamese is immaterial for the present purpose, for the suffering it has brought to the people is clear. The Chinese 'teaching a lesson' or 'invasion' of Vietnam is part of the same story. And finally, if the mounting tension between Vietnam and Thailand is not peaceably resolved, a violent encounter between these two countries could, God forbid, escalate into a major war involving their respective powerful allies and perhaps the whole of Asia, if not the whole world. In that event, the pain would be even greater than ever before.

Distortion of Asian spirituality: the root cause

Why are the people in Asia suffering so much pain? What is the root cause of this pain? And what does it take to get rid of this pain?

I am prepared to say this pain is rooted in the Asian spiritual alienation itself. Therefore, in order to deal with it adequately we must 'enter the struggle at the level of spirituality.' as M. M. Thomas has pointed out.[14] By spirituality he means 'the structure of ultimate meaning and sacredness within which man lives and enters into a relationship with nature and with fellow men in politics, economics, society and culture'.[15] In a similar vein, C. S. Song perceives spirituality in terms of the 'totality of being that expresses itself in ways of life, modes of thinking, patterns of behaviour and conduct, and attitudes towards the mystery that surrounds our immediate world and that beckons us on to the height beyond heights, to the depth below depths, and to light beyond lights.'[16]

While agreeing with the encompassing character of spirituality as defined by Thomas and Song, I would simply specify it as the divine or sacred dimension of human life. This divine dimension is experienced most fully at the traumatic moments of life and death. It is also experienced when people meditate, contemplate, suffer, celebrate and grieve. As such, it is at once personal and communal, at once temporal and spatial. Experiencing the sacred or the divine, people become aware of their power and limitations, their freedom and compassion, their identity and obedience. Because of its profundity, the experience of the sacred often defies verbalization. In that case, a certain object most vital to that experience – such as the sun, the sky, the land, a mountain, a river, a tree or a piece of stone – is lifted up to signify the divine experience. And when the experience is articulated, such sounds as Yahweh, Om, God, Dhamma, Allah are the result.

This human experiencing of the divine is precisely what authentic religion is all about. Spirituality, therefore, is identical with religious vision, that is, the fullest expression of the divine dimension of human experience. It is precisely this religious vision which orders the human community. That is, it constitutes the community, unites its members, underlies its history, motivates its historiography, emanates its power and authority, and provides its sense of identity and integrity, honour and destiny. When this ordering religious vision is concealed, forgotten, distorted or abused by the community, particularly by its ruling elite, injustice and oppression prevail. People are overtaxed, their dignity is robbed, their wives and daughters are raped, their sons are taken away, their land is snatched, and their very life is threatened. This is substantially the human condition in Asia today. The distortion of the Asian spirituality, the concealment of the Asian religious vision, has brought about the massive pain and suffering among the people.

Perverted kind of western spirituality

But that is only half the picture, for at the very least the western imperialist onslaught has certainly precipitated the distortion of Asian spirituality and the concealment of Asian religious vision. Among other things, the privileged status of the missionaries and their converts in the eyes of the colonial rulers – one of the scandals in church history – was far from bearing witness to Jesus Christ the suffering Lord. Even today the situation has not changed very much. The 1977 workshop report of the All-Asia Consultation on Theological Education for Christian Ministry in Asia, in which 110 Christian leaders participated, had this to say:

> The Churches have continued to support intentionally and unintentionally the exploiters and those in power, and neglected the needy far too often. The majority of churches are middle class institutions preaching a gospel identified with middle class values. When the Church does minister to the poor, the effect is very often that of an other-worldly religion.[17]

Recently another remarkable group of Asian Christian leaders met in Manila to examine the patterns of domination and people's power in Asia. While recognizing and affirming the positive signs of Christianity in Asia, they have, in the spirit of repentance, stated:

> Because the Church is often found on the side of political powers against the people, it very easily participates in programmes and structures which not only cause injustice and oppression but which also reinforce the suffering of the people.[18]

The two quotations above are cited in order to illustrate a simple point. As spiritual legacy from the West, the Christian churches in Asia have largely remained aloof if not alienated from the struggle of the poor and the oppressed. This is part of what I mean by spiritual alienation, mentioned earlier. But sad as it is, this aspect of spiritual alienation is no more than a footnote in comparison to the point which follows.

If the distortion and concealment of the Asian spirituality or the Asian religious vision is one side of the spiritual-alienation coin, the other side is what may be called 'western spiritual imperialism'. Strong words, but do not panic yet.

Let me explain. First of all, the western spirituality which rears its ugly head in Asia is not authentic western spirituality. In fact, it is a perversion of true western spirituality which is destructive even for the western world itself. Authentic western spirituality by nature does not become imperialistic. It would be welcome, for it would enrich authentic Asian spirituality and vice versa. I shall return to this subject in the next section. But before that, a few more words on western spiritual imperialism.

Put simply, the perverted form of western spirituality which has become imperialistic is nothing more than greed itself: the love of money (and profit) and the idolatry of the self. This greed leads to the concentration of wealth and power which has its own dynamics (the law of the market) and ideology (capitalism – both private and state).

The expression of this western spiritual imperialism takes many shapes and forms. Let us take note here of the four most obvious: the transnational corporations which buy off lands from the poor farmers and exploit their cheap labour; the doctrine of national security with its concomitant militarism and armaments race promoting the use of force to safeguard 'national security', benefiting the few elite at the expense of the life of the people; the western-supported patterns of 'mission and evangelism' which

pluck out their converts from their own culture, emphasizing individual conversions and life beyond death at the expense of
authentic Christian compassion and concern for social justice; and
the economic growth-oriented development with massive government (and church) schemes that eventually deprive people of the
lands and fatten the cheque-books of the economic and political
elite, making the poor even poorer still.

This, then, is the human condition in Asia today. The poor and
the oppressed are crying and dying in pain. They cannot participate in the economic and political power structures, they are out
of their reach. The land of their ancestors has been taken away.
Their families are breaking down, separated by economic necess-
ities and wars. They are deprived of the opportunity to produce,
or if they do produce, someone else enjoys the harvest. Their
precious culture and tradition have been suppressed. Behind all
this is the loss of a heritage, the general malaise of spiritual
alienation, the losing of the power of life. Yet the people survive.
They continue to struggle, in hope, to recover the power of life!

II The Christian Response, now and in the future

In the light of the above description of the human condition in
Asia, what has been the response of churches and Christians?
What are the prospects? And what should happen in the years
ahead?

I have no intention here to preach nor to bother you with a
theological exercise. Rather, I am trying to look at our history
and to probe, to hope, to dream and to pray that God may lead
the poor and the oppressed of Asia, along with the rest of his
people, to the promised land, into his Kingdom where love and
justice, freedom and compassion, dignity and celebration are not
only a dream but also a reality.

In his excellent article 'The Church and the Poor in Asian
History', C. I. Itty traces the early missionary-churches' 'alliance
with the ruling powers and the dominant classes'. In many countries, Christian participation in the struggle for freedom and independence is noteworthy. The churches have also been involved
in social services. Their work among the low castes, the tribal
communities, the marginalized and the oppressed sectors of society indicates their concern. And, finally, Itty lifts up the challenge of evangelical poverty in the face of expensive institutions

and methods of work of the churches. To him, evangelical poverty for the Christians would be in tune with Hindu and Buddhist spirituality which believes that voluntary poverty is a supreme virtue and a religious value. He concludes that:

> . . . the attitudes and concern of the churches for the poor during the missionary era were ambiguous, if not contradictory. However . . . there were lay leaders and charismatic movements which challenged the churches to recognize the wholeness of the Gospel, the liberating power of Christ, and to make a radical option for the struggle of the poor and the oppressed.[19]

As early as 1949, almost a decade before the creation of an ecumenical regional body, Dr Manikam of India and Dr S. C. Leung of China organized a conference of leaders of Asian churches in Bangkok. It was the era of the Chinese Revolution and national independence. The building of nation-states was a dominant theme. But concern for the 'majority of the people . . . who live in conditions of abject poverty and under oppressive systems' was clear. It was recognized that these people are demanding 'fuller participation in the life of society, at the level where power is exercised'. Such is the revolutionary ferment, the statement says, and the churches 'must welcome' it, for in it are elements which are 'an expression of the human dignity' affirmed by God's love in Christ.[20]

United concern of Asian churches

The Bangkok Conference came to three radical conclusions: God may be active in revolutionary events; what God does in the revolutions may be outside the Church, but may not be outside Jesus Christ; and if what God does may not be outside Jesus Christ, the Church has to make a response.

In 1958 the East Asia Christian Conference (EACC) held its inaugural assembly. At its Fourth Assembly in 1973 the name was changed to the Christian Conference of Asia (CCA). It is fair to say that one cannot talk about the Christian concern for the poor and the oppressed in Asia today without talking at the same time about the EACC/CCA, particularly since the creation of the Urban Industrial Mission work in 1968, exactly a decade after the First Assembly. The same can be said about the role of the World Council of Churches (WCC), particularly during the last decade when various sub-units of the Programme Unit on Justice and

Service have become more actively involved in Asia. But since we are dealing specifically with Asia, let us focus on the EACC/CCA, mentioning WCC and others only in that connection.

For the EACC in 1958 the concern for development was seen in terms of economic growth, 'accompanied by a determined will to distribute equitably the new wealth created by this economic development'. The role of trade unions and peasant organizations as well as that of women was recognized. In 1964 EACC focused on lay training for their effective participation in the struggle of the Asian peoples for new life and new societies.

By 1968 the EACC began to talk about 'the dehumanizing factors inherent in the process of modernization and secularization'. It affirmed, for example, the necessity of 'revolutionary change in power-structures' as well as the necessity to create a new ethos of values, attitudes and personality structure. Furthermore, it saw that 'the organization of the masses on the basis of their demands and rights, and the involvement of these people in mass struggles, are necessary to secure a just share of power for them'. Even 'civil disobedience in cases where the law and the distribution of power are manifestly unjust' was also approved by the 1968 EACC Assembly. It was this Assembly which authorized the creation of the Urban Industrial Mission desk which has loomed very large in people's struggles and people's movements in Asia.

Promoting people's power

Initially inspired by urban industrial mission work in the West, Asian UIM has now come of age. Its present scope includes the rural concern as well. Thus a new name: Urban Rural Mission (URM). In terms of ecumenical collaboration and solidarity, URM is an integral yet very distinct part of the Urban Industrial and Rural Mission (UIRM) network, loosely but effectively 'coordinated' by the UIRM desk of the Commission on World Mission and Evangelism of the WCC.

What is UIRM or URM? What is it doing? How does it operate? The 1977 booklet, *Struggle to be Human*, is an excellent introduction to UIRM. A few quotations will help:

UIRM is clearly a story-telling sign of the presence of God in this world, its cities and its industries, its rural lands and people's movements (p. 50).

Motivated by the biblical message and the earthly ministry of Jesus Christ, UIRM has this to say:

> The event of Incarnation is the visible historical happening which fulfilled God's promise of Immanuel, God with us. Christ's earthly ministry was to bring justice and love to the poor and the oppressed; he identified himself with the homeless, the hungry and the poor, and he proclaimed their salvation. The salvation he brought was comprehensive and extended to all people. But Christ has shown a particular concern for the nameless and the powerless people to the extent of saying that even Solomon in all his glory was not arrayed like them, and in his life Christ fulfilled Mary's Song of Magnificat: 'He has filled the hungy with good things and the rich he has sent empty away.' . . .

A just society is possible

The final report of Jae Shik Oh as URM secretary of CCA, before he took on the position of CCA secretary for international affairs, reflects best the URM experience in Asia. As he anticipates Asian URM in the 1980s, three symbols loom large for Jae Shik Oh: people, land and power. URM in Asia flatly rejects the greed-based development syndrome for it 'has forced the majority of the people into the periphery'. He says:

> We have stuck to modest methodologies as a realistic approach to building people's power. We have emphasized local involvement rather than working on the national or international level. We have taken the process seriously, paying detailed attention to each step of tactics and strategies. We have dealt not with the nations as entities, but with people. We have subscribed to positions of particulars, rather than to universal statements.

The goal, of course, is to achieve a just society. But Asian URM believes that the method of achieving that goal is first and foremost the 'sharing with the people in their suffering'. For that is what Jesus Christ did. Professing Jesus Christ as Lord, we really have no choice but to obey his most important command: 'Love one another, just as I loved you. The greatest love a person can have for his friends is to give his life for them.' That's the way of the Cross, the true meaning of sharing the cup of suffering.

Sharing this cup in love and faith, in life and death, brings true victory, creates real unity and establishes new community – where love and justice, freedom and dignity, friendship and communion are the order of the day. Sharing the cup of suffering therefore is the key to recovering the power of life.

But sharing this cup of suffering is by no means romantic. In fact it is very costly. Loneliness, persecution and even death itself are no strangers to those walking this path. Therefore, an ethical courage is required, for no one should underestimate the massive, well-organized and technologically sophisticated powers of the oppressors of people. Equally true, however, is the fact that, in spite of the odds and the risks involved, God has ordained men and women with such ethical courage to grace history. In truth, He sent his own Son to set the example. Their actions constitute the sign of hope, the power of life over death and the advent of the Kingdom of God. As disciples of Christ, can we do otherwise than walk with them?

Alan Saw U · *Justing Love*

Alan Saw U, 'Christian Mission within the Socialist System', in Oh Jae Shik (ed.), *Towards a Theology of People*, Christian Conference of Asia 1977, pp. 72–74, 77–79

For a wealthy man Jesus simply asked him to share his wealth with others. Had the man been a learned man, Jesus would have requested him to share his educational knowledge and wisdom with others. This social principle of Jesus Christ applies to all people from all walks of life who are endowed with particular skills, power, personality and authority.

Jesus Christ is simply requesting us to work in solidarity with each other by sharing whatever we particularly possess for the benefit of others. We ought to be reminded that this kind of sharing is directly concerned with the 'Eternal Life' and the 'Kingdom of God' that we have been recklessly and meaninglessly preaching and talking about without really knowing the real implications from the bottom of our hearts.

Jesus in his life and mission spoke very clearly about concern for both people and society . . . to make and keep human life more humane. He takes into account the total life of the people and their societal condition and his act of salvation is the liberation of the people from all bondages that dehumanize them to a fuller human existence and a more abundant life . . . a life that will free the people from the situation and condition that keeps them in bondage under the elements of the world. For this kind of saving act, Jesus chose the way of solidarity with the weaker sections of the society in their struggle for authentic humanhood.

The Gospel of Jesus is really a historical story of practical dynamic socialism. The Gospel gives us the vision of the creation of a new humanity. It activates us to participate in a socializing process of life that will lead to a more just and righteous human community . . . a community of equality, love, peace and joy. This community of equality, love, peace and joy is what Jesus meant by 'Thy Kingdom come on Earth.' In other words, the Kingdom of God can come on earth only through our concrete involvement in community affairs and our socializing actions to create a more righteous human relationship where each will live for all and all will live for each. This kind of a community in solidarity will surely be a sign and a foretaste of the Kingdom of God.

'Saving Act' calls for 'Socializing Act' and Socializing Act in turn calls for 'Socializing Love' – a love that has concrete social concerns for others around us. It is a kind of love that will enable us to treat all as our equals. This type of love demands justice. It is not a simple love but a 'Justing Love' – a love that does justice to others. Then this love will move us to work in cooperation with one another for the common concern of building a just human community. In brief, the Gospel requires of us to work in and for justice.

The biblical mandate for missionary action is a mandate for social action. It calls for us to do justice. Our lack of responsibility in doing justice to others will surely lead us to injustice because we will find ourselves oppressing others.

Whenever there is injustice, it is definitely sure that something is wrong with the human relationship. We can tell at once that there is lack of love and solidarity that give birth to unjust social structures and these structures are keeping us in bondage. Here we can clearly see that these unjust social structures are simply the things that have been institutionalized by us. These unjust social structures are the elements of the world because they are the fruits and the results of the absence of love which is the central theme of Christ and Christianity.

What are the forms and patterns of the elements of the world that are keeping us in bondage, that are dehumanizing and barring us from attaining a more abundant life that Christ promised us? That has become a real challenging issue to all of us today. This question also brings us to the point that only in the concrete understanding of social life of our country lies the possibility for us to explore concretely under what kind of elements of the world we are in bondage. Only then we may be able to find ways and means to liberate ourselves from the bondages of the world we are living in.

Christ promised to be with us always. He will also be with us in our struggling to liberate ourselves from the elements of the world of which we are in bondage.

We must intelligently participate in every realm of social life around us in order to manifest a just human relationship at all levels of life. This is a duty and the only way of life for all Christians.

In the light of this theological understanding, what follows are the analyses, implications and strategies of such a Christian social involvement in regard to our Burmese context.

Situation

As a purposeful involvement in social life is based on a sound knowledge of current social happenings, we must try to understand and systematically analyse the social problems around us.

The progressive knowledge of man and its consistent application gives birth to the phenomenon of chains of rapid social changes that lead to social revolution. It carries with it both humanizing and dehumanizing factors at the same time.

We, the Christians of Burma, are now being alerted by the philosophy of the Burmese Way to Socialism and its interpretation of Burmese history as a sequence of social class struggles within society. Its goal is the creation of a humane society, without the dehumanizing factors of modern social development efforts.

Since March 2, 1962, to wipe out the exploitation of man by man and to work for the restoration of basic human rights, the present government has instituted the 'Burmese Way to Socialism' with its basic philosophy of 'The System of the Correlation between Man and His Environment'. It has been striving to move towards appraising, appreciating and anticipating the basic needs of the people at the grass-roots level by far-reaching and gradual social, land and educational reforms. The ceiling on ownership of business enterprises, the nationalization of banks, foreign estates and big national companies and the eradication of landlordism and feudalism and other such measures, have gone a long way to promote human dignity and social justice for all . . .[21]

Realizing the fact that the prevailing injustices are not unavoidable, but have been brought in, institutionalised and perpetuated, the only possible and sure way of concrete action to create a more righteous socialist order is to commit ourselves to work with the people for liberation from oppression. We seek motivation for this commitment on the one hand in the proper understanding of the Christian religion and on the other hand, in the philosophy and ideology of the Burmese Way to Socialism.

To combat 'Structuralized Individual Selfishness' calls for a movement to help us strive forward, along with the people, in the process of socializing the revolution within the present socialist system. This kind of movement requires us to immerse our lives theoretically and practically in the struggle of the people with the following objectives:

(a) To build up a socialist consciousness among the people at the grass-roots level and help them discover the present socio-political realities and the corresponding implications for their individual responsible action.

(b) To start a process of education and conscientization of the people to discover the root causes of the problems they are facing; to ask themselves how they could solve their problems relying mainly on strength that comes from united action and the socio-economic programmes of the government.

(c) To stimulate the people about the importance of their solidarity with one another and to motivate them to join hands with others in the same plight to liberate themselves by standing up together for their rights and privileges through legal process, taking up their due places in the respective socio-political structures of their constituencies.

Strategies

The importance of these objectives will be evident if we briefly analyse the social, political, cultural and economic situation in which we are living.

From the beginning BCC-URM refused to be simply a movement of protest; it did not therefore try to make the reform of the church or the bourgeoisie the main targets of its action-reflection. Instead it decided to sponsor an experimental social action training with the hope of helping young men and women from various communities in different parts of the country, to help them equip themselves with the needed techniques and skills as demanded by the needs of their communities and to prepare themselves not to work for the people but to work and live with the people and share their daily life. Through this process we intend to change and transform the society for equality and justice. We assume that with changes taking place in the society, the institutional church and the bourgeoisie will then gradually realise their irrelevance and would inevitably follow or face even further irrelevance and ultimate extinction.

Content, style and organization of training methodology are largely determined by the problems we are facing and are flexibly tailored to the needs of the individual participants.

The training courses have the purpose of developing 'change enablers', equipped with a perspective of social change and a knowledge and techniques to –

(a) conduct structural analysis of the socio-political reality.
(b) understand the conditions responsible for increasing injustice and oppression.
(c) gain insights into the inter-action of religion and socialism.
(d) discover in detail the type and approaches of social involvement which will make concrete contributions to the real transformation of society.
(e) grow in spiritual motivation demanding commitment to social involvement.
(f) free them from all preoccupations that make them unfit to identify themselves with the grass-roots people; their social status, their mentality and their philosophical orientation.

We firmly believe that: 'For the promotion of social justice people should be given the chance to fend for themselves and grow within the possibilities of their own situation. Only then will they have the opportunity of growing as a self-determining community and not as others outside the area of their community would want them to grow.'

In the light of the above concept the role of the young people who are trained to be 'change enablers' for social transformation is basically to catalyse, energise, and stimulate people to think, act and grow on their own. They are given provisional skills to nurture a core of leaders and a strong mass base and abilities to inspire actions of the masses with a belief in themselves rather than depending on the 'change enablers.'

Through this slow and long-term manoeuvre from bottom up within the government apparatus, it is envisaged that we may be able to help build human communities which are self-reliant; communities composed of a people who can critically think and plan out; democratically decide and act on their own problems.

Conclusion

In a country of a one-party political system, people have to be conscious of being political entities and responsible citizens. We Christians too must remember that, like others, we too are citizens of the country we belong to.

We must be in the world and yet keep ourselves free from the bondage of the elements of the world. We must always remember that as we are parts of the body of Christ, our individual selfishness and our individual and personal sin affect the whole body of Christ – the people around us and the social environment of which we are a part.

Material things are good things. They are not bad. They are all created by God. In fact, we are making them bad by using them for our own selfish gain through our own selfish means. We do not think of mutually sharing them with others.

We must share the material things with others so that this material world might be presentable in the sight of God.

Our fellow citizens of other faiths and no faiths are compelled by 'social feelings' to work towards the goal of socialism. We Christians are compelled by both 'social and spiritual feelings' to work towards the goal of socialism. We must be more sensitive to injustice and oppression and must be even more active than others to work for the realization and implementation of the themes and plans of socialism. We must do twice the work others do in order to manifest the socialist order. To do so requires us to relinquish our status quo and deny our self-centredness and selfishness. We will then be poor, but by being poor we will have the chance to be productive in transforming society for a more just and righteous order.

6 · Indonesia

In Indonesia successive waves of Hindu, Buddhist, Islamic and Christian cultures have been superimposed on a diversity of animistic and mystical practices. Orthodox Christians first arrived from India in the seventh century but Islam, first introduced in the twelfth century, steadily extended its influence until 1900. It remains in varying degrees the faith of 80% of the population. The Dutch, who arrived in 1615, did not obtain complete control until early this century. Their oppressive methods, e.g. in the use of forced labour (until 1917) in the intensive cultivation of plantations for export, brought continuing revolts, in which Muslim Hadjis were often the leaders. Ethnic and geographical divisions would combine with religious and ideological differences to produce almost continuous conflict in one or other of Indonesia's regions throughout this century, quite apart from major war against the Japanese and the Dutch.

Non-denominational Protestantism became the colonial state church after two centuries of the Dutch Reformed Company Church, and in 1942 there were still 428 ministers, the majority Indonesian, on the civil service payroll. Traditions of quietism and dualistic beliefs regarding church and world marked both Protestant and Roman Catholic Churches alike.[1] But despite harsh repression by the Dutch in the 1930s the Student Christian Movement (GMKI) then became a centre for Christian nationalist organization. During the Japanese occupation and the attempt, 1945–49, by the Netherlands and her allies to reimpose colonial rule, Christians fully participated in the resistance and later protracted guerrilla warfare. This was a conscious and courageous option taken by countless Indonesian Christians, strengthened in part by the work of such seminaries as the Sekolah Tinggi Theologia (STT), Jakarta, which since 1934 had sought to relate theology to Indonesian society and culture. Identification with the long revolutionary struggle was to shape all subsequent Indonesian theology and those who laid the basis for this combined a full political or military career with their writing and reflecting.

Johannes Liemena, founder of the SCM and later a Cabinet Minister in many administrations in the 1950s, strongly influenced the participation of Christians in nation-building over four decades. The church stands amidst society as a signpost, he regularly insisted, 'with both feet in Indonesian soil . . . contributing both in effort and thinking to the development of society and nation'.[2] Because the aims of the church and those of the revolution are parallel, because the church finds her self-reliance and ecumenicity as the nation finds independence and unity, the church may fully participate in the revolution.

Tihar Bonar Simatupang, later Chief of Staff of the Indonesian Army, has been perhaps the most prominent of church leaders and theologians since writing his 'Journal from Banarang' during the War of Independence. In numerous writings he has sought to relate the life of faith to the work of nation-building, the history of present events to eschatology. In his collected articles up to 1967, Simatupang wrestles with the question 'how can we live in the midst of hopes and change as Christians who know that ultimate hope is not located in the processes of history, but in the God of history Himself?'[3] It is one history, he affirms, and the church is in the frontlines because to participate in God's plans is to enter Indonesia's struggles. This requires, he believes, both 'a body of theological thinking born out of a common involvement', and an ecumenical laity confessing this theology in their life-witness.[4] A close colleague of Simatupang, Peter D. Latuihamallo, was MP in the 1950s and later Rektor of the STT. He has written extensively on the relation of politics to mission, which, he says, is always carried out within a continuing revolution against all levels of domination. Because Christ's deeds of salvation always bring revolutionary change, there can be no neutral zone for the church. And personal life in particular is challenged by political and social emancipation.[5]

The most significant model for local theology in Indonesia has emerged in groups related to the Indonesian Christian Council (DGI). It is that of a 'double wrestle': the wrestle to understand and receive the grace that is in Christ, and to confess this in worldly action. From the time of revolutionary struggle, to participation in parliamentary government (1950–58), and during the deepening crisis of guided democracy (1959–65), a significant section of the church would maintain this theological wrestle.

A central issue was the nature of the 'Panca Sila' State,[6] which rejected Islamic control in favour of a religious pluralism. In the continuing social and religious tensions since 1950, Christians have seen in the Panca Sila principles a guarantee of religious freedom. The prospect of fuller toleration and dialogue between Muslim and Christian, outlined by W. B. Sidjabat in an important study,[7] has only sometimes eventuated. Amongst Christians who have in recent years worked and written on these issues, Fridolin Ukur of the Institute of Research and Study, Jakarta, insists that it is dialogue, in everyday Indonesian life, a dialogue in action, that is required. Eka Darmaputera, a Jakarta pastor and writer, describes a positive, not static tolerance which comes from work for the common aim of human development and against common evils of poverty and need.[8] Guidelines from the 1970 Conference of Roman Catholic Bishops declared in similar vein that the meeting point of religions is concern for a just and civilized humanity.

The related concern of Indonesianization appears in the work of regional writers like B. A. Abednego (East Java), F. H. Sianipar (North Sumatra) and W. Mastra (Bali) – Mastra in particular leading his church in the recovery of symbol and art-forms by which the gospel is experienced in Indonesian culture.[9] Judo Poerwowidagdo of Yogyakarta's Duta Watjana Seminary has similar objectives in his theological work. For Catholics, Indonesianization has been a continuing issue since the formation of the Catholic hierarchy in 1961. Amongst those giving it special attention, Felix Danuwinata focusses on development of an Indonesian priesthood, and on the encounter of Indonesian religions with the problems of human development. It can be said, in fact, that whether the initial point for theological reflection has been the Panca Sila State, Indonesian culture and religion, or the worship and mission of the church, problems of justice and development have became central in the last 15 years and now provide the primary context in which theology's 'double wrestle' must be carried out.

In the years prior to 1965 both Catholics and Protestants had their own Christian political party in which many of their most capable clergy and lay people were active. The events of 1965–67, which resulted in the replacement of these experimental democracies by military rule, stand out from the frequent uprisings and civil wars Indonesia has experienced since 1948, in the degree to which they have left major divisions in Indonesian society. Apart from the bloody elimination of almost 3 million alleged Communists, 100,000 political prisoners were still detained in often inhuman circumstances in 1975. The army has replaced the tentative pre-1965 socialism with a highly dependent capital-intensive economy, along with a military presence which dominates national institutions and local communities alike.[10]

In circumstances such as these it is easy to see how the issues of justice and development have become of central theological (as well as political) concern. The immediate response of churches to the turmoil of 1965-66 is seen in the letter of the Emergency Annual Synod of the Christian Church in East Java (December '65) and in the Message of the DGI of September 1966. This called for 'positive and creative efforts to restore the life of state and society' and for both criticism and self-criticism regarding injustice and oppression. The Catholic Church which already had a number of mass organizations involved in social action declared in 1966, 'her responsibility for the improvement of the social structure and for economic development, in which (her) supernatural vocation will be transparent'. Although many churches along with the DGI have for example maintained emergency services since that time for detainees and their families, it has been left to small groups or individuals to raise the prophetic questions regarding the larger issues. Latuihamallo has often voiced reservations concerning the role of militarism in Indonesia; Cardinal Darmowijono was strongly critical of government abuses in the 1971 election; and Simatupang, who had resigned in criticism of Soekarno's policies in 1959, wonders (1974) whether the army's heavy involvement in the development process will not lead to a more and more rigid militarized state. Poets and novelists had long contributed to the nationalist movement and to social protest and in the period after 1965 some of the most eminent writers would be imprisoned for their criticism; among them Muchtar Lubis, Promoedya Ananta Toer, Iwan Simatupang, Sitor Situmarang and W. S. Rendra.

The function of religious leaders in social criticism is expressly outlined by Danuwinata in 'Religion's Tussle with the Problem of Development'.[11] Religion, he declares, must both resist all

attempts to absolutize particular patterns of development and also
distance itself from all totalitarian authority. In order to attain a
humane society as well as a religious community which is truly
liberating, Danuwinata writes, there is required thorough empir-
ical study, repentance for collective social sin, and a commitment
to people where society is most inhuman. A specifically Christian
response to these demands is made by another Jesuit, Robert
Hardowirjono (Yogyakarta),who has been like Danuwinata an
advisor to the Indonesian Conference of Bishops. Since 1972 he
has made many contributions to the reshaping of Christian ministry, both of priests and laity, and to the understanding of ecumenism and mission in a developing society. He places these
(1976) in the context of a 'dialogue of life', which involves a
genuine experience of deprivation and oppression, a commitment
to bring about social justice, and an organized 'action and reflection in faith', which he declares is a constitutive dimension of
evangelism. The extract printed here comes from a lengthy two-
part study of these themes published in 1977.[12]

The biblical basis for such a position is explored in the work of
Liem Khiem Yang, Rektor of the Sekolah Tinggi Theologia, Jakarta. 'Enacting the Acts of God' (1973) is a careful study of New
Testament teaching on the present activity of God in our midst.
This he maintains gives a different model for our doing of theology, for both Jesus and Paul move from a discernment of what
God is doing to an enactment of that in immediate concrete
situations. He then pleads for a co-operative, and embodied,
theologizing which will make this possible.[13] Along with his colleague Liendert Oranje, with students and community workers,
he later (1974–76) implements the model in such suffering communities as Klender and Cheng Kareng. This 'Hidup Bertheolo-
gia' (Living Theology) appears now as an early example of the
'more concrete theology' called for by the Conference of the DGI
at Sukubumi in 1972, and of the 'dialogue of life' later described
by Hardowirjono. Albert Widjaja, lecturer in economics and
active in the Institute Oikumene Indonesia,reflects in his paper
'Beggarly Theology' (1973) on the implications of such approaches
for an emerging indigenous theology and part of this is included
here. His more recent writings include economic studies of workers' participation and the operation of multi-national corporations,
and a study of the relation of the Kingdom of God to the renewal
of the environment.[14] Another area of 'living theology' in which

both Yang and Wijaja have been involved, arises from the experience of urban and rural frontier ministries.

These had multiplied to meet the urgent social needs of the early 1970s and soon included a range of ministries in social action, development motivation and community organization in which theological reflection is an integral part.[15] In the related programmes of lay training, Ardi Soejatnoe and Wismoadi Wahono of the East Java Lay Training Institute, D. R. Martimoe and Pontas Nasution of the Institute Oikumene, have written important articles. Josef Widyatmaja, who directs a Social Welfare Foundation in Solo, is one example of the many lay-people and pastors now directly participating in community action and development. Regular and co-operative biblical and theological reflection is integral to their activity, and Widyatmaja's own writings arise from a continuing teamwork with neighbour villagers and attempt a rewriting of the gospel from within their experience.[16]

Other frontier ministries focus more especially on human rights issues and important documents have emerged from these. The Conference of Indonesian Secular Priests in 1972 issued a lengthy statement (edited by the author, Y. B. Manganwijaya), entitled 'The Solidarity of the Church with the Indonesian People, especially the Poor and Discarded'. In 1974, 1976 and 1977 other Christian groups issued documents critical of government policies and advocating a restoration of human rights. Yap Thiam Hien of the DGI Department of Service and Development has written of his experience in prison, where Muslim, Christian and allegedly Communist detainees shared together in Bible-reading and prayers. He testifies to a personal experience there of repentance and liberation, which, he declares, frees him to work now for the liberation of those who suffer.[17] Discrimination against non-indigenous minorities such as the Chinese has been the concern of writers like Chris Hartono and Yahya Wiriadanata, and women's rights have been given strong articulation by Christian women scholars like T. Omas Ihromi, B. Simorangkir-Simandjuntak, and Henriette-Marianne Katoppo. Katoppo places these questions in the context of the overall tasks of the development of people in Indonesia and of the formulation of a genuinely Indonesian theology. Extracts from her book *Compassionate and Free* follow. As well as many articles in secular journals, she has published a number in ecumenical publications, on theology and social issues related to contemporary Asian women.[18]

Robert Hardowirjono · *Serving the Faith by Promoting Justice*

Robert Hardowirjono, 'Service of the Faith in East Asia', *Teaching All Nations*, 1977, no. 2, pp. 112–17, 120–21

There is a 'spiritualistic' tradition which warns us that liberation and development, earthly well-being and human justice are not *the Kingdom of God.* They are ambivalent, and often lead men away from God. In the emphasis on social justice there lurks the danger of neglecting God to serve men, and of diverting the Church from its task of preaching Jesus Christ. Eschatology and the perspective of eternity relativise and de-emphasize the world and temporal prosperity. Involvement in social action and political struggle can scarcely be called Christian apostolate.

Human values of development and justice, on the other hand, are not realized in the abstract, but within social and economic realities and concrete human relationships. And it is within these relationships that the service of faith is to be realized. It is essential to be convinced that there is a *legitimate*, even a *necessary horizontalization*, since the Son of God became man, and the risen Lord is met and served in needy man.

Hence, the cause of human development and justice is our concern, not because injustices resulting from imbalance in the developmental process might lead to an explosion of violence, nor because Communism might take over and our countries might be lost to the 'democratic' camp, nor even to ease our consciences and find relief in an uncomfortable situation.

We are interested because human development and liberation are *intrinsic* to human wholeness and *salvation*, essential to the incarnate Person of Jesus Christ and his risen life, to the love that lies at the heart of the Christian reality, to the rights and dignity of every human person and the human community. *Salvation* having a personal and interior dimension, the total liberation of man in order to be genuine would have to include the economic, social and political dimension.

Says the decree on *Our Mission Today:*
'The Christian message is a call to *conversion:* conversion to *the love of God*, which necessarily implies conversion to *the*

love of men, which necessarily includes conversion to *the demands of justice.'*[19]

Since *salvation* is concerned with all the aspects of human activity and involvement, our experience of it cannot be separated from these areas of life and from active engagement in them, so that they may be progressively humanized, liberated and enriched.

The *history of salvation* means that salvation *takes place in history.* Hence, our service of faith, which is the proclamation of salvation, embodies itself in the events, aspirations, the signs of the times and the 'historical contents' of the present process in East Asia. Our Christian message, if presented as an answer to the needs of our peoples, will announce freedom to reach God, freedom from personal enslavements. Again, it is a call to conversion in a faith committed to God, to man, and to the transformation of society, so that men will uphold *the dignity of the human person,* provide the opportunities for development and progress, and promote that quality of life enabling them *to reflect their sonship in God.*

In the spheres of the 'secular' and the 'profane', God and his Christ are active in the Spirit, expecting our 'partnership' in the shaping and reshaping of human history and human destiny, our 'participation' in His on-going act of creation and re-creation. All God's gifts are also our tasks. It is essential to defatalize history. Providence is not fate. And in the Christian vision there is no Providence of which we are not part.

Our service of faith requires us to avert from people 'certain *false images of God* which prop up and give an aura of legitimacy to unjust social structures,' and from '*ambiguous images* of God which appear to release man from his inalienable responsibilities.' In certain regions in East Asia, within the atmosphere of certain religious beliefs, this is very important. We have to help people to rediscover *the true God,* 'who, in Jesus Christ, chose to share our human pilgrimage and make our human destiny irrevocably his own.'[20]

As true as faith implies much more than justice, and the deep causes and consequences of unbelief cannot be simply reduced to the social level, our problems in East Asia have roots that are not just social and technological, but also personal and spiritual: 'men are hungry: but hungry not for bread, but for the word of God.' Unbelief, *contemporary theoretical and practical* atheism, *reveals itself as one of the main causes of injustices.* While injustice, if it is tolerated and left unchallenged, generates new forms of atheism.

The God of love reveals Himself in *His Son Jesus Christ.* For any theology of development and promotion of justice, therefore, a *christological* foundation is essential.

In creating the world, God's plan was to entrust to us a world to be built and brethren to be loved. In order to become *images of God* in Christ and through Christ, 'the Image of the invisible God' (see Col. 1, 15 and 2 Cor. 4, 4), we too must become *co-creators.*

Christ also came to reveal the *sin and failure* of human enterprises. He is the bearer of a message from a God who *reconciles* all men. Christ is, moreover, Himself the supreme reconciliation. He recapitulates past history and opens up a new future for sinful humanity.

Hence, the Christian is one who follows Christ in announcing *the reconciliation* to be found even in the conflicts and ambiguities of human history. He is *actively* waiting for the Christ who will come again. This Christian message of 'creation' and reconciliation in our days has to be embodied in our efforts for human development and the promotion of justice.

The Christian is one who has, in his life, come to know the person of Jesus Christ and his Gospel. He has been given some experience of the reality of the living Christ. And henceforth he meets his brother in a love and concern that finds its foundation and energy within that faith and his experience of Christ. In his suffering brother he would encounter Christ, waiting for him to relieve him from his suffering, and to be lifted up in the freedom of the children of God.

The Church of Christ the Incarnate must be a servant Church, *in forma servi,* like Christ himself. Her mission primarily is a mission of service to mankind.

What are we then? A *'Church for the poor'?* or a *'Church for everyone'?* We easily accept that God in Holy Scripture always appears to be on the side of the poor, the weak, the little ones; and that Jesus also particularly loved the poor.

He identified Himself with the people of his time and his country. He made not only their religious and spiritual interests his own, but also their physical needs, their sicknesses, social injustice. *'To identify oneself'* does not only mean to look at with sympathetic consideration, with compassion and understanding, but: *to make it one's own* And this does not only imply to understand and to share, but also *to remedy,* to help in creating better living conditions.

Through participation in the Incarnation and through the communication of God's love, our development work is an integral part of the Church's mission, and therefore constitutive to our service of faith.

Yet at the moment one concludes that the Church – and we are that Church! – today should side with the poor, not merely by words, but by *deeds,* people begin to object that the Church is for everyone, rich as well as poor, and hence should not take sides with the poor and reject the rich.

Of course there is *no tension* whatsoever between the salvation of the poor and the salvation of *all.* God's plan of salvation is for all men. But the point is that *because* it is for *all* men, it has to consider especially the poor. Only when the *'last ones'* are saved, will the entire humanity be saved, like the ill in the Gospel. The poor should be the sign that salvation is for all . . .

Development work, the promotion of justice, is essentially a Christian *witness of life and of deed.* It speaks the profane language of the oppressed and the deprived in our countries. But, if understood in the Christian way, it is formed and experienced from a religious dimension, the dimension of the Gospel. The proclamation of the word would remain empty and ineffectual, even incredible in a certain sense, without the witness of the deed, of concrete practical love and fellowship.

Since for the Church in East Asia poverty is a question of life or death, the lives Christian *leaders* live must be, in appearance and reality, close to the lives of the masses. In BISA II[21] it was keenly felt that the Church should revise her own life style and institutions, in order to first realize within herself whatever she has to say about social justice. Because without justice inside the Church our message will never be credible.

All the way through our theological reflection *the mystery of Incarnation* has been the underlying source and inspiration. *Dialogue* with our fellowmen in their actual life-situations is as a matter of fact the way we live for ourselves 'dialectically' the life of Christ Incarnate within us.

Our *service to faith* is that dialogue, since the Church is to *evangelize the Asian 'revolution', and at the same time she is to be evangelized by the Asian 'revolution'.*

(a) Let us start asserting that in the context of that service, dialogue with adherents of other living faiths and religious traditions is imperative in order to understand their deepest needs and aspirations. Religions are the keystone to East Asian cultures. And – since God through His Spirit is guiding humanity towards its fulfilment in Christ the new Man – 'inter-religious dialogue is the response of Christian faith to God's saving presence in the religious traditions of mankind and the expression of the firm hope of the fulfilment of all things in Christ.'[22] Especially the 'great' Religions have become transforming agents in the plurality of cultural and religious situations of our countries, and at the same time have been themselves transformed by the local cultures.

(b) As it has often been stressed, we as the Church should speak with a voice echoing the life of our continent. This is the only way we may become an *epiphany*, a living proof that faith in Jesus Christ can help our nations to build an East Asia which will be truly human.

Hence, we *all must participate* in our common mission of humanization, by being a constructive force, by becoming involved in our society. We must also be *prophets* and have the courage to proclaim genuine justice, which means taking sides with the deprived majorities. Our cooperation with other agents of development implies in itself that we should also provide *a critical force* with regard to oppressive structures and institutions and be the intrepid defenders of *human values*, of integrity and liberty. We should be concerned with both *'micro-evangelization'* (individual conversions) and with *'macro-evangelization'* (the reform of structures), well-balanced according to the local circumstances.

(c) At the same time, we must *learn to listen* to the people among whom we live. Since everywhere we find ourselves confronted with the guiding presence of the Spirit, God speaks to us through events. This is why *'the signs of the times'* are the realm of our apostolic discernment in the Spirit. The experience of East Asia's growth and development, with its failures and critical situations, is an interpellation, contains God's word addressed to us right now.

Just like Israel at certain moments in her history, our communities are now passing through a period of *repentance*, individual and collective, to prepare us – as Christians and as Jesuits –

for a radical *transformation* of our way of life. We may have to abandon our role as defender – consciously or unconsciously – of the *status quo*, and impelled by the force of the Spirit, eventually become *the prophetic community of faith* our countries need.

Mere goodwill and dedication are no longer enough. To be able to identify the structures which obstruct the total development of man, to look beyond the complex phenomena of society, and to recognize the forces which give logic to seemingly unrelated events, we must have *the facts analyzed critically.*

Spiritual discernment, although indispensable, cannot replace profound and serious study. This is required to understand and solve the economic, social and cultural problems of society. Neither is it sufficient to point out that sin is the deepest cause for oppressing structures and injustice. In order to find our way through this complex reality, we need *the human sciences* no less than philosophy or theology.

Says *Pope Paul VI:*
'Mere denunciation, often too late or ineffective, is not sufficient. There must be *an analysis* of the *deep rooted causes* of such situations and a firm commitment to face up to them and resolve them correctly.'[23]

Scientific investigation is essential in order to clarify for ourselves which *concrete forms of injustice* we have to deal with in our countries, and what exactly in the real life of our people is meant by 'justice' as an ideal to be realized.

Seen in the light of the problem of *inculturation* also, the patterns of a prosperous and just society for each of our countries are still to be devised. And for this purpose the free expression and the appreciation of cultural values at all levels of society, especially those of the most oppressed and voiceless, appear as indispensable.

It is to be expected, therefore, that in our action for justice in the framework of serving our faith, there will be a multiplicity of responses, according to the particular life situations of each country.

All this is even more necessary, since the wording of *Our Mission Today* and other documents seems not specified or appropriate enough to be considered as concrete directives for our specific apostolate in our regions.

Let us keep aware, that – in thus scrutinizing the signs of the times, and in faithfully responding to them in the light of the Gospel, i.e. in view of man's total fulfilment in Christ – we are working on the *incarnation* of our faith in human society with the perspective of its full *redemption* at the end of times. We meet our fellow men precisely where they are, i.e. in the very problems of their lives rightly understood. This encounter with man deep down in his 'joys' and 'hopes', but still more in his 'griefs and anxieties', and particularly with 'those who are poor or in any way afflicted', this exactly is what the Son of God meant to bring about by becoming man.

This is essential in our *solidarity with the poor*, which should be understood in a much deeper sense than merely 'living among the poor.' Here precisely we continue in ourselves *the mystery of Christ Incarnate. . . .*

Albert Widjaja · *Beggarly Theology*
A Search for a Perspective toward Indigenous Theology

Albert Widjaja, 'Beggarly Theology', *South East Asian Journal of Theology*, vol. XIV. 2, pp. 39–45

I Introduction

The term 'beggarly theology' in the discussion below will be distinguished from the 'theological begging'. The latter term refers to a theological pursuit which more or less imitates, borrows and transfers from other theological work. Such a theologian tries to explore and interpret the meaning of Christian existence, through the structure and content of a borrowed theology. He has the profession of receiving. Theological pursuit thus described is found among the theologians or church leaders of the third world (or of the 'younger churches'). They believe that the theology of Martin Luther, Karl Barth, Rudolf Bultmann, Billy Graham, Paul Tillich, Gerhard von Rad, or Reinhold Niebuhr, are 'the theology' indispensable for the development of Christian faith. Any deviation from these systems of theology is considered shallow, untheological, and even perhaps sinful or secular. The theology of these great men often receives a special status, almost equal to the Scripture. The practice of theological begging has been one of the major outcomes of the western missionary endeavour. And it is not least promoted by the western seminary theologians, who educated the church leaders of the third world. Most problematic of all, we the third world churchmen tend to perpetuate such practice.

The 'beggarly theology', however, is different in the sense of the spirit of the beggar, not in the sense of the profession described above. The true spirit of the beggar can be discovered when he encounters a garbage container. He faces the garbage with a sense of anticipation. He believes that something will come out as invaluable, even though the garbage as a whole is considered junk by the society. He has an attitude of respect to the things which society rejects or depreciates. Similarly the beggarly theology takes its own experience and native culture seriously, even though such cultural experience is considered pagan, secular, and inferior by the western missionary theology. He has an independent spirit which is not motivated by rebellion or national pride, but by a desire of being sincere to his Christian commitment. He realizes that to be true and faithful to Jesus Christ, one has to be detached from the demand of conformity to the man-made theology. He wants to be genuine in his Christian life and witness. But such genuineness requires uninhibited acceptance of the demand of the Gospel and whole-hearted encounter with the challenges of his culture and society. The beggarly theology hungers after the righteousness of the Kingdom of God, not the wisdom of the western theology. In His Sermon on the Mount, Jesus said: 'Blessed are the poor in spirit for theirs is the Kingdom of God. Blessed are those who hunger and thirst for righteousness, for they shall be satisfied ' (Matthew 5:3, 6). The beggarly theologian seeks a new orientation, because he wants to be genuine in his commitment to Christ, and far-reaching in his witness.

The term 'beggarly theology' may be confusing for many people. It may be charged as emotional, indecent, and unscholarly terminology. These charges may be made by those who forget that the majority of the third world people are poor. These charges may come out of pride with their identification with western theology which often substitutes for holiness cultural cleanliness. The confidence in the power of the Gospel is replaced by the complacency of the power of wealth. Freedom in Christ is replaced by conformity to the existing social order. Even with such opposition, the beggarly theology continues its work, because it is not designed for the western world. It is for the third world whose true problem has often been ignored.

The beggarly attitude is an attitude of identification with the struggle of the dispossessed, of the lost, of the disintegrated ones who are caught in the modernization process. The beggarly attitude seeks to accompany those whose 'souls hunger after the living bread, and their spirits thirst for the living water.'[24] The beggarly theology does not seek, however, to bring revolution nor to tear down the social order; it seeks the path of gradual but decisive transformation of human hearts and human relations as done by the early church.

The beggarly theology does not say that culture is more authoritative than the Gospel. On the contrary, it does say that on the one hand the beggarly theology rejects any form of conformity; and on the other hand it maintains serious confrontation between the Gospel and the culture in which it lives. It does not flee from its society. Yet it wants to move beyond the trivialities of the society in the light of the Gospel. Realizing its poverty in theology, in culture, etc., the beggarly theology gives special attention to its relation with God who promises: 'For the needy shall not always be forgotten, and the hope of the poor shall not perish forever.' (Psalm 4:8). The beggarly theology emphasizes the need of repentance when it is confronted by Christ. It is by this experience that a new and substantial theology can be gained.

In short, the beggarly theology offered here basically reflects a search for fundamental perspectives through which a truly indigenous theology is to be developed. The beggarly theology, however, is not 'the' indigenous theology! It is one among many approaches to indigenous theology. Yet it is indispensable for an indigenous theology. It does not stand in false hope, because it seeks to be a disciple of Christ who is our hope. As Paul says: 'Though he was rich, yet for your sake he becomes poor, so that by his poverty you may become rich' (II Cor. 8:9 cf. Phil. 2:5–6, Rev. 2:9). An indigenous theology from a poor church is indeed possible. The resources are right 'here', not 'there' in overseas places.

II A Perspective for Indigenous Theology

The current discussion about indigenous theology may be a fad for some and fruitless for others. Yet it may always be significant for the third world churches. It reflects a constant struggle to free themselves from the letter of the 'law',[25] and a constant quest to live with the Gospel in a deeper way.

Indigenous theology is not a theology which merely adjusts western theology into the thought-form of the indigenous culture. Nor is it a ramification and elaboration of certain fundamental aspects of western theology to meet the presupposition of the native culture. Indigenous theology is a theology which seeks to be genuine in its commitment to the demand of the Gospel, seeks to be original in its perception of the challenges of the world in the light of the Gospel. It attempts to be relevant to the society, yet faithful to its Lord.

Theology is a tool of the church. It serves to deepen and clarify the church's faith in Christ. At the same time such theology serves to shed light upon the consequences of that faith for the Church's responsibility in the society, both in evangelism and social witness. As Christ himself came to the world with a task to accomplish, so the church has the task to continue His work. Thus theology has to keep its perspective in tension between the world and the Gospel, not in a peaceful continuation as that of the western liberals nor in arbitrary friendship and hostility as that of the evangelicals . . .[26]

Our point here is that we are deeply entangled in the ways of the world in which we live. We try to perpetuate the status quo and cannot go beyond it. The common sense and the traditional theological reason often control our reason in its attempt to understand the illumination of the Holy Spirit in intuition. In that case, reason can't grasp the newness of the Gospel. Theological endeavour then only repeats or elaborates the things which have been said by others. Or, it merely conforms to the norms of the culture. If reason wants to grasp the novelty of God's revelation, and if reason wants to do justice to God's ways which are different from man's ways, then reason should not allow common sense and the traditional theological reasoning to dominate its work. This is not to say, however, that one ought to suppress or to feel as if our reason and experience are empty. What it says is that reason has to develop a critical attitude toward the status quo. The person has to be aware and willing to admit that he has been deeply socialized with his culture and religious background. Then, at the same time he needs to be critical of them. This critical attitude means that we have to question what is obvious, final and popular; scrutinize what is simple and assumptive; juxtapose what is contradictory and paradoxical; and probe what is unfamiliar and profound. Only by a critical attitude can man open himself to the new revelation of God. He will allow God to judge and transform his life and faith. He will no longer be peaceful with his old stereotype faith. By such self-criticism, one can shake his hang-up with the western theology. At the same time, the indigenous theology can be developed without blindly conforming to his culture.

III The Relevancy of Beggarly Theology As Indigenous Theology

When the Protestant Reformation abolished the monasteries and established the concept of the priesthood of believers it tried to recast the nature of dynamic relationship between the Gospel and the world, the contemporary historical experience of the society. It tried to place Christianity in its true calling; that is, to identify with the world and yet to transform it for the sake of God's Kingdom. To do so, requires a new perception of the ways of God and a thorough-going involvement in the experiences of the society. Beggarly theology's emphasis is to give the society a special place in its theological endeavour. It identifies with the people of all walks of life. It goes to all the streets of its own society, and not to Geneva, New York, Oostgeest, Barmen, Harvard, or Heidelberg. The beggarly theology does not pretend to be holier, wealthier, or more civilized than thou toward its own society. It wants to live deeply with the agony of the world in which it lives. It moves out of the pietistic ghettoism. It tries to bring the message of God in the most intelligible, concrete and dynamic way. It also provides a basis for the Church to be involved in the development programme of the society.

The pursuit of an indigenous theology is also a sign of a mature church. A church is mature when it realizes that the church is fully responsible for its own life and task in the world. A mature church is a church which does not need to go to 'mother church' to ask an explanation of what God wants to say to the church. A mature church makes for dialogue and mutual admonition. A mature church can meet God directly, without human mediacy. In arriving at such consciousness, the church feels the need to be equipped with a thoroughly developed Christian faith which is rooted in its environment. Such is the indigenous theology which is seeking a genuine and comprehensive faith. The indigenous theology is a search for an authentic path of a mature church, a path of true servanthood to our Lord Jesus Christ.

H. Marianne Katoppo · *Liberated in Asia*

H. Marianne Katoppo, 'Liberated in Asia', *Compassionate and Free – An Asian Woman's Theology*, WCC Risk Book 1979, pp. 22–4, 33–46, 63–5

As we've seen, Indonesia is a vast, multicultural society structured on traditional patterns. It is also still very much influenced by concepts of cosmic balance, of kinship, common soil and so on. In a society such as this, woman may be subordinated, exploited, oppressed – but she will never be so completely the Other that she has somehow become in the western capitalist technocracies.

She is the partner in production, the co-ancestor of future generations. Without her, there is no cosmic balance. Alienation on the western scale can, therefore, never occur.

Marriage is important, because it not only ensures the procreation of the tribe but it also maintains the cosmic balance. An unmarried man is just as pitiful as an unmarried woman – and just as unacceptable.

Production is, and always has been, a joint affair. Since there has never been a system of the guilds, parents have passed their knowledge and skills on to their children. Some employment opportunities have perhaps been more open to men, others to women. Women are weavers, women are goldsmiths or silversmiths, working together with men. Agriculture always was a joint venture, not in the least because it had mystic connotations.

One should not confuse the situation in which a high-born woman like Kartini[27] found herself, with the daily life realities of the average Javanese woman of her time. That woman would not have had time to go to school, to grow dissatisfied with her lifestyle. She would be far too busy. She had a great freedom of movement and she was quite independent. In 1887 (when Kartini was eight years old) the Dutch missionary Poensen writes: 'It is the (Javanese) woman who takes care of the rice, which she has planted, harvested, dried and gleaned. She cooks the rice and the vegetables . . . she buys the household equipment . . . she sells the home-grown products . . . she dyes the cloths which she has woven, and sells them.'

Twenty years later Kruiyt, another Dutch missionary, was also impressed by the presence of the Javanese woman in various different spheres: in the market, in the shop, pounding the rice in the village, making batik, brewing herbal medicine, and so on. Woman being such an active factor in the village economy also made her an important member of the community. In this community, each action had been predetermined by tradition, and each member had a special function to fulfil for the good of the whole. To be wife and mother was inseparably connected to this function, and was imperative for the well-being and the continuity of the community.

An aristocratic Javanese woman, on the other hand, did not have to contribute anything to the economic life of the community. Married off at 15 or 16, she lived a very restricted life with little to do except please her husband (who often had scores of concubines to please him, anyway) or look after her children – and she invariably had a retinue of servants to do that, too.

Perhaps a woman like Kartini was oppressed, but she herself was also an oppressor, a fact not taken into account by biographers emoting over the poor little Javanese princess. She proved this conclusively when she agreed to marry the Regent of Rembang, *on condition* that she should be the head wife. Women's liberation in Asia, then, should definitely not model itself after Kartini . . .

In Indonesia, the working woman's life is essentially rural, as 85% of the population live in villages. Nearly 95% of the female work force is engaged in agriculture, or in industries such as textile-making, batik, and foodstuffs.

The greatest problem in rural areas is the absence of adequate sanitation facilities as an effective measure to ensure community health. People often live at subsistence levels. Statistics show that 85% of all the female children under five in Indonesia are undernourished.

Seen in the overall context of poverty, this may not be surprising. There are entire villages where children are cretins because of malnutrition. However, the malnourishment of female children may be attributed to the fact that they are often the ones who get the least food; fathers and brothers get first priority . . .

In preparing this chapter, I came across an article by the Dutch theologian Maria de Groot.[28] She called it 'The Breakthrough of the Gospel in the Life of Women', and uses the story of the healing of the woman in Luke 13.

This woman was 'bent double and quite unable to stand upright', besides being possessed by a spirit that left her enfeebled. Jesus laid his hands on her, and immediately she raised herself up. And she glorified God.

And that, says Maria de Groot, can only happen after you are raised up. 'You can sing the prescribed song. You can participate in the community where only men have the leadership and can speak. But you do it as someone who is bent and distorted. Only if you are lifted up by the power of Jesus and in the space of the kingdom of God, then your own song awakens.'

People often ask me why I am so concerned about the sexist language and sexist practices of the Church. What's wrong with calling God 'Father', what's so tragic about women not being allowed to be ordained? The good work goes on anyway, and *that* is important, isn't it? Besides, my church has accepted women ministers almost from its inception, so why should I worry about other churches? In Indonesia, churches are distinct from one another not so much through denominational as ethnic and cultural factors. As a Minahassan woman, perhaps I should be aware of subtle differences in culture, and not poke my nose into relationships I don't understand.

Maria de Groot has said exactly what I would like to have said. As a woman, I too have felt bent and distorted. As a matter of fact, I still often feel that way.

And it is the power of Jesus which liberates woman, in the space of the Kingdom of God. So that woman can stretch herself to her full length, and glorify God.

Raising up woman

This is what it's all about: liberation, power, glorification. How good is the work which is being done by bent and distorted people within a structure that leaves them no room for 'stretching to their full length'? Are we so fearful, have we so little confidence in the power of Christ and the Kingdom of God, that we don't want all God's people stretching to their full length? Are we like the oppressors, who keep dangerous prisoners in tiger cages?

Maria de Groot also points out that, in Luke 13, the head of the synagogue really couldn't appreciate Jesus' healing the woman at all, as it was a sabbath day – and she sees a direct analogy with the attitude of today's church leaders, who are not overly enthusiastic either with 'women on the sabbath and on Sundays, raised to their full height, taking the word and singing their own song, proclaiming from their own corporate recovery'. In other words, they are very critical of women participating in salvation.

Jesus calls these spiritual leaders hypocrites and throws the question right back at them: 'If you free on the sabbath your ox and your donkey to let them drink, what then have you to say of my act regarding this woman? Is she not a daughter of Abraham?'

Jesus lifts up the woman to what she is. A daughter of Abraham, faced with the hypocrites who taught that they were the sons of Abraham. Yet who failed to grasp the essence of their own Torah. The woman is a daughter of Abraham, she does not have to become it by one or another achievement. For 18 years she has been bound by the power that Jesus calls Satan. And the hand of Christ is sufficient for complete liberation: there is no need for anything else. No approval of authorities, no proof from the woman's side. She is the daughter of Abraham, she is released.

And here I think of the words of another woman theologian, Nelle Morton: 'While forgiveness must be permitted to bring its *shalom* into our lives, the *shalom* woman cannot do those whom she forgives the disservice of allowing them to remain in anti-shalom positions. While she loves and forgives the ones who sin against her, she can no longer permit the sins of sexism (and racism) to continue wherever they become identified.'[29]

In the previous chapters it has already been pointed out that Asian women's self-image is less than satisfactory. In the case of Christian women, this poor self-image is preserved by the church's tendency to give male chauvinism a theological and quasi-divine legitimation, so that there are churches where women have no awareness at all of being created in the image of God, *imago Dei*.

They are burdened by the thought that they are 'the devil's gateway, who caused man, the image of God, to sin' – as Tertullian so kindly stated, and some men are so fond of repeating.

At best, women are comforted by the thought of being a helper, something which is drummed into them at catechism lessons and wedding ceremonies. That *'ezer* in the Hebrew means 'help' in the sense of mutual action, or the cooperation of subject and object where the strength of one is not sufficient, seems to escape the good leaders' attention.

The importance of raising woman's awareness of her self-worth cannot be over-emphasized. Always accepting that God transcends all human understanding, we could make use here of the feminine aspects of divinity, and also of the meaning of the symbol of Mary, in order to restore woman's true image of herself. This is women's contribution to whole theology, which, as Nelle Morton says, 'as full human experience, is only possible when all the oppressed people of the world can speak freely out of their own experiences, to be heard and touch one another, to heal and be healed' . . .

It is no coincidence that lately more importance is given to Mary, both in Catholic dogma and in Protestant thinking.

Asian Catholics, for example, are beginning to see her no longer as the 'fairy queen oozing out sweet piety', but rather as 'the mature and committed (Asian) woman, the peasant mother who cheerfully wears herself out to feed and clothe her carpenter son; the worker's wife wearing holy furrows on her face . . . an image reflected in millions of Asian village mothers today.'

Protestants, if they have learned to overcome their initial fear of 'mariolatry', might find their sign of hope in her as the first fully liberated human being, whose Magnificat is central in the theology of liberation.

Protestant thinking definitely has a blind spot where Mary is concerned. In the Federal Republic of Germany, a woman theologian drew up a list of instances in the Bible concerning 'Jesus and women', to be studied by a women's group. Looking over the list, I asked the group whether they had noticed a significant omission. Nobody had – and everyone was much surprised when I pointed out that there was not a single reference to Mary, who was after all, the first, and perhaps the most important, woman in Jesus' life!

There is a cartoon by Joe Noonan on the wall of the World Council of Churches' editorial office in Geneva which provides food for thought. It depicts Joseph and Mary. She is obviously pregnant, and wears a halo round her head. Joseph – a young man, not the superannuated version which became so popular after the third century (to account for Mary's perpetual virginity, no doubt) – asks her: 'When you're the Mother of God, will you still be my Mary?' the caption reads: 'Do we ever think that they loved each other? "Joseph my husband" – "Mary my wife." A child listens. And grows. And becomes the lover of humankind.'

Jesus did not grow up in a vacuum. What strength did the man Jesus draw from the woman of the Magnificat? What gentleness?

Thinking of Mary, I do not exult in her supposed purity, for that is too narrow a perspective which does her no justice. I see her in the wider context of love and self-giving. I admire and appreciate her sensitivity to social injustices and her readiness to take moral risks for the sake of a needed social change.

That is on one level. On another level, I see Mary as the pre-eminent model of humanity, growing into the full image of God. As the receptive Virgin (receptive to the action of God) and the creative Mother (sharing the mission of bringing the good news of salvation to the world), she is the model not only for woman, but also for man. She is the new human being (man-woman), receptive before God, who calls him/her to be *imago Dei*.

Human liberation often seems to be grim and joyless struggle. The Magnificat shows otherwise. And I exult in the fact that this Asian woman, this Mary, upon her encounter with God bursts out into this great song of thanksgiving and joy given to God, who liberates through the oppressed themselves. Through Mary, women in some special way personify the oppressed, although she represents all oppressed peoples, not just women.

Mary is the truly liberated, fully liberated human being: compassionate and free.[30]

7 · Sri Lanka

Sri Lankan history is still being moulded by the Sinhalese Buddhist culture established in the third century BC, and by Tamil Hindu culture which arrived in the first centuries of the Christian era. Other major cultural forces resulted, in the modern period, from the colonization of the lowlands by the Portuguese and the Dutch (sixteenth century) and by the British (eighteenth century). In each case, a distorted Christianity provided justification for conquest and introduced successively Roman Catholic, Dutch Reformed and Anglican beliefs and practices. Each colonial power also claimed to have a civilizing mission despite their brutal punitive campaigns and the slow destruction of Sri Lanka's cultural and religious traditions. By the 1850s, British colonial administration was directed largely to economic gain, by means of a plantation system with indentured Indian labourers. The result has been the enrichment of planters and foreign shareholders at the cost of the valley and village economies, and of the severely exploited plantation workers. The change to a competitive capitalist society, along with an English education system, largely through Christian schools, also produced a Western-educated, middle-class elite which still holds much of the political and economic power.[1]

In the 1930s the prospect of independence led to the exploitation by rival economic classes of Sinhala-Tamil differences and in 1943 to the first communal riots in Sri Lanka's recorded history. But independence was declared in 1948. Sharp inequalities in Ceylon society had already been addressed by Christians like G. K. Ekanayake and James Pieris during the early decades of this century. Their work in labour organization and legal reform, sometimes in association with Buddhist groups, would later be taken up by Peter Pillai and F. O. Tambimuttu in the programmes of Catholic Action, Young Christian Workers and the Social

Justice Movement, all of which were founded in the mid-1930s. Economic liberalism and Marxist revolution were alike rejected by Pillai,who in the 1940s and 1950s applied Catholic social theory to an array of economic problems.[2]

The Buddhist Sangha (monkhood) had throughout the colonial period provided the one remaining centre for cultural continuity. In the wake of independence, the pent-up grievances of two centuries found expression in the strongly nationalist and anti-Western, Buddhist-Sinhalese resurgence, commencing in 1950. The privileged positions of the Christian (largely urban) middle class, of the English language, and of some ethnic minorities (also partly Christian), all came under attack, as did the church as a legacy of empire and partner with Britain in the destruction of Buddhism. Positively, the renaissance recalled the ancient Buddhist and Sinhalese virtues and renewed the call for 'One land, one faith, one people'. Yet this in turn, led to linguistic and racial riots throughout the country in that and successive years. Discrimination against Tamils continues in, for example, language-use and the franchise and Tamil plantation workers remain destitute victims of a system which still enriches British tea companies. Large numbers of industrial workers, however, are in scarcely better position.

Early Christian response to the Buddhist resurgence was expressed by the Anglican Archbishop Lakdasa de Mel who in 1956 renewed his proposals for indigenization. His own diocese, Kurunegala, had been self-supporting from its inception, and a centre for indigenized architecture and worship. His support for Yohan Devananda led to the establishment of the Devasarana Aramaya (Ashram) in 1960, which has had a seminal influence in Christian-Buddhist-Marxist dialogue, in urban and rural ministries and in people's education and theology. S. J. de S. Weerasinghe was another who wrote (in 1958 and 1961) of the justice of Buddhist accusations and the consequences of a different understanding of Christianity rooted in a cultural heritage.

The Christaseva Ashram, formed in Jaffna in 1939, increased its activities from 1958 in the areas of interfaith dialogue and of studies in religion and society. Founded by S. Selvaretnam, the Ashram also had the leadership of Daniel T. Niles who made major contributions to world ecumenism and to the theology of mission until his death in 1970. In the late 1950s and early 1960s, Niles stimulated both churches and community groups, throughout Sri Lanka, to grapple with inter-religious and social issues in for example his series of Conferences at the Ashram and at Uduvil College. But his main contribution to a contextual theology lies in the implications for Sri Lanka of his numerous books on the biblical foundations of mission. In the weightiest of these, 'Upon the Earth' (1962), Niles stresses that Christ himself is already present and at work within every secular or religious setting. The Christian church is therefore a pilgrim company on the road to a new world and wholly involved in the life and history of their people. The selfhood of the Christian church, he had said in the 1959 John R. Mott lectures, is to be found in its mission within a particular nation and in its secular engagement, with those of any creed. 'The decisive difference for Christians is simply that the *total* life of man is seen to be the centre of divine concern'.[3]

The Ecumenical Institute for Study and Dialogue was founded by the National Christian Council in 1963 and in the work of Lynn de Silva and, more recently, Aloysius Pieris SJ and Wesley Ariaraja, has provided basic resources for inter-religious co-operation and for the growth of a localized Christian theology. The extract by Pieris here included comes from his lecture to a conference of Third World Theologians in Sri Lanka. Since the mid-1960s, his writings on liturgy, ecumenism and on Buddhism have explored interfaith relationships in 'the depth of the secular'. In earlier sections of this lecture he describes how a 'humble participation in the non-Christian experience of liberation' – his example is from Buddhist spirituality – can enrich both Christian theology and a radical concern for Asia's poor.[4]

A number of theologically aware pastors and lay people wrestled with the nature of Christian presence in Sri Lanka in the 1960s.[5] Charles Wickremanayake combined evangelical passion with socialist convictions and advocated a closer Christian identification with Buddhist and Hindu communities. In association with Yohan Devananda, and a large 'People's Committee', he issued a challenging Manifesto (of 36 pages) to the Church of Ceylon in 1970, calling for drastic changes in life-style and church management and a new participation with those of other religions and ideologies in building a society of justice. In a sustained theological commentary, the writers detail the changes required of the church once it is recognized that 'God intervenes decisively in the events of the nation' and also 'purifies his Church'.[6] A less radical volume issued in 1968 [7] examined the role of the Christian community in Sri Lankan society and included papers by Donald Kanagaratnam of the Pilimatalawa Seminary and Kenneth Fernando of the Suddharsana Centre. Kanagaratnam has elsewhere written of his work in grounding Christian and theological education in Sri Lankan communities. Fernando's writings have outlined the biblical understandings of, for example, salvation and the kingdom of God, which require a dedication to Sri Lanka's people and to a 'humanizing of the revolution'. In Celestine Fernando, pastor and editor of the *Ceylon Churchman*, generations of aware Christians have known a mentor in relating Christian theology to a wide range of social and political issues. It is central to Celestine Fernando's thought that only a permanent intellectual and spiritual revolution will enable Christians to support all Sri Lankan movements for a radically new society and, within it, for a transformed church.[8] A Christian thinker and activist who has spanned the same period in his writings is Bryan de Kretzer. In verse, meditations and occasional articles he reflects a deep nationalism influenced both by Sinhalese-Buddhism and by Christian understandings of incarnation and mission.

Economic difficulties mounted during the same decade and the precarious coalition of Marxist parties which Mrs Bandaranaike now led was unable to establish an integrated and self-reliant economic policy. Although major reforms in land-ownership and rent-controls were enacted, unemployment increased rapidly and contributed to the alienation which erupted in the 1971 nationwide insurrection. Yet disparities in income remained the most serious source of conflict.[9]

The National Christian Council had issued statements in both 1968 and 1970 regarding Christian responsibility in society, and the Bishops' Conference of the Roman Catholic Church called in 1970 for 'enlightened cooperation with the new government'. This was the second term of Mrs Bandaranaike's Marxist coalition, formerly opposed by many Christians, Catholics in particular, not only on ideological grounds but also for the nationalizing of Christian schools in 1960. A minority of Christian groups, although critical of the government's mixture of socialist ideology and capitalist values, strongly supported the attempts to eliminate the worst economic injustices, and the Anglican Bishop Wickremasinghe had for this reason also welcomed the election results. Prominent amongst such groups was the Christian Workers' Fellowship, which since 1958 had fostered participation in the workers' movement and study of the gospel within contemporary society. Wickremanayake, Devananda and Ainslie Semarajiwa (later of the Centre for Society and Religion) were among those who have assisted in its development. But it is Jeffrey Abeysekera and a team of worker-theologians who have developed the group to be an inter-religious and radical force in labour and industry. Abeysekera had written the paper 'Building Lanka with the Marxists' in 1965, following some years at the Devasarana Aramaya. In 1968 the Fellowship issued the results of a lay study series in a detailed survey of Christian social thinking along with a full analysis of Sri Lankan society.[10] In publications, worker-cells and workers' masses the Fellowship expresses a strong commitment to socialism, to inter-religious co-operation in direct action, and to theological reflection. Sacramental sharing is, for the Fellowship, a powerful model for the just sharing of all things and of a reconciliation that only comes through conflict.

Other student and worker groups have contributed to the body of Christian thought, emerging from encounter with the cultural and economic realities of Sri Lanka. The SCM has proved a seed-bed for socially and theologically aware Christians, as has the Young Christian Workers. Such rural settlements as those led by Leonard Pieris and Nicholas Rose for example are also engaged in the doing of theology, and two books published by Devananda demonstrate how the elements of a local theology are emerging from People's Committees, collective farms and dialogue with both Marxists and Buddhists. Farmers, students, officials and scholars have joined in village labour and in theological reflection, and the Manifesto mentioned earlier is one of many documents that arise from the Aramaya's 'living with flesh and blood neighbours'. Devananda's volumes[11] depict a 'theology which witnesses to spiritual experience through an ever increasing involvement in (local) secular realities'. Devananda is one of a number, including de Kretzer, Ashley Halpe and George Perera, whose poetry reflects similar concern.

The conservative United National Party returned to power in 1975 and has since set about dismantling socialist policies and welcoming the return of foreign investment. Vast increases in the cost of living have only deepened existing inequalities however, and led to recurrent disturbances in both rural and urban areas.[12] The context for Christian theology is also shaped by continuing traditions of positivism and fatalism in Sri Lankan culture and by the persistence of strong caste divisions. Along with racial and economic tensions, these provide sharp stimulus to a confessing Christian theology.

The writings and addresses of C. Lakshman Wickremasinghe, Bishop of Kuranegala, show a deep awareness of such elements as these. He has built on de Mel's work in shaping self-reliant Christian communities able to express the Christian faith in terms of their own culture and the structures of society. Many movements for economic justice or community development, many experimental centres and ministries, have benefited from his leadership over the last twenty years. In his sermons, and monthly pastoral letters, these and other contemporary issues are related to a 'fresh awareness' of Jesus' innovative and prophetic work in the present. The extract following is from one of many lectures Wickremasinghe has given, often to international meetings, which outline a local theology of dialogue, politics and development.[13]

Equally forthright public statements along with exhaustive analysis of Sri Lanka's economic and social problems have come from the Centre for Society and Religion, Colombo. Based on the earlier work of Peter Pillai, the Centre is led by Tissa Balasuriya, former Rector of Aquinas University. Balasuriya's theological writing has appeared in numerous articles and in two books where the twin concerns which shape his thought are the renewal of Christian spirituality and Christian participation in the social process. These he sees to be intimately related. If evangelization is a process of incarnation then, he maintains, we must allow 'the Asian revolutionary temper' to evangelize us. If we place our faith in Jesus Christ, this necessarily involves us in the praxis of his love, in his pedagogy, and in his permanent contestation of the existing order.[14] Closely associated with the Centre's work are Bishop Leo Nanayake, Michael Rodrigo and Ainslie Semarajiwa who have also contributed to Sri Lankan Christian thinking.

Similar work is done by the Satyodaya centre in Kandy, led by Paul Caspersz. Satyodaya's involvement in social development is more localized perhaps, but Caspersz himself has produced lengthy studies of Marxism and Religion, of Sri Lanka's Tea Economy and on Asian Theology. He, like Balasuriya, has paid particular attention to ideological questions and to the rethinking of christology within Sri Lankan realities.[15] Extracts from two articles in the latter category are chosen for inclusion here.

Aloysius Pieris · *The Asian Sense in Theology*

Aloysius Pieris, 'The Asian Sense in Theology', *Dialogue*, new series vol. VI,
nos 1 and 2, January – August 1979, pp. 44–47, 49–51

To predispose ourselves to receive the *Asian Sense* into our Christian consciousness, certain inhibitions inherited from the local
churches of the West need first to be eliminated. Consistent with
the methodology so far pursued in our investigation, this review
of our theological past must also be made (a) from the *Third-
World point of view* in general and (b) from the *Asian point of
view* in particular. The content of an Asian Theology however
does not concern us here. All we hope to achieve by this critique
is to discover the *Asian Style of doing Theology*.

A Third World Critique of our Theological Past

In the course of our discussion we met two 'secular' movements
engaged in liberating us from our 'poverty'; both have originated
in the West; the first is *Marxist Socialism*; and the other is the
development ideology associated with Capitalist Technocracy. The
West is also 'spiritually' present through the Church which, for
the most part, is an extension of Western Christianity. Thus the
Church too reflects, in her own *theological* self-understanding, the
ideological conflicts of the West.

*The Asian Church, for the moment, has no theology of her own,
though the cultures that host her teem with them.* She is today
caught between two 'theologies' which are as 'Western' as the
secular ideologies just mentioned. The first is the *Classical European Theology* which, in its various brands, is officially taught in
all major institutions of the Asian Church. The second is the *Latin
American Theology* which is also making itself felt in certain
theological circles. These theologies, of course, are diametrically
opposed to each other, as are also the secular ideologies mentioned above.

Classical theology in the West which went through the mill of
renewal since the 19th century is said to have made a major
'break-through' in the middle of this century, climaxing in modern
theology with its openness to the 'world'. The chief centres of this
renewal were the French and German linguistic zones, according
to Mark Schoof, because, to quote his own words, it was there

that 'the theologians seem to have the necessary scientific tradition and sufficient creative energy at their disposal'.[16] One major source of inspiration for Catholic renewal of European theology is traced back to Protestant Germany according to this author.

This close-range view of European theology justifies Schoof's title of his thesis: *Breakthrough*. But an Asian looking from a critical distance sees quite another picture. The real break-through in Western theology came with the Latin American critique of that same 'scientific tradition' which Schoof proudly alludes to. The openness to the world which European theologians achieved up to the sixties by dialoguing with contemporary *philosophies* is only a mild reform compared to what the Latin Americans achieved from the sixties onwards. The latter effected a complete reversal of method. They seem to have done to European theology what Feuerbach did to Hegelian dialectics. They put theology back on its feet. They grounded it on theopraxis. What was formerly revolving round a Kantian orbit was made to rotate round a Marxian axis.[17]

For us Asians then, liberation theology is thoroughly Western, and yet, so radically renewed by the challenges of the Third World that it has a relevance for Asia which the classical theology does not have. The Ecumenical Association of Third World Theologians (EATWOT) which is now holding its Asian Consultation here is perhaps its first tangible fruit in Asia. In the Churches of the East this *new method* has already begun to compete with the traditional theology. What the Latin Americans claim, and what we Asians must readily grant, is that it is not perhaps a new theology, but a theological *method*, indeed the *correct method* of doing theology.

The features of this methodology peculiarly relevant for us in Asia can be selected from Sobrino's presentation. The first feature is that the Kantian attempt to 'liberate reason from authority' paved the way to a theological preoccupation with harmonizing 'faith with reason' while the Marxian attempt to 'free reality from oppression' did not receive theological attention in Europe until the South Americans made an issue of it. Thus the use of 'philosophy' to explain away 'suffering' rationally or to define God and His nature in such a way as to justify the existence of oppression and injustice was understandable in a European socio-political context, while substitution of philosophical speculation with 'sociological' analysis to *change* rather than explain the world of

injustice has become the immediate concern of liberation theology. Such a concern cannot come within the 'scientific' purview
of European theology, whether Protestant or Catholic.

The second feature, quite important for Asians, is the primacy
of praxis over theory. Spirituality, for instance, is not the practical
conclusion of theology but the radical involvement with the poor
and the oppressed, and is what creates theology. We know Jesus
the *Truth* by following Jesus the *Way*.

Thirdly, this Way is the Way of the Cross, the basis of all
knowledge. Thus, the growth of the World into God's Kingdom
is *not* a 'progessive development', but a process punctuated by
radical contradictions, violent transformations and death-resur-
rection experiences – what Sobrino calls the 'ruptura epistemo-
logica' – scripturally founded in the 'Transcendance of the
Crucified God.'

Fourthly, we see that it is not a 'development theology' such as
would justify and perpetuate the values of an 'acquisitive' culture,
but a 'liberation theology' demanding an asceticism of renunciation and a voluntary *poverty* that sneers at acquisitiveness. This
resultant 'spirituality' is not self-enclosed, motivated as it is by the
desire to bring about the kingdom of God here on earth. What it
inculcates is not merely a *passive solidarity* with the poor in their
poverty and oppression, but also a *dynamic participation* in their
struggle for full humanity. Indeed, a dynamic following of Christ!

Finally, the encounter of God and Man, i.e. the interplay of
Grace and Liberty, is seen as Man's obligation to use all his
human potentialities to anticipate the kingdom which, nevertheless, remains *God's gratuitous gift*. This explains the liberation
theologian's political option for socialism, i.e. for a definite social
order in which oppressive structures are changed radically, even
violently, in order to allow every person to be fully human, the
assumption being that no one is liberated unless every one is.

This theology, and also its European predecessor, receive their
contextual significance in Asia precisely in relationship to the
aforesaid Western ideologies with which they are very closely
connected. Our earlier criticism of how these ideologies operate
in Asia has clearly situated the two theologies, too, in the context
of Eastern religiosity. Hence our task is to complement the Latin
American method with an Asian critique of classical theology
. . .

Let me then put things back in focus. In all the non-biblical

soteriologies of Asia, *religion* and *philosophy* are inseparably in-
terfused. Philosophy is a religious vision; and religion is a philosophy lived. Every meta-cosmic soteriology is at once a *darśana*
and a *pratipadā*, to use Indian terms; i.e. an interpenetration of
a 'view' of life and a 'way' of life. In fact, the oft-repeated question
whether Buddhism is a philosophy or a religion was first formulated in the West, before it reached Peking *via* Marxism. For in
the Buddha's formula, the four-fold salvific *truth* incorporates the
Path as one of its constituents while the Eight-fold *Path* coincides
with the realization of the Truth.

Here let me refer to the current trend of *using* 'Buddhist techniques' of meditation in 'Christian Prayer' without any reverence
for the soteriological context of such techniques. For the naïve
presupposition is that the (Buddhist) *Way* could be had without
the (Buddhist) *Truth*. It is time to impress on our theologians that
in our culture the *method* cannot be severed from the *goal*. For
the word 'technique', now misused in task-oriented cultures to
mean a mechanical action which, when done according to set
rules, produces predictable results, must be traced back to its
original Greek sense. *Technē* is not a mechanical action, but a
skill, an art. In our traditions, the art of doing a thing is itself the
thing done. The *goal* of life, in Buddhism, is the *art* of living it.
The perfection to be achieved is the style of achieving it! The
obvious corollary is that the Asian method of doing theology is
itself Asian theology. *Theopraxis is already the formulation of
Theology*.

Thus the mutuality of praxis and theory which defines the Asian
sense in theology is the missing ingredient in the Theology of
Religions which we have uncritically accepted and which hampers
our task of acquiring the Asian style. . . .

Hence our conclusions:

(i) Our theology is our way of sensing and doing things as
revealed in our people's struggles for *spiritual* and *social* emancipation and expressed in the idioms and languages of the cultures
such struggles have created.

(ii) Theology then is not mere God-talk; in our cultures, God-
talk *in itself* is sheer 'nonsense.' As evidenced by the Buddha's
refusal to talk of Nirvana, all words have *Silence* as their Source
and Destiny! God-talk is made relative to God-experience. The
word-game about nature and person or the mathematics of one
and three have only generated centuries of verbosity. It is word-

less-ness that gives every word its meaning. This inner *Harmony* between *Word* and *Silence* is the test of Asian authenticity, indeed it is the Spirit, the Eternal Energy which makes every word spring from Silence and lead to Silence, every engagement spring from renunciation, every struggle from a profound restfulness, every freedom from stern discipline, every action from stillness, every 'development' from detachment and every acquisition from non-addiction. Since, however, Silence is the *Word Unspoken* and the Word is *Silence Heard*, their relationship is not one of temporal priority but dialectical mutuality. It is the Spirit of Buddhist wisdom and Christian love. If there is Harmony between our Speech and our Silence, whether in worship or service or conversation, the Spirit is amongst us.

(iii) The same *Harmony* reigns between *God-experience* which is Silence and the *Man-concern* which makes it heard. One is not temporally prior to the other. It is, rather, the mutuality between Wisdom and Love, Gnosis and Agape, Pleroma and Kenosis, or as the Buddhists would put it, between 'Knowledge that directs us to Nirvana and the Compassion that pins us down to the world.'[18] For liberation praxis is at once a withdrawal into the meta-cosmic and an immersion into cosmic.

(iv) The most subtle point of this dialectic is between *authority and freedom.* The magisterial role in the Asian Church has to be earned by the Master's *competence to mediate liberation.* Authority makes no external claims. Authority is competence to communicate freedom. He who lacks competence uses power. 'With whose authority . . . ?' asked the power-thirsty clerics from the Son of Man who submitted himself to that very power in order to vindicate his authority. His *authority was His freedom* available to all who touched Him. It is a self-authentication derived from a liberation-praxis; it is a man-concern testifying to a God-experience: the two prongs of a liberation struggle.

(v) To regain her lost *authority*, therefore, the Asian Church must abdicate her alliances with *Power.* She must be humble enough to be baptized in the Jordan of Asian *Religiosity* and bold enough to be baptized on the Cross of Asian *Poverty.* Does not the fear of losing her identity make her lean on Mammon? Does not her refusal to die keep her from living? The theology of power-domination and instrumentalization must give way to a theology of humility, immersion and *participation.*

(vi) Hence our desperate search for the Asian Face of Christ can find fulfilment only if we participate in Asia's own search for it in the unfathomable abyss where Religion and Poverty seem to have the same common source: – God, who has declared Mammon his enemy (Mt. 6:24).

(vii) What then is the locus of this praxis? Certainly not the 'Christian life lived within the Church in the presence of non-Christians'; rather, it is the 'God-experience (which is at once the Man-Concern) of God's own People living beyond the Church' and among whom the Church is called to lose herself in total participation. That is to say, *theology in Asia is the Christian apocalypse of the non-Christian experiences of liberation.*

Paul Caspersz · *Jesus of Nazareth and Human Liberation*

Paul Caspersz, 'Jesus of Nazareth and Human Liberation', *Satyodaya Bulletin*, nos 74 and 75, April – May 1979

In the present stage of our knowledge of Jewish history, it is difficult to determine precisely the dates and the duration of the successive waves of foreign rulers on native Jewish soil. If it is difficult for us today, the determination of dates was impossible to Jews like Jesus in Jesus' time. To them it was also much less important than the preservation of memories. Transmitted orally by parents to their children and their children's children in a time during which human memory was much more retentive than it is today, these memories stored up the history and the myths of the people, gave them an identity and a culture.

These memories of Jesus certainly went back to the Egyptians, the Assyrians, the Babylonians, the Persians, the Greeks, the Ptolemies and the Seleucids who successively and with only short periods of intervening precarious independence, conquered and ruled his people. The slavery in Egypt probably began after the Hyksos rule in Egypt was overthrown by native Egyptians in the sixteenth century and the Seleucid domination was finally ended by the Hasidim and Hasmonean rulers in the second century. Hellenic influence continued in the Hasmonean court. Numerous intrigues in the palace made the government very insecure. Finally in 63 BC began the era of Roman domination.

Soon after Herod I's death there were frequent liberation uprisings of the people and of all these during the impressionable years of his boyhood and youth Jesus would doubtless have heard. In Jerusalem itself these uprisings were put down with great cruelty by the Roman governor of Syria, Quintilius Varus. In the Jordan valley the rebels rallied round a slave of Herod called Simon; in Judea around a former shepherd Athronges and his four brothers; in Jesus' own district of Galilee, Judas who probably later founded the Zealot movement plundered the arsenal of Herod at Sepphoris, only three miles from Nazareth, where Jesus lived. From Nazareth Jesus could see Sepphoris. Since he was neither deaf, nor blind, nor dumb, Jesus would have heard, seen and spoken of these things. From what the Gospels tell us about his later life, it would have been impossible for Jesus not to react sensitively to so much human and national tragedy.

The foreign rulers, from the time of the pre-Exodic Egyptians, humiliated the upper and middle-class Jews and economically exploited everyone under their domination. The burdens of slavery, taxes and forced levies fell most severely of all upon the common people. But the common Jewish people were crushed also by their own ruling classes. These classes united in the Great Council or the Sanhedrin (Hebraized form of the Greek *synedrion*, 'sitting together') which was the body of seventy-one persons – chief priests, elders and scribes – who met under the ruling high priest to decide religious, legal and internal Jewish civic matters that did not pertain to the Roman governor.

The Sanhedrin or Great Council of the Jews stood for power: political, religious, economic, ideological. In the hearts of the seventy-two there was hatred and contempt for the Roman rulers but, in practice, for the sake of the selfish interests of their class, they connived with the Romans to keep the common people at bay. That the three Synoptic evangelists make it quite clear that Jesus was first condemned by the Sanhedrin (though it is Hyam Maccoby's view that it was not by the Sanhedrin at all but by the Chief Priest's Court) before, for various reasons, they took him to the Roman Court, must be always recalled with shame and fear by priests and religious who belong to the class from which the Sanhedrin drew its membership. Shame, because the veils they draw before their eyes prevent them so often from giving true judgements about events and people. Fear, lest again in the name of a rule they condemn themselves to inaction or they condemn

a person who outside the rule brings deliverance to a people
. . .

At the bottom of the social ladder, with no room even on the lowest rungs, were the common people, the am-haares, the people of the land. They lived both in rural and in urban areas. In the former, some owned small parcels of land, but others were the exploited tenants of the rich absentee owners or were so landless and so bereft of economic power in the feudal society of their time that today they would be called the rural proletariat. In the latter there were the artisans, small-scale producers of food, text-iles, perfumes and jewellery, those who worked in the building industry (the Temple was rebuilding between 20 BC and 62 while Roman overlords and native aristocrats built grand mansions for themselves). Many of this class of wage workers in the towns would today be called the urban proletariat. Finally, both in the towns and in the villages of Jesus' Palestine, there were the slaves.

If a too facile and simplistic two-class analysis of society, such as is so often made by superficial Marxists, does not do justice to the complex social reality of modern societies, still less is it adequate to understand the society of Jesus' Palestine, about which our information is in any case so remote and so scanty. However, there can be no doubt that Jesus faced in his country a social situation where the great majority of people was common and poor and felt oppressed or at least deprived in a land which they held to be sacredly their own. They were, as we have seen, oppressed and deprived not only by the hated Roman conquerors but by the social system which was managed for the benefit of the wealthy and the powerful sections of their own people.

In this social situation the young and enthusiastic Jesus had to make his fundamental guiding option. It would have been pre-posterous for him to have sought a place in the Sanhedrin class. But might he not have looked for a reformist role within it or at least on its fringes, keeping the system going but smoothing its roughest edges, as the Pharisees, Nicodemus and Gamaliel, sought to do? Jesus, however, was not to be content with reformism. He was a revolutionary leader of his people. He opted to be squarely with the poor, the lowly, the outcasts of the people. What he did in the Nazareth synagogue was make his option public.

The incident in the synagogue at Nazareth (Luke 4) and many other sayings and actions of Jesus recorded in the four Gospel accounts make it impossible for anyone to doubt the presence, and even the centrality, of a fundamental option to be squarely with the dispossessed in Jesus' life. That Scripture scholars may question the authenticity or the validity of the evangelist's own interpretative rendering of one or the other action or saying is both possible and legitimate. But our argument does not proceed from this or that text. It is built on the evidence of the accumulation of such records and this evidence then becomes unbreakable.

What is important is to see in the fundamental option taken by Jesus his clear awareness and his deliberate exclusion of the opposite. Jesus' decision to take an unequivocal stand with the poor and the outcasts of society was made in a climate of conflict with those who did not grant that the practice of true religion consisted in working for the liberation of one's fellows from the structures of injustice and oppression.

The existence of the opposite, the acceptance of conflict, the assumption of the role almost of an agent provocateur is evident in the Beatitudes with its series of powerful subversive paradoxes. It is evident again in the portrayal of the Final Judgement of humanity in Mt 25. Jesus has come to serve, not to be served. The rich think that they do not need service, they can command it. He has come not for the just, but for sinners. Not the proud self-righteous religious leader but the lowly publican makes the sincerest prayer. Not the ostentatiously rich donor but the poor widow makes the richest offering. Mary's Magnificat is the community song of the liberated poor.

It is evident also in many of the parables which traditional spirituality and traditional novitiate and seminary training have used for other purposes such as the invitation to repentance and penance. The Father accepts and re-invests the outcast son while he seeks to make the self-centred elder brother see the inapplicability of accepted social norms of behaviour in a situation where openness to the dispossessed should be paramount. The parables of the lost coin and the lost sheep must likewise be re-evaluated in the light of Jesus' fundamental option.

That Jesus took his fundamental option with full knowledge of its consequences is proved by the daring things that Jesus did. Among them are the occasions of table-fellowship with the hated, feared and despised tax-collectors, with prostitute women (was the box of alabaster ointment a gift from her employer the previous night?) and with sinners of all kinds. By these actions Jesus knew that he was acting in defiance of the culture and customs of respectable Jewish people. By their means he forced people to take sides between the old society with its social taboos and the new where the only law would be love. Incidentally the prayer, 'Give us today the bread we need', was probably taught by Jesus with undertones that this bread should be eaten in the company of the wretched of the earth.

Whether the followers of Jesus in history and in our time have taken the position Jesus took is a question that has to be asked and answered. More than by anyone else this is a question that has to be answered by the leaders of the Jesus community – the Bishops of Rome and Canterbury, by the other bishops, by priests, religious and lay leaders. Jesus' fundamental option was not just a theoretical one. He had to translate it into a programme of action precisely in the areas of the oppression and exploitation most acutely felt by his people. These areas, as we have seen, were national subjugation by the Romans and economic exploitation by the prevalent Jewish social system and, embedded in the latter and legitimizing it, the falsification of religion by its official exponents.

Martin Hengel has well summarized the three options available to Jesus in face of the humiliation of subservience to Roman imperialism: armed resistance in the manner of the extreme nationalists, connivance in the manner of the priestly Sadducee aristocracy, passive endurance in the manner of the am-haares. In face of the evils of the national social system itself, the options available to Jesus were not different from those available to us in our situation in our own country today: revolutionary retaliatory violence, connivance with the oppressing forces and not bothering at all about the evils of society because religion is held to be about something else.

The greatness of Jesus is not that he excluded connivance, escapist submission or mere indifference – many other leaders in Jesus' time and ours do this – but that he transcended the way of liberation by violent resistance. He did not reject violence, he went beyond it. By precept and by action he showed that there is a more revolutionary way than violence to establish the society of love and sharing of the goods of the earth where each would give according to one's ability and receive according to one's needs. This was not a pacifist way. Jesus accepted the role of conflict, he even provoked it, as his famous Sabbath cures show. The conflict was between his ardent passion for interhuman justice and the vested interests of his foes in maintaining the status quo. He tore off the mask of piety from religious practices that worked against interhuman justice and kindness or which were just neutral in a situation of injustice. He called Herod a fox and knew that what he said would be taken back to Herod. He seems to have made a joke of paying taxes and probably even encouraged non-payment of taxes to the Romans.

But Jesus was not facile in dividing society into two classes: the poor who are always blameless and rich who are always wicked. In the parable of the workers given work at different times of the working day, yet paid the same wage, Jesus seems to have been well aware that there often surfaces an upsetting unexpected lack of solidarity among the poor: so today we have the phenomenon of workers in Germany and Britain being more intolerant of immigrant coloured class-brothers than the middle classes of their countries, and international solidarity of the working class is perhaps more distant than when Marx dreamt about it. . . .

What was the difference between Jesus and the Zealots? Basically, the Zealots, like the great Jewish prophets of old, were not revolutionaries, but reformists, in that they had confidence in the Jewish social system centred ideologically upon the Law and practically around the Temple. As against the Law, Jesus propounded the freedom of the children of God. As against the Temple, Jesus worked for the worship of God in spirit and in truth and, practically, in effective love of humanity. Like Marx, Jesus is sure that man can achieve a society free from alienation. Jesus, however, thinks far more positively than Marx about society as it should be. While Marx thinks that the way ahead to the new society lies in the use of the very tactics of the oppressor to ensure his down-fall, Jesus envisages not merely a revolutionary goal for society but a revolutionary strategy for the attainment of the goal.

In the programmatic manifesto he issued at Nazareth, it is significant that, according to some good manuscripts, Jesus omits the last line of the Trito-Isaian text: to proclaim 'a day of vengeance for our God' (Is. 61:2). Jesus was indeed capable of sarcasm, anger, rough language against the unjust, but he probably preferred to leave these passions out of his official proclamation at Nazareth. Jesus has the fullest confidence that the day of full justice will come. In fact, in some of his actions and sayings, Jesus seems to want his followers to know that with him this day of deliverance has already come. Elsewhere there is evident in the Gospels a tension between the not-yet and the already. In the period of tension, just as at the end, there should be no room for vengeance. The followers of Jesus have therefore the assurance that though the goal cannot be reached without revolutionary fervour, revolution does not necessarily include lies, vengeance, torture for dissidents, exile, murder and character assassinations.

No wonder the crisis deepened for Jesus more than it did for Marx. It led Jesus finally to the shameful death by crucifixion. Jesus did not die a natural death. He was killed for his views and for his revolutionary claims. Throughout his short public life he had maintained a critical stance towards society: towards the Roman rulers, towards the Council of the Jews, towards the people whom he never romanticized. His criticism shook society to its foundations. In a final desperate bid against the revolution, all classes combined against Jesus and killed him. They hoped everything would be over and that society could continue its blunderings again. But Jesus lived on.

Soon after his death, however, two powerful tendencies arose which ever since have endangered his essential message of human liberation. One was the institutionalization of his prophetic movement in a hierarchical Church. The other was the deification of his person to the detriment of his message. The two tendencies coalesced when the Church began to claim power and privileges in the name of the power and the privilege of its founder who once was Jesus of Nazareth but who is now God.

The task of Jesus' followers today is not to live in society according to a belief that Jesus of Nazareth is God. It is rather to live in society according to a faith that God is Jesus of Nazareth. They do not know God other than in Jesus of Nazareth. Then the liberation message becomes irresistable and invincible because it is the message, the central message, perhaps the only message, of Yahweh, God of Justice.

C. Lakshman Wickremasinghe · *Alienated Church and Signs of the Times*

C. Lakshman Wickremasinghe, *Mission, Politics and Evangelism*, Church Missionary Society, May 1979, pp. 6–11

From a political perspective, we can see two features of significance for the church in the contemporary history of the nations in Asia. One is the change in the self-understanding of the generality of people who are deprived, marginalised and oppressed. This awareness is not present with the same intensity of awareness everywhere and always, but it is widespread. They have certain aspirations which have become explicit: for the basic benefits which the privileged alone enjoy, for a better recognition of their dignity as human beings, and for opportunity to share in decisions which affect their future. They have also become more aware that their present state is not due to fate but to other people more powerful than they are who are being unjust to them. Their expectations have also risen; they see opportunities to satisfy their aspirations which were not available hitherto. But those whose expectations have risen are also frustrated, because they see that the system allows only a few of them to benefit from these opportunities. Among quite a few there is a seeking for religion which will enable them to overcome injustice rather than acquiesce in it. But other attitudes also continue to jostle within them – a sense of powerlessness, individual and family self-seeking, and inferiority before the elite. Therefore, the elite can still divide them or manipulate them. Self-reliance and mass solidarity are only fitfully realised as a result.

A political satire being staged currently in Sri Lanka makes this situation clear. The central character is a cripple, who represents the crippled section in society, those deprived of their full humanity. He wants fulness of life and he believes he can get it at the top of a mountain which has a rare gem with supernormal power. But since he is a cripple, he needs the help of others to carry him there. It is the politicians who offer to carry him there. They need his help to direct them to the top where they seek the same gem which they believe will give them power to rule society. In short, they need his vote to achieve power. The cripple is not sure whom to trust of the politicians offering to help him, as he feels all will manipulate him for their own ends once they reach the top and not serve his needs. He is aware then of what he wants and how he can satisfy these wants and shrewdly assesses his would-be helpers. But as a cripple he is helpless to some extent and open to manipulation.

The other picture which we can see from a political perspective is the alienation of the church from these masses. It is alienated because for the most part it is captive to the elite groups who rule the nations of Asia and to the middle-classes who support them. Whatever exception there may be, the Protestant churches at least are in this situation. Whatever congregations, institutions and projects may be evidenced among down-trodden groups, the leadership dominating the church and the patterns of church enterprise indicate this link with the upper and middle classes and predispose others to move up the social ladder. The way resources are used and personnel are trained, and the mentalities, life-styles and reactions of church-members to industrial conflicts, all reflect this class bias. This is vividly illustrated in an incident which took place recently in Sri Lanka. Many textile workers were dismissed by the new management of a state corporation after the new government assumed power. Those who belonged to certain trade unions were not re-employed. One of these who was a Christian was willing to join another trade union allied to the government and to accept the stringent conditions imposed for readmission. He approached me with the help of the local clergyman and other fellow-Christians. He said that God had deepened his faith in adversity, and he wanted me to speak to a highly-placed Anglican in the corporation to re-employ him on the grounds of being a fellow Christian. Even though his personal faith had been enriched, he was concerned only with himself. In another parish there was another Anglican who had been dismissed for the same reasons. He met me at a parish function in a state of inebriation. He made a nuisance of himself. But when I spoke to him, the point he made was simply this. He said that all had been dismissed unjustly. He was not asking me to help him regain his job. He wanted justice, namely that all be re-employed and without such stringent conditions for readmission. If the church helped them to achieve justice, he would have more respect for its leadership. But the leading parishioners merely complained that he was drunk and abusive. Here were sad indications of captivity to elite values, spiritual encouragement for self-seeking and alienation from those who were oppressed.

The significance of these two features for the church is this. In discerning the signs of the times in our midst, we see the change in self-understanding among the down-trodden masses as the way in which the Lord of history is passing judgement on our present social system and its values, and the groping fitful struggle by them for a more just social order as the way through which he is bringing to birth a new order of life which will better reflect the values of his kingdom. He is disturbing and he is reshaping. What sense then do we make of the alienation of the church from these masses in whose midst the Lord is at work? Is the existing type of mission in which she has been engaged for the most part a reflection of disobedience to her Lord? A biblical paradigm that speaks to our situation is found in the book of Jeremiah. Jeremiah points out in chapter 29 that the people of God have been captive to temple, to cult and to the land. The Lord is at work on the other hand in stirring the king of Babylon to alter the historical situation and take the people of God out of such ideological enslavement into a foreign land. There they must seek the welfare of those among whom they are destined to live and seek the Lord so that they may find him and understand afresh his purpose for them. They were being asked to undergo a basic change of perspective: to hear the word of the Lord in penitence.

In recent years we know that the church has begun to experience a change of direction. It has begun to take note of its class bias and alienation and change its attitudes and pattern of mission. A variety of projects geared to development have been undertaken in Asia among the down-trodden masses in the urban, rural, plantation and coastal sectors. In her preaching and teaching, the church has sought to make people aware of the need to liberate the poor from their misery and servility and the rich from their greed and arrogance. Clerical and lay personnel have been trained to fit them for leadership in these activities. Church resources have been diverted to implement these new aspects of mission. Donations have been obtained from rich sponsors and in some instances evangelism has accompanied these ventures. In some instances also prophetic witness has been reactivated. Unjust practices have been exposed; appeals have been made and moral pressures exercised more than before on politicians and administrators to repeal unjust laws and to provide new policies and facilities to effect reforms. In all this, foreign agencies like CMS have collaborated with both funding and personnel. In England, they have made appeals, registered protests and exercised moral pressure on multi-nationals and on the government when any policies have contributed to further deprivation of the masses in Asia.

One concrete instance might illustrate this trend. In the town of Kurunagala there is a valuable piece of coconut and paddy land owned by the descendants of a convert to Christianity through the work of pioneer CMS missionaries. Income in cash and kind from the land has been given for church work at regular intervals. It could have been sold as housing property but was donated to the church to run a farm for drop-out youth and others. Now it is a flourishing farm with thriving animal husbandry units. The tenant cultivators were given ownership of part of the paddy land, and the balance cultivated by the farm with double the previous yields. Both unemployed youth and social misfits have benefited from the farm. There have been attempts to help neighbouring colonists with good seed paddy for their paddy cultivation and good strains of cattle for their domestic cattle. The quality of service and care shown by those who manage the farm has drawn some of those brought into contact with it, into profession of the Christian faith. A clergyman with the necessary gifts has been released to manage the farm. When local funds proved insufficient, a foreign Christian agency provided the required funds to facilitate further development and self-support.

There have not only been church-managed projects. In many places there have been community projects in collaboration with people of other faiths. Elsewhere, Christians have joined in movements engaged in such ventures as Sarvodaya under Buddhist inspiration, and the Gandhi Sevagram (Society) under Hindu inspiration.

The whole approach can be described as developmentalist or reformist in perspective. It seeks to protect the poor from the rapacity of their oppressors, and from servile dependence on their patronage; and to convey to the down-trodden a better sense of their worth as human beings. It also exposes wrong-doing and injustice by the elite, and seeks to alter their attitudes and practices by an ideology of benevolence based on religious commitment. Christians find their inspiration in the ideal of a righteous ruler and the legislation relating to the Sabbath Year and the Year of Jubilee in the Old Testament along with the courageous exposure of wrong-doing in high places by the prophets. In Jesus, they also see a similar trend, with his commendation of generosity and warning of the evils stemming from riches, his rebuking of the establishment for its callous laws, and his conversion of the oppressor Zacchaeus to a new way of operating his finances. Buddhists and Hindus find their inspiration for this social ideology in their own scriptures, ranging from the tradition of the righteous ruler and the virtues of detachment in oneself with kindness and compassion for other beings, to the concept of the welfare of one being found in the welfare of all.

But the limitations of this approach have become obvious, at least to many in Asia. The landowner, the money-lender, the profit-making capitalist, the elite, those moving up the social ladder, will support this type of reform so long as their own living standards and dominant power are not radically affected. Though certain numbers from among the down-trodden have benefited from a variety of projects and reforms, on the whole it is the rich and those with skills who have improved their condition, while the poor and unskilled have become relatively marginalised. Also, the sense of inferiority and powerlessness among the masses has not been significantly erased. What is more, those who have operated the reforms and the projects have become a new cadre with money and influence, especially due to massive foreign aid. Clergy and laity, including the missionaries, even though working on behalf of the oppressed masses, have become a new elite, though an elite working on behalf of the oppressed masses. Those in the church who have sought to break through class alienation have continued it in a more subtle form. It is only occasionally that patrons have become servants; that community workers have learnt to share fully in a life-situation with down-trodden groups; that there has been commitment to people rather than to schemes of development. There are of course exceptions. Where identification with the poverty and powerlessness of the poor have been genuine, activity has matured into a quality of living. Such lives have borne witness to a religious vision and commitment and have borne fruit; others associated with their projects have been inspired to live likewise. These exceptions are signs pointing to this compassionate idea; they do not set aside the limitations of this approach for contemporary Asia.

To overcome these limitations, another approach has been advocated in more recent times by radical sections in the church.[19] It can be described as the neo-Marxist approach. It is Marxist in that it accepts the basic Marxist insight of a conflict of class interests between oppressors and oppressed. For the down-trodden to fulfil their aspirations, they must in the first instance organise mass pressure to compel the elite to make alterations to the present unjust social system and finally take over the levers of power to establish a just social order. The alienation of the masses from the church can be overcome, they feel, not merely by improving their living standards and empowering them with skills through a variety of development projects, but primarily by taking their side against their oppressors and organising with them to establish a just social system.

The focus of activity is not on projects. They are fostered only if they arise from the felt needs of oppressed groups. The role of the community agitator is to build awareness of the fact of oppression and the reasons for oppression and to generate a sense of people's power or mass solidarity. Particular issues such as lack of basic amenities or low prices for their produce are raised among those oppressed and support is mobilised to confront the oppressors and wrest concessions from them, whether they be landlords, profiteers or corrupt officials. It is a process of agitation and mass education. Links are forged with Marxist parties seeking to gain political control of the levers of power, to radically change the unjust social system. A recent incident will serve as an illustration. After the devastating cyclone in Sri Lanka, massive government aid was provided for relief and rehabilitation, with assistance from foreign agencies. In several instances government officials at the local and regional level appropriated a good part of the financial assistance and diverted the free food and materials to the local traders who sold them at maximum prices. The ordinary people felt powerless in the face of this callous oppression. But a group of community agitators from the peasantry, associated with a Christian clergyman, raised these issues with local groups of farmers belonging to an island-wide Peasants' Congress, in a particular region. They organised a series of work-camps where they helped each other to rebuild their homesteads and to repair irrigation works for the next cultivation season. They pressurised government officials to provide implements and vehicles; they obtained donations from peasants and well-wishers in other areas. Finally, they drew up a petition exposing the corrupt practices of officials and profiteers, obtained signatures on a massive scale, printed and distributed the same. They handed a copy to the central authorities, prepared to send a delegation and held a mass meeting with the help of certain Marxist parties. Here was a mobilising of support around a felt injustice, a display of people's power and a raising of mass-consciousness in a rural area.

An alienated church in Asia must opt also to foster and support community agitators of this type to serve in rural, urban, coastal and plantation sectors. They are as important for the mission of the church as parish clergy, community workers and evangelists. They may not be listed among the functionaries in the New Testament documents; they are essential functionaries in contemporary Asian Christianity. They are a sign that an alienated church is serving where the Lord is judging and reshaping contemporary Asian society and the company of Christ's disciples within it. They bear witness to the prophetic function of the church to make unpopular options and to face the harsh consequences of suffering and dying as martyrs for the cause of Jesus. They point to a religious vision that empowers people to resist injustice and the powers of evil, rather than simply acquiesce. '. . . he who understands and knows me, that I am the Lord who practices a steadfast love, justice and righteousness in the earth; for in these things I delight, says the Lord.' (Jer. 9:23–24)

Christians find their inspiration for such tasks in the song of Mary with its themes of radical displacement of the proud, the mighty and the rich by the humble, 'the poor' (meek) and the hungry. They see Jesus by his birth and lifestyle identifying himself with the common people; exposing and condemning their ecclesiastical oppressors, and confronting them finally with an active protest in the heart of the establishment, within the temple; and then weeping over the impending destruction of Jerusalem. He bears witness to a community where justice and love prevail. His counter-community of disciples which evolved into the early church in Jerusalem had an egalitarian economy which distributed according to need and discouraged private property. The experiment did not survive and Jesus had also to bear the harsh consequences of his confrontation with the establishment. But the ideal and the perspective have continued to inspire future generations. The Buddhists find their inspiration in the community of monks with its egalitarian economy and in the Buddha figure who exposed and undermined caste and class privileges in Brahminic society in his era. Hindus find inspiration in Gandhi-ji who used organised non-violence as an instrument of protest and confrontation to secure justice. Marxists find inspiration in their red heroes who in life and death under repressive regimes have been unflinching in their dedication to the cause of liberating the oppressed masses.

These community agitators may not always succeed in their efforts. The divisions among the masses, their self-seeking in a crisis, the pervasive power of the oppressors, mistakes in judgement, make progress uncertain, fitful and slow. Political reaction may decimate their numbers as in Korea and the Philippines. The Marxist parties with whom they seek to co-operate may manipulate them while seeking power and marginalise them once they have seized power, as in China. They also have their own limitations. Some community motivators may be alienated from the people among whom they work due to undue money-power. Others aggravate conflict when more conciliatory methods can achieve their goals in a particular situation. Nonetheless, where the commitment is genuine and the identification deep-seated, they pay in their own persons the human cost of transforming an unjust society; they bear witness to the goal of peoples' power among down-trodden people. The quality of life evidenced bears its own fruit, as others are inspired to do likewise. In the Christian community agitator, such a quality of life commends the claims of Jesus Christ with an effectiveness no words can convey.

8 · India

Christianity has a longer history in India than in any other Asian country, with Syrian Nestorian Christians active in South India since the fourth century. With the coming of Portugal and later France, Roman Catholicism was established and Protestantism followed in the seventeenth century, initially through the work of East India Company chaplains. The earliest attempts to indigenize the forms of Christianity, those of Robert de Nobili, belong to this period. But despite seven centuries of Mogul (Muslim) rule and a hundred and fifty years under Britain, the ancient Hindu-Sanscritic culture remained overwhelmingly dominant and would have a determining role in the growth of Indian Christian theology. Leaders of the Hindu Renaissance like Ram Mohan Roy and Keshub Chandra Sen incorporated many Christian features into a reformed Hinduism and stimulated the first attempts at an indigenous Christian theology. These were made by Brahmobandhav (1861–1907) who was both a Sunyasi and active nationalist, and restated Thomistic belief in Vedantic terms. Sadhu Sundar Singh (1889–1929) and A. J. Apassamy (b. 1891) amongst others, lived and wrote of a personal Christian experience in the tradition of Bhakti devotion. For Sundar Singh this was described as 'the water of life in an Indian cup'.[1]

The nationalist movement which emerged in the formation of the Indian National Congress (1885) did not become a mass organization until the advent of Mahatma Gandhi. In strongly rejecting Western civilization and many of the forms of Christianity, Gandhi nevertheless accepted Jesus as the 'personification of the moral and spiritual principle of non-violence'.[2] While being 'Great Soul' for the masses of India and the pivotal leader in the struggle for independence, Gandhi became for countless Christians the model for Christian presence in Mother India. C. F.

Andrews is only one of many non-Christians thus influenced, but S. K. George (1910–1960) articulated most clearly the Gandhian challenge to Christianity. In three books and many articles he reflects extensively on Gandhi's life and work and presents Satyagraha especially as the manifestation of Christ's redemptive suffering and love in practice. The cross was here reclaimed, George declared, as not only a working principle for life but also as a science of mass action for a new social order. George's own commitment to inter-religious understanding, to Christian theologizing and to social justice shaped a life which in poverty and suffering resembled the same cross.[3]

The Christian significance of Indian nationalism was the subject of many books in the early decades of the century, notably by S. K. Datta, S. K. Rudra, K. T. Paul and C. F. Andrews. At the height of the struggle for independence, a group of lay theologians argued forcefully for the expression of Christian theology in Indian terms. Prominent in the group, and themselves prolific writers, were P. Chenchiah, who pictured Jesus as a new creation, the 'man in our history', and V. Chakkarai whose theology of the cross related Bhakti tradition with a social action directed to eliminate all inequalities.[4] The group reflected strong nationalist aspirations along with a deep appreciation of Hindu tradition and had strong influence, P. Chenchiah in particular, on Paul D. Devanandan.

Devanandan (1901–62) was, like all those mentioned above, a widely-read layman. He was also founder of the Christian Institute for Study of Religion and Society (CISRS). Dialogue for him no longer meant an adaptation of Hinduism, but the exploration of God's continuous activity in his world, by which 'all men "not merely Christians" are involved in the great redemptive movement in history'.[5] The Spirit which works outside the church in the Hindu Renaissance for example is also transforming the church, Devanandan believes, for a total mission and for full participation in nation-building. The Indian expression of Christianity requires the transformation of society, he wrote in 1961, because at the core of the gospel is the resurrection which is in itself the pledge of the transformation of grossly material reality.[6] This was to be central to the thought of Devanandan's partner at CISRS, M. Mammen Thomas, as was his recurring emphasis on 'the hope of glory'; that glorified community at the end, which is even now conditioning the present. Devanandan and Thomas had (like many others) been strongly influenced by the YMCA and the Student Christian Movement (SCM), in which they were long-time leaders, by the Youth Christian Council of Action (Kerala) and by the Christian Ashram Movement. Thomas, like their early colleague A. K. Thampy, had also been active in Marxist movements in Kerala. If the principal contribution of the SCM, under such leaders as A. Rallia Ram, was in biblical theology and Christian nationalism, the contribution of the Ashrams such as Christakula (Tamilnadu), Manganam (Kerala), and Sihora (Madya Pradesh) was in the development of an indigenous Christian worship, evangelism and service.[7]

But strong influences were also being felt in post-independence years due to vast political and economic changes in the nation. The new constitution (1950) brought together 562 states and 6 major religious bodies in a secular, pluralistic state and established the National Congress in power. It would be led until 1967 by Jawaharlal Nehru. His attempts at large scale modernization and the elimination of extreme poverty failed to achieve self-sufficiency in food or to eliminate a neo-colonial dependence on foreign markets and foreign aid. Nor would his administration prevent the continuing concentration of wealth in the hands of land-owners and caste-groups which now formed horizontal alliances to gain their ends. A weakened Congress party split in 1969 and that section led by Indira Gandhi, relying increasingly on divisive and non-democratic processes to stay in power, in 1975 declared Emergency Rule.

During this period, the Roman Catholic Church moved from its pre-independence hesitancy regarding nationalism or the values of Indian cultures to a fuller participation in national concerns. Inculturation becomes the deep concern of many seminaries and centres, notably the National Biblical Catechetical and Liturgical Centre in Bangalore, the Vidyajoti Institute (Delhi) and the Indian Social Institute (Bangalore).[8] The Indian federation of Catholic Students (AICUF), like the SCM, has become an influential training ground for Christian reflection in the Indian context, often in situations of human desperation and struggle.

The major work of M. M. Thomas also belongs to this period (since the mid-1950s), although it is impossible to summarize adequately his wide-ranging contributions to a living theology in India (his own phrase). In numerous articles he has outlined the biblical and historical resources for Indian Christianity, or analysed the dynamics of nationalist and revolutionary movements. His chapter 'Criteria of an Indian Christian Theology'[9] has stimulated creative responses throughout Asia. Indian Christian social thought and contemporary spirituality are central interests as are the ecumenical movement and the place of the gospel in a secular pluralistic state. As we have seen above, he sees in the resurrection of Christ the ground for both dialogue and social action, and with many colleagues he has developed the CISRS to become the foremost Indian centre for research, publication and education in both these fields. Significantly, the institute works in close association with a wide range of community groups and people's movements, of every religious or ideological persuasion. In major studies he has examined Christian dimensions in the thought of leaders in the Indian Renaissance or in secular Indian ideologies and the relation of Christian salvation to processes of humanization or to the renaissance of other faiths. The prophetic core of faith remains for him in the life, death and resurrection of Jesus Christ, as the power to join God's work of active loving service in all society and history.[10]

Many lay-theologians, Christian activists or scholars have been closely associated with the work of CISRS or in other Indian ecumenical agencies. Among those who have contributed to the same living Indian theology are three more laymen: T. K. Thomas in, for example, studies of various Christian themes in contemporary Indian literature; Samuel Parmar in the areas of development and social justice; and D. A. Thangasamy, in his writings on church renewal, secular lay ministry and ecumenical mission in India.[11] A series of volumes (1967–75) issued by the National Christian Council India have included papers by many who were actively exploring 'a theological dynamic'.

The volumes and many articles of Paul Verghese (Paulos Gregorios) should also find mention here although only some deal with the Indian context. Notable here are his series of Bible studies, e.g. 'The Gospel and the Hungry', and recent papers on an Indian hermeneutic. In a number of books he outlines the basis for a Christian community and ideology able to live and act in today's India.[13]

E. V. Mathew (1917–71) was also closely associated with such people as Thampy, Thomas and Chandran. Described by his colleagues as a 'prophet of Christian secularism', Mathew continually urged the churches to promote secularism in India, as the only way in which communal divisions could be reduced and politics desacralized. Yet he affirmed the heart of his beliefs in the conviction that God had acted decisively for the renewal of man and of society, in Jesus of Nazareth – 'the transcendent in the secular'. The demand on the Christian therefore was no less for radical personal change than it was for revolutionary change in unjust social and political structures. Amongst many writings on the Christ event, church renewal, and law and politics, the extract reproduced here outlines a Christian approach to law in the context of revolution.[14]

The deeper political and economic conflicts of the last decade have also led many Christian groups to share courageously in the movements and struggles of local communities. And from this participation lively theology has emerged. At the centre of a number of reform and worker movements in Kerala stands Joseph Vaddakan, Catholic priest and former Gandhian activist. His identification with poor labourers and evicted tillers, for example, and his co-operation with both communists and non-communists in resisting the brutality of landowners and government officials has led to his suspension from traditional priestly duties. In his writing Vaddakan declares that poverty, 'the greatest sin', can be eliminated only when love is expressed in political action and his autobiography ends in a moving climax with the image of a mass 'outside the church' where Christ's feeding of the poor is again enacted and again rejected by 'the temple'.[15]

Urban and industrial ministries in many Indian cities have long been following the same path of full solidarity with people in their local struggles. They have frequently experienced the same rejection of which Vadakkan speaks and yet have made rich contributions to a living Indian theology. This is especially so in the case of the Ecumenical Social and Industrial Institute, Durgapur, and the Bombay Urban and Industrial League for Development.[16] Kuruvila Abraham, Director of the ECC, Bangalore, and an authority on Marxism, has written a number of articles concerning the struggles in India for peace and justice as the context for biblical and theological interpretation. Others providing valuable treatments of these themes include T. M. Philip of United Theological College, Bangalore, and Victor Premasagar, until 1979 of the Andra Pradesh Theological College.[17]

After leaving Durgapur for St Paul's Cathedral, Calcutta, Subir Biswas pioneered the joint action in a new metropolitan plan for Calcutta and with his co-workers transformed the Cathedral into a welfare and action centre for those living and dying in bastees or refugee camps. One of the most capable theologians in India until his death in 1977, Biswas in his rare writings pictured the new theology now required as one of pilgrimage, praxis and incarnation. His volume of meditations on 'the daily struggle in the city' reflect on the silent, powerless God who is nevertheless present in all struggle, all change.[18] At the Tamilnadu Theological Seminary, Madurai, Samuel Amirtham and Y. David have worked with many others, Christian and non-Christian, to form a living Christian community grounded at all points in the life of the larger community of Tamilnadu. A meaningful human community is one of the pre-conditions for a living theology, Amirtham believes, and this requires a direct involvement in particular struggles where Christian theology is experienced directly as saving gospel. Amirtham's writings include many Old Testament studies – of the presence of Yahweh or the relation of prophecy to politics – as well as essays on e.g. the challenge to theology of new religious movements in religion or development.[19] Many of these thrusts are reflected in the extract printed below.

Amongst many Christians involved in both organization and theological reflection within the movements for mass education, M. J. Joseph, formerly of the NCCI staff, is author of many recent articles and meditations. Joseph works closely with the staff of CISRS, which is now directed by Saral Chatterji, until 1976 Principal of Serampore College. Writing with specialized knowledge of economics, Chatterji has authored and edited many volumes on the themes of modernization, religious values in development and revolution and church-state relationships in India. In shorter form, he has dealt with aspects of Indian political process, Christian participation in people's movements and 'conscientious living in modern India'. In his concern to desacralize and humanize social revolutionary forces, Chatterji carries forward the thought of such people as S. K. George and M. M. Thomas.[20]

Perhaps the most eminent of Indian Catholic theologians, Samuel Rayan of the Vidyajoti Institute, Delhi, has produced a wealth of writing since 1965. Much of it has appeared in ecumenical contexts and has interpreted Vatican II reforms or discussed issues for Indian theology and spirituality. Rayan's volume on the Holy Spirit and many shorter meditations reveal the depth of his own spirituality, but in recent years his attention, like that of so many others, has been focussed upon the Christian commitment to social justice. 'To God's radical love and Jesus' own radical obedience' wrote Rayan in 1974 at the conclusion of a lengthy study of Jesus and the Father, 'correspond the radical demands they make on us, that we . . . risk our life for the liberation . . . and well-being of the broken neighbour and of the oppressed and dishonoured masses'.[21] The excerpt following gives one particular application of this understanding. Similar thrusts are seen in the work of Rayan's colleague, Sebastian Kappen, who has given much of his attention to interpreting the manhood of Jesus. His fullest treatment is contained in the volume *Jesus and Freedom* (1978). Bishop Paulose mar Paulose, of the Nestorian Church, is also concerned with the radical demands of Jesus' continuing mission. These are outlined in his Joshi Memorial Lectures on 'Mission' (1978) where he discusses in India's historical context the church's participation in 'God's revolutionary strategy'.[22]

E. V. Mathew · *The Role of Law in a Revolutionary Age*

E. V. Mathew, 'The Role of Law in a Revolutionary Age', in J. R. Chandran (ed.), *The Secular Witness of E. V. Mathew*, Christian Literature Society/ Christian Institute for the Study of Religion and Society, Madras 1972, pp. 117–25

Certain Aspects of the Christian Teaching on Law

The confusion that is constantly noticed in Christian teaching on law arises from the fact that Torah has been mistranslated as Nomos. 'Law' in the Bible meant revelation and not a rational human inference from the nature of things. The idea of law as a self-evident principle that could be gathered by human reason is mostly a contribution of Greek philosophy and Stoicism to Western political thought. But the essence of the biblical understanding of law will necessarily have as its basis God's continuing revelation in the world and Christ as the Lord of the world. So it is to be highly regretted that many Christians think of Christian faith as one that replaced law by love. Many seem to think that to see God as the Law-giver is obsolete, as we should think of him only

as Father. A refreshing contrast is found in the statement of a
Scottish bishop at the beginning of the nineteenth century. 'The
law was predicting the gospel and both are to be viewed as con-
stituting one beautiful and consistent scheme of salvation.' Vidler
tries to improve upon this by saying that 'there is Gospel in the
Law and Law in the Gospel, both being the work of one God –
not of a bad God and good God, not of a stern God and a tender
God, but of one God who is at once and always both severe and
good.' He raises the question, 'For what is God's promise to
Abraham but good news of blessing which is assuredly to be
bestowed upon all the families of the earth?' God's scheme of
salvation is by way of call, election, covenant and promise. It is
not exactly like a human covenant as it is not a bargain but a
blessing. Neither does it rest on man's compliance. God alone
initiates it and so He will fulfil it. Nor is the scheme one for
individuals but for all the families of the earth. It is in the background of the scheme of salvation. He gives Law and promulgates
it to a people whom He has already chosen, redeemed and
blessed. The people will have to respond continually to the deliverance He is bringing about by His law. They are addressed by a
Personal Being to personal beings. Emil Brunner states, 'The law
is the gift of God. The Bible knows nothing about a general moral
law of reason . . . The Law is given. It does not float in the air
like a general idea above reality, it enters into history as a personal
reality.' Further, law is not given to Israelites for their own benefit
but that through their obedience all the nations of the earth may
be blessed. The servant nation has to minister to other nations by
the fact of its election and the gift of law. The badge of election
and the supreme gift of law only point to their true role as the
despised servants of God. The Law of God is addressed to every
nation and to every man. The universal quality of the Decalogue
makes it speak to every society and touch a responsive chord that
almost knows no barriers. The response is confined not only to
societies of Judaeo-Christian tradition, but to other societies in
the world. In every society that is in the process of secular deliverance from all religions that claim totality of obedience to their
value system, the Law of God offers true organizing strategies.
Two characteristics of the Torah are specially noticeable.

(i) God's law preserves freedom and maintains order. The natural tendency of man is to disrespect God's laws and to set up his
own value systems. This natural tendency requires to be curbed.

The very fact that it was necessary to promulgate law for the Israelites and declare it to them shows that there is no law in them. In this respect the Law of God is calculated to bring home to everyone how sinful and rebellious humanity is. At no point in the history of man does law become unnecessary; law reveals to man his sinful, rebellious, disobedient and covetous nature against which law's enforcement agencies must ceaselessly operate.

(ii) Law as revealed in the Bible does not identify itself as a static principle, blindfolded and tyrannical in its impartiality and cruel logic. It is a strategy, an institution of great potentiality to establish juster relationships among men and enforce them with its might. At the same time man will tend to forget the true source and basis of law, viz. the one and only God and His changing will. Instead, human nature in its passionate search for all-time solutions and for immutable principles resisting all change will seek in law's role of preserving order and certainty an answer, a satisfaction to its own inner craving for stratification. Law has quite often been used for these false ends by the very pedestalling of it. Law must preserve order but must also reveal its partial and ambiguous character. It has to run with life and respond to its realities. Law must constantly undergo judgement before the great tribunal – life. Law, in pointing to its inadequacies and to its proper role as a servant of mankind, also holds out the promise of its fulfilment not by itself but outside of itself – Christ is the end and fulfilment of Law. Christ, by taking upon Himself our manhood and our Israelhood, with all its weaknesses and disobedience, and by submitting Himself to perfect obedience, fulfilled Law. But in the process He was destroyed by the custodians of Law. This is what constantly happens in human history. Unless law remains true to its role, as servant of the people to establish a juster order among them, without elevating itself in the place of life, it will become the enslaver of man.

However it cannot be denied that an underlying dichotomy between law and gospel has been read by many into biblical revelation. This, to say the least, is unhappy. It degrades law in the scheme of God's salvation to a stepping stone on which Christ and the Gospel could be preached. God gave man the law and, regardless of what men do with it by misformulation and misinterpretation and mishandling, it continues to be one of the richest gifts of God. Jesus Christ is the fulfilment of law and not its destruction. He continues to be its fulfilment and law is in the hands of Christ. Gospel and Law cannot be separately dealt with.

Therefore the following dimensions of the biblical perspectives of law require special emphasis.

(1) Law reveals the nature of God and man. The dividers of law and gospel carry a false division right into the nature of God. Law reveals that the God of Israel is always the redeemer of His people. He does not murder but protects the life of even the offender. He is faithful to the last even to the point of fulfilling the covenant by taking upon Himself the obedience of Law imposed on man by an act of complete self-emptying. He strikes at all the legalism of law by allowing Himself to be destroyed by the custodians of law. Law in turn reveals man in his sinfulness, his propensity to make false gods, to absolutise legalism and ideologies in place of the living, active God of History thereby qualifying himself for punishment, who prostitutes and elevates sabbath to manipulate his neighbour denuding it of its purpose as the servant of man, who steals what is really due to the other and who indulges in such selfish unconcern about the life of the other as to cause the neighbour's gradual loss of the gift of abundant life received from the Maker. Law reveals man in absolute need of God whose uncompromising love validates law. Without law man is alienated from God, from life itself. Man may then be tempted to reject the gospel, the goodness of the event, that fulfils the law.

(2) If the charismatic characteristic of law is emphasised in the Bible it is only to bring to the fore the essential servanthood of leadership. There is no valid leadership acknowledged in the Bible whether it be of men or of institutions that does not fulfil itself in servanthood. 'He that desires to be your master, let him be your servant.' Israel's leadership of the nations is to minister to other nations. Jesus came to minister and not to be ministered unto. Law's charismatic and purposive leadership establishes itself only so long as it retains its essential servanthood of ministering to the needs of the people for their welfare. Love is the law of life, love that does not degenerate to sentimentalism. When law forgets this essential servanthood in the reality of change, it sets itself up as a false god. It will not then hesitate to crucify the Lord of Life who came to fulfil law.

(3) Responsibility – There is no suggestion anywhere that the purpose of law in biblical understanding is to punish free choice of evil. The purpose of law is apparently not retribution for its

own sake. The law in the Bible is forwardlooking. This is in contrast to the common view that legal responsibility is a matter of moral blameworthiness and this ushers in free choice of evil. It has to be borne in mind that the responsibility imposed on the criminal is responsibility for the acts and situations to which he had no real responsibility. In this sense the punishment he undergoes is vicarious. The example that comes to one's mind is the large number of juvenile thieves caught and arrayed before the judge awaiting punishment. Analysis of their previous history will show that many have resorted to crime as a result of their helpless economic condition, childhood influences of bad company, desertion by parents and other causes over which they at no time had any effective choice or control.

Community's responsibility for crime must reflect in its attitude of forgiveness to the prisoner, realizing that law's institutions cannot at the same time pronounce judgement and extend forgiveness. Solicitous care of those who have been dependent on the prisoner for their maintenance and careful planning for the rehabilitation of the prisoner on completion of sentence will have to be seriously undertaken. Harsh and unconscionable punishments and excessive imposition of bail amounts need constant checks by a vigilant public, conscious of its responsibility in crime. Law's symbols and rhetoric should eschew the notion of personal rejection of the offender.

The worshipping community has special responsibility in this field. With the eye of faith it sees the intricate pattern in which society as a whole is interlocked in sin. Sin, guilt and confession will no longer remain the individual's affair. Instead everyone will realize that he is interlocked in the sin of the other and that all are in common need of confession and redemption.

Christian responsibility will become one of sharing of human guilt. It will refuse to be identified with ideological action because it carries its own justification. Responsible action does not lay claim to knowledge of its own ultimate righteousness. The refusal to be the divider of good and evil and sole dependence on God's grace for justification will be the marks of Christian strategists for responsible historical action. Responsible action motivated and limited as it is by commitment to God and neighbour will include readiness to share both guilt and freedom. Lawyers and jurists, being specialists in the motive mentality of law in the realm of reconciliation and responsible action, are marked out to carry on relevant dialogue in the worshipping community.

(4) Justice in the Bible – This righteousness of God is spelt out in the Bible not as a vertical concept of justice blindfolded, holding the scales in just equality between man and man. God's will stands for the establishment of justice in the land but it is much more comprehensive than the technical justice and rights of natural law. Justice or righteousness includes within itself in its very basic definition a particular regard for the undefended ones of the earth, to rescue them from the clutches of those that are stronger than they. God vindicates in history those who cannot themselves rescue their own rights. 'He hath showed strength with his arm; he hath scattered the proud in the imagination of their hearts. He hath put down the mighty from their seats and exalted them of low degree. He hath filled the hungry with good things; and the rich he hath sent empty away.'

A dynamic perspective of law must necessarily integrate all the insights that the Christian perspective emphasizes.

(a) Reality of the revolutionary change that is brought about by the moving spirit of Christ, the Lord of Revolution who holds in His hands all the institutions of man and relativizes them. Sabbaths are made for man, to serve him and not to effect mastery over him.

(b) Law in its role as means of preservation, as call to judgement and as guidance to renewal, shows sufficient ability to be demythologized while constantly conserving order and freedom. True order lies along the movement of change. The rights and the freedom of the person are realized in horizontally relating and relevantly submitting to the freedom and rights of others.

(c) The bias towards the oppressed, the disinherited and the unequal, integral to the understanding of divine righteousness, will save law and justice from technical legalism and formal positivism and move it towards its leadership by servanthood in a society of interlocked responsibilities.

However in an age of specialization law, to be judged and renewed, requires that the tools of understanding on the basis of insights referred to above should come from within the situations of law and law-making. For this end, it must be recognized that inter-disciplinary relations need far greater strengthening than is usually conceded, for a better understanding of the complex and rapidly changing society. The lawyer now cannot function in isolation, as also the politician and the theologian. The continuous and vast output of modern legislation raises serious anthropological enquiries. So the tools of judgement will have to be effectively shared among the theologian, the lawyer and the law-maker. How else will it become possible to reckon with the reality of the forces unleashed by specialization and of employing them in the perspective of the whole man and of a world society? We need a total view of the situation, however inadequate and however much it may need to be modified and refined as knowledge and specialization by experience increases. We need this as a basis for strategy of action. A dynamic christologically-centred, changing programme of involvement, while affirming and promoting the integrity and sanctity of the human being in a community of persons will save law and its strategies of self-creation from absolutizing and elevating itself in place of the true Lord of history and of situations. A true perspective of law and its role in a revolutionary situation can come to us only when we accept with sincere contrition of heart and of intellect the interlocking nature of human responsibility and of the provisional nature of our enlightenment, derivable from involvement within situations of law and the making of law. Yet it is by involvement alone that we will be known as our neighbour's keeper, which is our true destiny.

Samuel Amirtham · *The Church: The Bearer of Salvation*

Samuel Amirtham, 'The Church: The Bearer of Salvation', in M. Zachariah (ed.), *The Church: A People's Movement*, NCC, India 1975, pp.35–43

The Church, the Prophetic Agent of Salvation

It has now come to be widely accepted that the church has to play a *prophetic role* in God's plan of salvation. And by this one commonly means the uncompromising demand for social justice and scathing condemnation of religious and social injustice. There is a tendency to set in contrast the prophetic role against the priestly role. The priestly is degraded to a mere meaningless formal, cultic and ceremonial aspect of religious life. This is not completely true to the Biblical tradition. The prophets and priests very often stood close to each other and in the same tradition, e.g., Samuel, Jeremiah and Haggai. In the Bible both the prophet and the priest proclaimed condemnation and comfort. The Priest is the one who links God to man and man to man. He offers the world to God in worship and helps the church to adore her Lord. The priest offers forgiveness, in the name of God. He gathers the individual worshipper to the congregation. Therefore the misuse of the priestly role should not lead us to negate the importance of this role. Emilio Castro observes, 'The church in performing the priestly function of joining the life of the individual with society is performing its specified vocation and is rendering an important service to society. It disseminates information, stimulates conscience, summons people to a vocation, purifies intention, inspires courage and nourishes hope'.[23] The church has a *priestly role,* a reconciling role.

The prophetic role in the Bible is a *varied role.* One of the dangers of being a prophet is to become a false prophet: This happens when he takes the word received in an earlier context and offers it as the word for *today.* In Jeremiah's time, the word received by Isaiah of a previous century that Jerusalem would not fall was proclaimed by the false prophets (Jer. 7:23) as God's message in their situation. A prophet becomes a false prophet not so much because of the non-genuineness of his message (it may have come from God), but because of its non-contextuality, i.e., it was not meant for that context. The church stands in danger of being a 'false prophet' in this sense.

It is here that we must remember that there are different paradigms of liberation and the prophetic role in each has been different. In the Egyptian Exodus paradigm of salvation when people were oppressed and despondent, the prophet was the leader in the struggle. He was the one who conscientised the people, planned the strategy, negotiated with Pharaoh and achieved liberation at the end. In the liberation from the Philistines, Samuel the prophet discovered and used a man called Saul who became the instrument of salvation. In the Babylonian Exodus paradigm where bitterness and anger was the mood of the people (Ps. 137), the prophet Jeremiah asked them to wait, to settle down, to marry and give in marriage, to pray for the welfare of the city. In this second Exodus the prophetic role of second Isaiah was to recognize Cyrus as the deliverer and to proclaim him as God's chosen instrument (Is. 45). The prophet also spoke of the suffering servant, who in total commitment to the will of God, became the bearer of God's salvation: 'On Himself he bore our sufferings' (Is. 53:4). The church's prophetic role therefore will be varied in different situations. Sometimes she may be called to be the bearer of salvation by drinking the cup of vicarious suffering, at other times she may be the leader in struggles of liberation, and at other times her task may be to identify and proclaim the agent of salvation whom God uses today. As I wrote in another context 'The church is called to discern in faith God's agents in world history and proclaim them to the world'.[24] The church has then a *discerning role*.

The prophet has also a *conscientising role*. We said that Moses had to make people aware of their oppression and challenge them to rise against these forces. He had to help them to understand the possibilities of the situation with God's help. To create a critical consciousness of the limiting forces in society and the awareness of historical possibilities of changing them is the conscientising role. The programmes in mass education and education for liberation organised by different groups in our churches are attempts along this direction.

But to be a prophet means to participate. Involvement and identification are the legitimation to be a prophet. The church must then seek a new identification with the people, particularly the down-trodden of the society. A statement from Latin America made by the bishops reads as follows: 'Christ our saviour, not only loved the poor, but rather being rich he became poor. He lived in poverty. His mission centred on advising the poor of their liberation and he founded his church as the sign of that poverty among men.

'The poverty of so many brothers cries out for justice, solidarity, open witness, commitment, strength and exertion directed to the fulfilment of the redeeming mission to which it is commissioned by Christ. The present situation then demands from bishops, priests, religious and laymen the spirit of poverty which, breaking the bonds of the egotistical possession of temporal goods, stimulates the Christian to order organically the power and the finances in favour of the common good.

'The poverty of the church and of its members in Latin America ought to be a sign of the inestimable value of the poor in the eyes of God, and obligation of solidarity with those who suffer'.[25]

In India the church has a very limited influence, though far out of proportion to its small size. In the way of the cross, the Indian church has the power of speaking and acting from its powerlessness. The church must learn to be humble, but also to be involved in the processes of society for the purpose of its transformation. C. T.Kurien observes, 'To be purposively and effectively involved in the contemporary struggles for the transformation of society is to get caught up with the world as it is, with all the risks of contamination that it carries. But as Dickenson rightly points out, "Churches must accept the dangers of contamination and compromise which being involved in history requires; indeed they are not contaminated and compromised as much if they do not act resolutely and consciously as when they do act". Because history is an all-inclusive and dynamic process, inaction and attempts to escape reality are in themselves of influence! The new involvement and openness are not merely matters for crucial decision-making on the part of the church. They will also demand new styles of operation for influencing and altering the power centres in society. These are not areas of good will and charity, but of power and politics'.[26]

Our country has become a land of institutionalized violence. Undernourishment, unemployment, infant mortality, uncontrolled population growth, social discrimination, oppressive exploitation, widening gap between the rich and poor, rampant corruption and communalism are all forms of violence. The church is called to join the positive forces in the country to over-come this situation.

The church should not however make one mistake, namely, to think that because the gospel makes her sensitive to these issues, she has also the solution to these problems. Biblical and theological insights should not become substitutes for patient study of issues, analysis of situation, and working out of solutions with expert knowledge. As Charles Elliott said in *The Development Debate*: 'Perhaps one of the greatest blasphemies the church offers its founder is to believe that it can somehow transcend the tough thinking of the technocrat and perceive levels of moral truth denied to other men by making a token intellectual nod at the complexity of the real world'.[27] The church therefore has to depend on and use the expertise and analysis of others and should be glad to cooperate with other forces for common purposes.

One more point can be made regarding the role of the church in this respect. In these days when conferences and services are falling into disrepute, I found it helpful to be reminded by E. Castro that the theological discussions in the church can have *a desacralizing role* on existing structures. Our thinking, speaking and writing also achieve something,

Take for example the subject of social ownership of property. It is a taboo for many a person to question property right as a fundamental right. Recently Bishop Geevarghese Osthathios of Kottayam has published an article, 'Theology of classless society', which has initiated some discussion on this subject. It is Biblical to hold all property as belonging to God and as being held in trust. That wealth should not go on accumulating in a few hands but be equi-distributed periodically is one of the fundamentals of the Jubilee Year. There is a great reluctance even to discuss these matters, probably because of fear of losing one's own property. The Communist Manifesto puts this matter succinctly: It reads, 'You are horrified at our intending to do away with private property. But in your existing society, private property is already done away with for nine-tenths of the population; its existence for the few is solely due to its non-existence in the hands of those nine-tenths. You reproach us, therefore, with intending to do away with a form of property, the necessary condition for whose existence is the non-existence of any property for the majority of society. In one word you reproach us with intending to do away with *your* property, precisely so, that is just what we intend'.[28] The church should initiate discussion on this and similar subjects. 'When private ownership is held to be a sacred right, the church's discussion of property ownership rights; because God is the sole owner of the earth, desacralizes the issue, destroys barriers and frees collective consciousness to create alternatives'.[29]

The church as a prophet has also the *kerygmatic role*. She is called to proclaim God's love and salvation among the complex situations of life of the individual and society. Many understand proclamation as a naive preaching of sin and hell. The Gospel is primarily about God's love, comfort and acceptance. But sin and hell also need interpretation: These words like sin and hell have not lost their meaning but their communicative power. The forces of sin today show their ugly teeth in oppressive structures as much as in the lack of moral content in individual lives. Father Vadakkan wrote once at the entrance of his church that poverty is the greatest sin. Hunger for power, affluence as the be all and the end all, bureaucratic corruption, revolutions which turn out to be oppressive in themselves, and self-sufficient secularism, self-righteous ideologies, are the modern idols and worship of these is demonic. Therefore salvation means to join the struggle to cast out these demons from our society.

M. M. Thomas's words are very significant here: 'It is precisely at this point that the victory of the Cross is relevant. The mission of the Church in this context is to be present within the creative liberation movements of our time which the gospel of Christ itself has helped to take shape, and so to be able to communicate the genuine gospel of liberation – from the vicious circle of sin and alienation, law and self-righteousness, frustration and death into the new realm of Christ's New Humanity where there is forgiveness and reconciliation, grace and justification, renewal and eternal life. It is this message that will liberate the liberation movements from the false structures of meaning based on idolatrous worship of schemes of self-redemption and thus redeem their creative impulses from self-destructive tendencies enabling them to achieve their inner rationale of human emancipation. Our message of Christ's salvation is ever the same, it is the call to men and nations to turn 'from idols to serve a living God' who has 'translated us from the domain of darkness into the kingdom of his dear son Jesus Christ'.[30]

The Church – The Community of Salvation

Theologically, in its very essence, the church is a *community*. God chose not individuals, but a people, the people of Israel. This is very significant for us today. From the beginning warring tribal groups were brought together as one community bound by covenants and covenant loyalty *(Hesed)*. God's way of salvation was not saving individuals and then making them into a group, but to call a people and within the covenant framework provide opportunities for persons to respond to His love. To be a person always means to be in a community. Israel gave us the concept of corporate personality in which the individual and society are inseparably bound together. It is in the psalms that we find the idea very vividly pictured. In them salvation of the individual and society are inextricably bound together. The agony and cry of the psalmist, his vow for praise amidst the congregation, (e.g., 22:22; 26:12; 5l:18-19) are evidence that at no place his thoughts were purely individual, or purely congregational. Salvation which commences in a very personal situation has social consequences. It leads into community.

A community has certain characteristics. It has a common bond transcending lesser loyalties. In the community it becomes possible for members to know and love one another, to the extent of mutual sharing and supporting. Community has to be of a sufficient size to make what sociologists call 'primary relationships' possible. The community does not devalue the individuals, on the contrary, because the aptitudes desires and needs of the individuals are taken care of, there is opportunity given for the individuals to develop and find their fulfilment and community needs in organization. A community builds up its own tradition and guards it. It reflects a common life-style. Mutual responsibilities become axiomatic within it. A community accepts persons not only with their strength, but also with their weaknesses, because a community calls for surrender and therefore commitment.

St Paul has given the powerful image of the body to describe the Christian community, the Church: 'For just as the body is one and has many members, and all the members of the body, though many, are one body, so it is with Christ. For by one spirit we were all baptized into one body – Jews or Greeks, slaves or free – and all were made to drink of one Spirit. For the body does not consist of one member but of many. If the foot should say, "Because I am not a hand, I do not belong to the body", that would not make it any less a part of the body . . . The eye cannot say to the hand, "I have no need of you" nor again the head to the feet, "I have no need of you". On the contrary, the parts of the body which seem to be weaker are indispensable, and those parts of the body which we think less honourable we invest with greater honour . . . Now you are the body of Christ and individually members of it' (I Cor. 12:12–27). 'Here there cannot be Greek and Jew, circumcised and uncircumcised, barbarian, Scythian, slave, free man, but Christ is all, and in all' (Col. 3:11). The Church is the Community of Christ, it is the community of the Spirit of Christ.

A caste-ridden church, a communalistic church, that takes pride in its own particular tradition, as we find it in the Indian church, makes the community claim of the church ridiculous. She is called to be truly a community of love, of forgiveness and acceptance. The evangelistic concern for repentance and forgiveness must be affirmed and deepened in this community. But this is to be proclaimed not so much in words, but by creating a community where this is possible. Amidst the crowded technological way of life and the ideological struggles of sensitive persons, this gains great significance. 'When one lives in situations of intense ideological struggle where the borderline between the battle of ideas and the battle of persons is hard to discern, or when situations of oppression are such that hatred befuddles conscience, or when actions become so ambiguous that one is constantly at risk of living hypocritically, one's well-being requires the encounter of man with man, openness to the mystery of the infinite and life in a community of forgiveness.[31]

Today we go in for large congregations and big gatherings. Indeed one of the attractions of 'conventions' is the mass meetings. While they may have their place, real community life is possible only in small groups. Only in such groups are personal concern and caring possible. Only so can all the members of the community learn to care for others. Otherwise it is the paid pastor who has this responsibility. Someone remarked that Jesus promised to be present where two or three are gathered in his name and not where two thousand or three thousand are gathered! Large numbers have no value for a community, indeed they may be a counter force. So the formation of small communities of faith, family churches and fellowship groups must be encouraged so that the church may be truly a community of love.

The church is a *servant community*. Archbishop Michael Ramsey draws a distinction between the *diakonos church* and the *doulos church*, and we may say, the serving community and the suffering community. To the diakonic nature of the church belong the acts of service, service to meet the needs of humanity. But the church does not exist only for serving the needs of the world. The Church exists to be God's *doulos,* to be bound to Christ, to witness to his Lordship and to suffer vicariously in this affirmation. While the church is involved in social service programmes and social action programmes, both of these must be remembered. When the church meets with misunderstanding, mis-representation of her intentions, rejection, biased criticism, etc., she may remind herself of her identity as the *doulos* community.

The church is an *open community* – open not only in the sense that it is open for all to join, but open to the needs and pressures of society. There is a growing tendency among certain groups of the church to meet together for devotional exercises. These tend to be exclusive fellowships and strengthen a sense of solidarity, identity and community among themselves while they are closed to the world. But in so doing they forget the needs of the world, the language of the world, and neglect effective communication to the world. They affirm community at the cost of relevance. The community becomes closed. The church must remember that she is called to be an open community to her Lord, to others and to the world.

The church is the bearer of salvation inasmuch as she is a *representative community*. Like Abraham, she is to be a channel of blessing to all. Her salvation has any meaning only inasmuch as through her God's salvation becomes available to the whole world. God's people are not just Christians, but people everywhere who are being saved by God. All those who are oppressed all over the world and are being liberated are, in a sense, Harijans, God's people. The church does not have exclusive claim for God's salvation but she remains the community of salvation as long as she witnesses to and is sustained by it.

Samuel Rayan · *The Justice of God*

Samuel Rayan, 'The Justice of God', in D. Preman Niles and T. K. Thomas (eds), *Witnessing to the Kingdom*, Christian Conference of Asia, 1979, pp. 10–15

The Justice of God

(a) That God loves us is the whole Gospel. That he loves us, loves our world, loves all men and women unconditionally, is the basic affirmation on which everything else is built, the source reality from which everything else flows. His love means that he gives us our own selves, gives us life, the earth, the sun, the rain and crops, fruits and food and happiness. His love is faithful and just, and his justice consists in the fidelity and care with which he makes abundant provision for our life, growth, and wholeness as men and women in the human community. In his love and justice he provides for the fulfilment of every man and woman.

(b) An aspect of his Providence is that we freely become providence one to another. We are, one to another, the concrete presence and experience of God's love and justice. It is the privileged vocation of each one of us to be our brother's keeper, to be the place of God's provident justice for the brother, to be a sacrament of God's love. So also this earth with all its riches and resources, as well as all the wealth of any kind we produce and create, is meant to be God's justice and love and providence to one and all.

(c) Four important conclusions follow. *One:* wherever a person is found without the means required to meet human needs, without resources for creative action and participative life in society, there injustice has been operative. *Two:* where people do not care and share but seek to dominate and oppress and where some have plenty while others do not have enough, there is injustice. *Three:* where there is injustice, the sign of God is abolished, and his personal experience is impeded, which amounts to a divine black-out leading to a progressive crystallization of atheism. *Four:* in all such circumstances it is the privilege and task of the churches to 'Gospel' people and situations with that divine Love and Justice which they have experienced in joyful faith. To neglect to do so and to choose to stay within the security of a ritual and legal religion unsoiled by proximity to the dust and sweat of real life would be disloyalty to the core of the Gospel of Jesus and refusal to be his church.

(d) Our response to God's unconditional love is obedience to his commandments: 'If you love me you will keep my commandments. If anyone loves me he will keep my word' (Jn 14:15, 23). And his commandment is that we should love one another: 'I give you a new commandment: love one another' (Jn 13:34; 15:17). We must here take note of the very special grammar of the thought of Jesus which gives to the Christian Faith its characteristic structure. Love is never a returning love completing the circle, but a new-creative love reaching out further to ever-widening horizons. 'As the Father has loved me, so have I loved (not the Father, but) you. Just as I have loved you, so you must love (not me, but) one another. If I . . . have washed your feet, you should wash (not my, but) each other's feet' (Jn 15:9; 13:34; 13:14). We are here at the heart of the Gospel and in touch with the specificity of the Faith. The only adequate response to God's unconditional love in Jesus Christ is to make our own his concern for people and to give all we have for their total liberation and wholeness as he gave his Son for the world's salvation. Now, love is something concrete;

it is deeds, not words. It means securing bread for the breadless, recognition for the marginated, dignity for the despised, liberation for captives and freedom for the downtrodden. It means making ourselves responsible for all who are dispossessed, stripped, broken and discarded on the roadside by a competitive society propelled by the single idea of grabbing ever fatter profits (see Lk 10:29–37; 4:18–19; Mt 25:31–46; 11:1–4; I Jn 3:16–18). In the face of these imperatives of the Faith the churches stand summoned to prove themselves neighbours and brothers to victims of actual and structural injustice not merely at the individual level but especially at the level of groups and whole masses of marginated and downtrodden people.

(e) For people are sacred. Men and women are made in the image of God. Men and women, not simply as individuals, but as community, are the only Image and Symbol capable of pointing to the Mystery of the Divine with any relevance and meaningfulness. It is in respecting, loving, serving, cultivating, liberating and waiting upon the mystery of this Image that we come to discover and experience the Divine with an ever deepening, creative sense of the Real. Men and women in community are the only place of life-giving encounter and communion with God. That is why besides this human Image of his which God has placed on the earth, no other image may be made. Attempts to put up other images are escapist tricks: images of our making can be manipulated whether they be rubrics or laws, liturgies or authorities, establishments or dogmas. But men and women, brothers and sisters, neighbours whom God has placed there as his own Image, make demands on us, and apart from meeting these demands there is no meeting with God. If then we are true and brave enough to follow up the consistency of biblical thought, we shall find that Man has in our Faith a surprisingly central place. Everything is for Man: the earth and the sabbath are for him; for him are all sabbaths, sacraments, laws, and institutions, whether sacred or secular; all authorities, parliaments, economic and political arrangements, all sciences and technological devices. Where therefore injury is done to men as individuals or groups, where his rights and freedoms are abridged, his creativity and growth are impeded, or he is denied due voice and place in society, the most sacred Reality on earth is being insulted and profaned, the Image of God is being humiliated and discarded, the Face of God is being wiped out and atheism built, the future of our earth marred, and the humanity of all impoverished. The question therefore of injustice, misery and oppression cannot but become a central human and Christian concern.

A Mission of Liberation

Hence we see Jesus defining his mission as well as his own identity in terms of people, of needy people and of services rendered to them; of captive people and their liberation; of dead people and people not allowed to live and their uprising. Jesus' basic redemptive service was a service of liberation, freeing people and enabling them to be themselves first, and then build their destiny and their future. He liberated people from ritual religion and ritual morality; he liberated them from the meshes of legalistic religion and legalistic morality and the shallowness of externalism. He liberated them from every sort of fear of gods and demons, of the powers that be, of one another, of themselves, and summoned them to live in love. He led them out of the depressing sense of guilt and the prisons of yesterdays by proclaiming the Father's universal and unconditional forgiveness, and by calling on them to make it their own personally by sharing it generously. He liberated them from burdensome traditions and from all oppressive powers symbolised in Satan and detailed in temple, priest, scribe and Pharisee, in Herod and Caesar, and the arrogance of the rich. He liberated them from isolation and individualism, by educating them to life as a sharing brotherhood patterned on the table-fellowship he enjoyed and recommended. In place therefore of the old exploitative, unbrotherly and classist society, Jesus initiated a movement of justice and love, of freedom and fellowship and celebration of Man and God. Today the movement is us. In us it seeks to be alive and active. We surely want to be the Jesus movement, but we are it only in the measure in which we as churches are a real fellowship and a home of freedom, in the measure in which we are a voice raised against injustice and a hand working to end the degradation and exploitation of the majority of men and women, in the measure in which we are good news to the wretched of the earth.

Jesus was rejected by the political and religious leaders of his nation and his church. They had him killed. They started plotting against his life the moment they discovered that he was no preacher of innocuous pieties, no dealer in religious platitudes, no traditionalist mouthing old words or quoting ancient authorities. They were upset and angry because Jesus spoke in God's name about the people and their problems, about the poor, the downtrodden and the working class, about the masses that laboured and were heavily burdened and were allowed no rest; they were angry because Jesus moved among these, ate and slept with them and championed their cause and their right to dignity and a fair deal. Jesus' words and deeds and life-style, his relationships and demands, the models he projected and the course he followed were all subversive of established systems, interests and value-sets of religion, of social life, of the economic set-up, of political power structures. When the powerful ones saw that Jesus was out to affirm people, to let the lower classes feel that they were not low and need not remain low, that their squalor and servitude were not part of God's plan, that they could serve God and be his children only by throwing away the yokes imposed on them, they opposed him and finally got rid of him.

That means the church has a stake in the real world of men and women, in the world of 'the vast majority', the world's poor. It has to get involved in areas where the life of the people is made or unmade, in social, political and economic affairs, not for the gain and power of its leaders, nor for the prestige of a minority community, but for the sake of man, of humanity, of the Image of God on earth, of justice, of the quality of human life on earth. It also means that the church, when it takes up the cause of justice, must be ready to take the consequences of its conviction and pay the price.

Ambiguity of Church Practice

Turn now from this ideal and call of the church to its practice in the matter of justice and sensitivity to the condition of the poor, and we meet with many a perplexing ambiguity. We have been very vocal about the poor justice meted out to Christians of Scheduled Caste Origin, and there is a thirty-year history of our 'fight'. But I guess we do not pretend that this is the only or the biggest case of injustice we have come across in this country. Is not this rather a small sector of a vast system of injustice in which the masses of the people are held captive? Have there not been cases of enormous atrocities perpetrated on the poor, the small farmer, the landless worker, the Harijan, the Adivasi? And we have chosen most of the time to keep silent. Our silence perhaps is not an example of ambiguity: it is an example of support for the status quo which has mechanisms of oppression built into itself. We have not only been silent, we are deeply involved in the system itself which is a system of individualism and competition with a view to maximisation of profit that can swell capital to be invested with accelerated competition for fatter profits. We are involved in this system and are supportive of it though perhaps unwittingly. We have not adequately questioned the moral basis and the human consequences of capitalism, landlordism, the big industry with sophisticated technology, an export-oriented economy etc. We have rather supported it with investments, or by letting ourselves be drawn into its dynamics by developing services that have to depend upon it continually. We have rarely stopped to ask what critical judgement our Faith has to pass on the system.

All our churches seem to have accepted without questioning the classist pattern of social structuring. We have settled down to the fact that rich and poor exist within the churches. There are places where the priest, the sisters, the lay teachers and the orphan students eat in four different places and not together; and the quality and quantity of food go on diminishing as the classes descend from priest to orphan. The intricate questions of justice and Christian fellowship implied in the situation are never raised. Nor is attention paid to the social models implicit in and proposed by our Eucharistic celebrations, or our faith in a Creator or in the Trinity, or the Lord's prayer which we say together but have not yet begun to live. If we really take them seriously, then we should share all the resources of the Christian community in order to make sure, as the early Christian communities made sure, that nobody among us is left in want and that no unfraternal classes and divisions exist in our midst. Can we demand fair distribution of national resources before making sure of fair and fraternal distribution of Christian resources which are considerable? Can we point to Government's duty without fulfilling our own within the churches?

We spend an undue proportion of our resources, which are by no means small, in the service of a minority of the wealthy and the well-to-do, be these Christian or non-Christian. Usually it is the representatives of this minority that control the levels of decision-taking, policy-making and priority-setting in the churches, just as in the Government it is often non-Christians and

non-scheduled caste people who settle the affairs of Christians of
SCO. We go out of our way to secure enormous funds to run
colleges, special schools, medical colleges and excellent hospitals,
all of which we know only the richer classes can afford. Aid goes
to the poor mainly in relief or in emergency cases. While thus we
serve the rich of all sections we want the Government to care for
our own poor. The churches seem to be saying something like
this: 'I am a rich Christian. So many (how many?) millions of
rupees come into my hands every year from funding agencies
abroad. With this I serve my class, the upper class, irrespective of
religion. Now here are the poor Christians. Government, you,
please, take care of them. You must if you are just.'

There are Christians of SCO who are well off economically,
and there are needy Christians who are not of SCO. This is true
also of all the non-Christian sectors of the nation. Should the
churches then seek a liberal interpretation of the provisions of the
Constitution and a wider application of this interpretation, or
should it bring a Gospel critique to bear upon the very provisions
themselves and the socio-economic presuppositions of these provisions? Thirty years of experience has shown that an approach of
privileges and paternalism does not improve the lot of long-op-
pressed sections of the people. Some of the groups tend to enjoy
being privileged and protected. But that is not redemption, and
we with our Gospel culture should be among the first to detect
the falseness of the situation and cease being pre-occupied with
laying claims to our share in the cake of privileges.

There is another, greater, ambiguity which clouds the question
in hand. We Christians are a casteless community. We are strictly
egalitarian. We do not accept the idea that some are low-born
while others are high-born for all are born of God through Jesus
Christ in the Holy Spirit. Those who have accepted Jesus in faith
have received the power to become God's children; their birth is
free of the stains and chains of the wilfulness and instincts of
human selfishness, the breeding ground of class and caste and
outcaste. Our Faith is that all men and women are created in the
image of God and are being renewed in the image of the Creator;
'and in that image there is no room for distinction between Greek
and Jew, between the circumcised and the uncircumcised, or between barbarian and Scythian, slave or free man. There is only
Christ: he is everything and he is in everything' (Col. 3:11;
Gal.3:27–28). Theologically therefore nobody is, nobody may be,

marginated in the Christian community, and there are no caste distinctions. Theologically, then, what could be the meaning of the term 'Scheduled Caste Christians'? It is perhaps an awareness of the incongruity of the term and its contradiction on Christian lips that leads us to grope for other phrases and to come out with 'Christians of Scheduled Caste Origin'. But our thought betrays us and the contradiction remains. It is ungracious (and the Gospel is all Grace) to keep harping back to distant origins and carnal divisions when Christ has abolished all divisions and united us into the New Man through the Grace of his Cross. If the correction of inadequate terminology was ever theologically or religiously necessary, it is necessary here. We know Christians recognize no caste linkage, for God has redeemed us from all such bondage into the fellowship of his Son. Is it right on our part to make that from which God has saved us the basis of claims to social and economic advantages?

When in the Constituent Assembly Christians through their leaders declined reservations, separate electorates and special privileges, they were at once overcoming the temptations of minority situation and caste awareness and underlining the redemptive universalism of the Christian fellowship. And if the Government cannot see caste distinctions in the Christian ranks, are they doing us an injury about which we should complain, or paying us a compliment over which we should rejoice? Is it impossible for us to understand the Government as saying, 'You, Christian churches, have solved in your measure the big problem of casteism and communalism with which we are still wrestling. You have such spiritual resources.' We could then press forward to try to solve the problem in a still larger measure! The Government is saying that in its view the Christian community does not marginate sections of itself; those who converted have escaped from the meshes of the caste system and the prisons of a closed society into the situation of openness and hope which characterises the Christian fellowship. But if caste has followed them into the churches what difference has conversion made? It depends on us whether we take up or decline the challenge of this stance, whether we turn it into grounds for anger or for hope.

The Task ahead

The basis and scope of our struggle, therefore, need to broaden
out. From concern for certain privileges for a particular group
within a denominational minority community, we should move to
the larger, catholic issue of justice for all the deprived, dispossessed and downtrodden masses of the people of the sub-conti-
nent. It will be more consonant with our Faith to take up or to
join those who have taken up the cause of all the underprivileged
and exploited. The basis of the struggle will be the rights of the
millions who belong to that class which has been working the
hardest for generations and centuries and remained the poorest,
also for centuries and generations. The fight will be against those
social and political mechanisms by which the fruit of the toil of
these millions is siphoned off and enjoyed by the few at the top
rungs of the social ladder. The fight will be against a conception
of life and of man which acquiesces in the existence of very rich
and very poor in the same national or ecclesial community. The
stand will be for a redistribution of resources in order to give
some substance to the ideals of equality, freedom and democracy.
For in a landlordist-capitalist system of high productivity and
cheap labour, these words are but hollow ideological gimmicks.
In sponsoring the 'rights' of Christians of SCO, the church is only
tackling symptoms and not causes. It will do well to devote its
energies to detecting the causes of widespread misery and
wretchedness, to attacking these causes, and to promoting action
for the implementation of such directive principles of the Constitution as call for distribution of the national community's resources to subserve the common good, and for prevention of
concentration of wealth and means of production to the common
detriment.

The concern of the church is not Christians but the poor; its
struggle is not for itself but for the liberation of all men and
women who are held captive. Not that its care for Christians of
SCO is unjustifiable: it is natural, it is perhaps the concretisation
and focal point of the church's universal concern. The New Testament too has such sectarian perspectives. Paul tells us to do
good to all, and especially to our brothers in the faith (Gal. 6: 10;
James 2: 15). This is an attitude evolved in the early Christian
community. The passages that directly reflect the mind of Jesus
are universal in scope as in Mt 25: 31–46, or in the story of the

Samaritan. It is such love and concern for the neediest, irrespective of religious affiliation, that can be the finest witness to the unconditional love that God has disclosed and given to the world in Jesus Christ. Every particular concern of the church must be seen as a symbol that seeks fulfilment, that is, transcendent realization, a realization always larger than itself on a higher or deeper plane.

The task of the church is to champion a whole new social order of true and not merely nominal freedom and equality and people's power. It will begin with itself becoming the New Reality, an egalitarian, socialist society based on freedom and animated by love and realized in shared resources as indicated in the celebration of its Eucharist. It will go on to identify with the poor and suffering and dispossessed masses of men and women everywhere, help awaken their humanity and dignity, help them organise themselves for effective action to bring about a total revolution in structures of the heart as well as in structures of society so as to forge towards the creation of the New Earth of God's dreams and God's promises. It will organise the poor rather than go claiming privileges or begging for benefits. It will take an open stand for justice and try to establish its credibility after too long a silence which has become an embarrassment to its members and its friends. Its call for a redistribution of national resources will be heralded by a reallocation of its own resources with a clear partiality for the poor and the down-trodden which marks the entire history of God's action on our earth. It will take upon itself afresh its responsibility for its poor, but as a concrete sign of its involvement with the plight of all the poor of this land. And finally it will try to make sure that all its ranks, especially those who have come into its freedom from an oppressive past, become catalysts of social change and not seekers of social security, become leaders of liberation movements in favour of all the oppressed of our country and not enjoyers of a separate paradise.

Notes

Introduction

1. See Koyama Kosuke, 'The Lord's Controversy with Thailand', in *Waterbuffalo Theology*, mimeographed edition, Singapore 1970.

2. Earlier discussions of this confessing task are found in 'Questions Relating to the Confessing Church in Asia and the Theological Task – East Asia Christian Conference (EACC)', *Confessional Families and the Church in Asia*, Colombo, EACC 1965; EACC – *Confessing the Faith in Asia Today*, Sydney, Epworth Press 1967, esp. ch. 4; M. M. Thomas, *The Acknowledged Christ of the Indian Renaissance*, SCM Press 1970, ch. 10.

3. Robert Schreiter, *Constructing Local Theologies*, Chicago, Catholic Theological Union 1977, p. 4. This work is still the most comprehensive treatment I know of resources and methodologies for the construction of local theologies.

4. See for example the major study by Nakamura Hajime, *Ways of Thinking of Eastern Peoples*, Honolulu, East-West Centre 1964.

5. The factors involved are sharply delineated in for example K. M. Pannikar, *Asia and Western Dominance*, Allen & Unwin 1954; K. Buchanan, *Out of Asia*, University of Sydney Press 1968, part II; Kim Yong-Bok and Pharis Harvey (eds), *People Toiling under Pharaoh*, Tokyo, Christian Conference of Asia (CCA) 1976.

6. The divergences are readily recognized in recent collections of Asian Christian theological writing, for example: Gerald H. Anderson (ed.), *Asian Voices in Christian Theology*, New York, Orbis Books 1976; D. L. Elwood (ed.), *What Asian Christians are Thinking*, and, with E. P. Nacpil, *The Human and the Holy*, Manila, New Day Press 1976 and 1978; Oh Jae-Shik (ed.), *Towards a Theology of People*, Tokyo, CCA 1977; Yap Kim-Hao (ed.), *Asian Theological Reflections on Suffering and Hope*, Singapore, CCA 1977; D. P. Niles and T. K. Thomas (eds), *Witnessing to the Kingdom*, and *Varieties of Witness*, Singapore, CCA 1979 and 1980.

7. The most recent discussion of these issues is contained in George Ninan (ed.), *Theology and Ideology*, Hong Kong, CCA – Urban Rural Mission (URM) 1980. Much of the material in this and following paragraphs has been clarified in a series of six consultations conducted by the

CCA in 1972–75. A major report appears in Oh Jae-Shik and J. C. England, *Theology in Action*, Tokyo, CCA 1973, second edition.

8. See for example, the interview with Ed de la Torre, *IDOC Bulletin*, May 1974; Ian Fraser, *The Fire Runs*, SCM Press 1975; T. K. Thomas (ed.), *Testimony amid Asian Suffering*, Singapore, CCA 1977.

9. Amongst many collections see esp. Charles R. Avila, *Peasant Theology*, Hong Kong, World Student Christian Federation (Asia) 1976; Emergency Christian Conference on Korean Problems, *Documents on the Struggle for Democracy in Korea*, Tokyo, Shinkyo Shuppansha 1975; Tissa Balasuriya (ed.), 'Theology in Asia – New Pathways', *Logos*, vol. 17, nos 2, 3, 4, 1978; Oh Jae-Shik, op. cit.

10. T. S. Avinashilingam (ed.), *Education*, compiled from the speeches and writings of Swami Vivekananda, Coimbatore, Sri Ramakrishna Mission Vidyalaya 1971, p. 74.

11. On the methodologies involved see further J. C. England, 'To Rediscover Theology in Life', in C. Ma. Lagunzad (ed.), *Experiential Theology*, Manila, St Andrew's Seminary 1975.

1. South Korea

1. Quoted by Ryu Tong-Shik in G. Anderson (ed.), *Asian Voices in Christian Theology*, New York, Orbis Books 1976, p. 169. Ryu's article is the best outline of Korean Christian theology available in English.

2. Although Kim Jae-Jun has written extensively since the publication of his collected works in 1971, very few of his articles have appeared in English. Apart from a number of translations in this editor's possession, there are articles on the history of the Presbyterian Church (e.g. 'A Historical Sketch of the Development of the Hankuk Theological Seminary' and 'The Formation of the Presbyterian Church in the Republic of Korea' mimeographed in 1963) and on contemporary issues facing Christians in Korea (e.g. 'Historical Manifesto of Korean Christians 1975', mimeographed 1975, ICUIS Document 2742).

3. *Mission Through People's Organization: South Korea*, IDOC Dossier, no. 7, 1974; 'T.K.', *Letters from South Korea*, Tokyo, Iwanomi Shoten 1976; G. Ogle, *Liberty to the Captives*, Atlanta, John Knox Press 1977.

4. See, for example, Stephen Cardinal Kim, 'On the Church and the Defense of Human Rights', in *Evangelism in Asia Today*, Manila, Cardinal Bea Institute, and Loyola School of Theology 1974, part II, p. 70.

5. Emergency Christian Conference on Korean Problems, op. cit. 1975, pp. 37–43.

6. Apart from numerous printings of individual writings, three volumes of Kim Chi-Ha's writings have appeared in English. Nicola Geiger (ed.), *Cry of the People and Other Poems*, Tokyo, Autumn Press 1974; Kim Chong-Sun and Shelley Killen, *The Gold-Crowned Jesus and Other Writings*, New York, Orbis Books 1978; David R. McCann, *The Middle Hour*, New York Human Rights Publishing Group 1980.

7. See his *Swischen Tiger und Schlange*, Evangelical Lutheran Mission Verlag 1975.

8. Mun Dong-Whan, 'Human Liberation and Christian Education', Seoul, Hankuk Theological Seminary Press 1979.

9. The two articles are in the *North East Asia Journal of Theology (NEAJT)*, nos 3 and 13. The two quotations which follow come from no. 13.

10. These papers along with others from a Korean consultation in October 1979 appear in Kim Yong-Bok (ed.), *Minjung Theology*, CCA 1981.

11. See e.g. 'Christian Koinonia in the Struggle and Aspirations of the People of Korea', in Yap Kim-Hao (ed.), *Asian Theological Reflections*.

12. The chapters by Hahn and Chung are in H. S. Hong, Kim Chung-Choon and Ji Won-Yong (eds), *Korean Struggles for Christ*, Seoul, CLS 1966; that by Min in Ryu Tong-Shik (ed.), *Christian Thought in Korea*, Seoul, Christian Thought Magazine 1975.

13. Cf. M. R. Pihl (ed.), *Listening to Korea*, New York, Praeger 1973.

14. Few of these writings have been published in English although translations of some have been mimeographed. Han Wang-Sang however has six meditations included in D. P. Niles and T. K. Thomas, *Witnessing to the Kingdom;* and Park Pong-Nang's 'A Theological Approach to the Understanding of the Indigenization of Christianity' appeared in *NEAJT*, no. 3, 1969.

15. Many of Kim's papers have appeared in *NEAJT*, nos 7, 8, 10, 12, 18/19, or in *Theological Studies*, Hankuk Seminary, nos 12, 13, 15, 16, 19 ('Theology of the Afflicted in the Motive of the Exodus Event'), 20 ('A Study of Psalm 22'), 21, 1971–79. 'Theological Reflection on the Crucifixion Day' appears in *Third Day*, April 1973.

16. Translated as 'The Contemporaneous Christ' in *NEAJT*, no. 3, 1969.

17. A number of memos written in prison by Kim Chi-Ha have circulated widely despite their proscription by the authorities. Available only in mimeographed form.

18. The Tong Hak, or Eastern Learning, an eclectic partly Christian religious sect, founded by Ch'oe Che-Un in 1859. A full study is Benjamin Weems, *Rebellion and the Heavenly Way*, University of Arizona 1964.

19. Full documentation of the movement is provided in Emergency Christian Conference on Korean Problems, *Documents on the Struggle for Democracy in Korea.*

20. Ahn Byoung-Moo, 'Minjung, Monjok, and the Church', *Kotokkyo Sasang* (Christian Thought), April 1975, pp. 14–19.

21. These two documents are given in *Documents on the Struggle for Democracy*, pp. 119ff., and 37ff. respectively.

22. This novel reveals the suffering of the people (minjung) in the Yi dynasty in the light of the contemporary situation (author's note).

2. Japan

1. For a full treatment of the work of Nakajima, Kakehi, Ken and Gan, cf. C. H. Germany, *Protestant Theologies in Modern Japan*, Tokyo,

International Institute for the Study of Religious Responsibility 1965, pp. 56ff.

2. On Abe Kozo and Kawada Hidenobu see C. H. Germany, op. cit., pp. 204, 205ff.

3. Suzuki's writings have been collected in *The Coming of God's Kingdom*, Tokyo, Shinkyo Shuppansha 1969, and *The Collected Sermons of Suzuki Masahisa*, Tokyo, Kyodan 1969. Articles in English have appeared in *Japan Christian Quarterly (JCQ)*, vol. XXXIII, no. 3, 1979, and *North East Asian Journal of Theology (NEAJT)*, no. 1, 1968.

4. Important writings available in English include Doi Masatoshi, *Search for Meaning*, Tokyo, Kyo Bun Kwan 1976; Cho Kiyoko Takeda, 'State Religion and Ideologies in Japan', in M. M. Thomas and M. Abel (eds), *Religion, State and Ideologies in East Asia*, Bangalore, EACC 1965.

5. Kitamori, *Theology of the Pain of God*, Tokyo, Shinkyo Shuppansha 1958, and Virginia, John Knox Press 1965.

6. Amongst Takenaka's longer writings are *Reconciliation and Renewal* New York, Friendship Press 1967; *Creation and Redemption through Japanese Art*, Osaka, Sosensha 1966; and *Christian Art in Asia*, Tokyo, CCA and Kyo Bun Kwan 1975.

7. See for example his volumes published by Shinkyo Shuppansha in 1964, 1965 and 1969. Also 'Zen Buddhism and Christianity in Contemporary Japan', *NEAJT*, no. 4, 1970.

8. The discussion is outlined in J. Phillips, 'Biblical Studies in Japan 1945–74', *NEAJT*, no. 15, 1975. See also Tagawa Kenzo, *Miracles et Evangile*, Paris, PUF 1967; three further volumes have since been published in Japanese. Arai Sasagu's *Jesus in His Time*, Tokyo, Iwanomi Shoten 1974, will be issued in an English edition in 1981. His *Die Christologie des Evangelium Veritatis* appeared in 1966, and *Primitive Christianity and Gnosticism* in 1971.

9. Takao Toshikazu, *Death and Rebirth of the Christian University* Tokyo, Shinkyo Shuppansha 1969, ch. 3, translated in *Risk*, vol. 6, no 1, 1970. Other writings in English include a comparative study of Yagi, Takizawa and Tagawa, *JCQ*, Spring 1973, and articles in Christian-Marxist Dialogue, *JCQ*, Winter 1975.

10. Some of Ichida's papers have appeared in *NEAJT*, nos 10, 13, 15. Kumuzawa's 'Seeking to Integrate Text and Context' in G. Anderson, *Asian Voices*, is a good brief introduction of Japanese Christian theology. A series of Takayanagi's studies appear in *Japan Missionary Bulletin (JMB)*, 1979.

11. Koyama, *Pilgrim or Tourist*, Singapore, EACC 1974; *Waterbuffalo Theology*, SCM Press 1974; *No Handle on the Cross*, SCM Press 1976; *Three Mile an Hour God*, SCM Press 1979.

12. See for example Shiina's *The Go Between and Other Stories*, Valley Forge, Judson Press 1970. Endo's work includes *Silence*, 1966, *Wonderful Fool*, 1974, and *A Life of Jesus*, 1978, all published in Tokyo by Charles E. Tuttle.

13. The Burakumin are an outcaste minority, suffering severe exploitation. Kamigasaki is the notorious slum district of Osaka. Hirata has for

example edited *On the Scene: Reality Ministry in Japan*, Kyoto, Kansai Urban Industrial Mission 1975. Fukada has edited *God's People in Asian Industrial Society*, EACC 1967, and since 1974, the *NEAJT*. Takenaka edits, with Oh Jae-Shik, *Church Labour Letter* which contains many of the documents referred to.

14. Cf. *JCQ*, vol. XLIV, no. 2, 1978; *Colleagues in Development*, no. 4, and *Gospel and World*, February 1980.

15. Hendrik Kraemar, *A Theology of the Laity*, Westminster Press 1959, p. 147.

16. Jacques Ellul, *The Presence of the Kingdom*, Seabury Press 1967, pp. 20-21.

17. Cf. Masaaki Hiraoka, a student spokesman in 1969: 'Even if ninety-nine were to be happy, if there remained one that was oppressed, that person would be the basis of our understanding.' Quoted in Takao, 'An Alliance of Egoists', *Risk*, loc. cit.

18. Takao, 'Representative Critical Approaches to the Contemporary Japanese Situation', *JCQ*, Spring 1973.

3. China – Hong Kong – Taiwan

1. Although the principles were enunciated by the late nineteenth century and partially applied by some missions in the 1920s, it is not until 1950 that the Three Self Movement is formally organized. The three 'Selfs' are self-support, self-propagation, and self-government. See F. P. Jones (ed.), *Documents of the Three Self Movement*, New York, National Council of Churches of Christ in the USA 1963.

2. Cf. Ng Lee-Ming, 'The Promise and Limitations of Chinese Protestant Theologians, 1920–1950', in *Ching Feng*, vol. XXI, no.4/vol. XXII, no. 1, 1979. The following paragraphs are partly based on Ng's series of articles in *Ching Feng:* on Hsu Po-Ch'ien, vol. XXI, no. 1, 1978; on Chao Tzu Ch'en, vol. XIV, no. 1/2, 1971; on Wu Li-Chuan, vol. XX, no. 4, 1977.

3. Article by Chao in *The Chinese Recorder*, 1938, p. 347. See Winfried Glüer, *Christliche Theologie in Chine*, T. C. Chao 1918–56, Gutersloher Verlaghaus 1979.

4. Cf. Hans-Ruedi Weber, *Asia and the Ecumenical Movement, 1895– 1962*, SCM Press 1966. Journals published by a number of seminaries were the vehicle for much of this discussion, e.g. the Nanking *Theology Quarterly* (1913–63), *Nanking Seminary Review* (revived 1939–61), *The Ginling Union Theological Seminary Review* (until 1957).

5. Y. T. Wu, 'To Look at Reality from the Christian Point of View' in *Tien Feng*, no. 98, 1947. See Ng Lee-Ming's lengthy study of Wu in *Ching Feng*, vol. XV no. 1, 1972, for this and the following paragraph.

6. F. P. Jones, 'Theological Thinking in the Chinese Protestant Church Under Communism', *Religion and Life*, Autumn 1963, contains useful information.

7. Ting Kuang Hsun, 'Christian Theism', *Student World*, vol. LI, no. 4, 1958, pp. 373f. and 382f. It also appears with other Three Self Documents referred to in F. P. Jones, op. cit.

8. *Kwang Ming Er Pao,* 1975.

9. Chao Fu San, 'The Chinese Revolution and Foreign Missions in China Seen through the May 4th Movement' has appeared in English in *The Churches and Social Change,* Saskatchewan, Prairie Christian Training Centre 1979.

10. Two issues of *China and Ourselves,* nos 19 and 20, 1980, published by the China Program of the Canadian Council of Churches, are largely devoted to this series. There are also mimeographed documents: 'Facing the Future or Restoring the Past', Toronto, November 1979, and 'Retrospect and Prospect', the opening address at the Third Chinese National Christian Conference, Peking, October 1980. Ting's booklet *How to Study the Bible,* has been published by Tao Fong Shan Ecumenical Centre, Hong Kong, January 1981.

11. See M. Bernt, *The Diakonia Function of the Church in Hong Kong,* St Louis University Press 1970.

12. Amongst those writing frequently in *Ching Feng* are Philip Shen (e.g. 'Our Theological Tasks in Relation to Our Theological and Cultural Heritages', vol. XXI, no. 4, 1978), Teresa Chu (e.g. 'A Realistic Perspective', vol. XXII, no. 1, 1979). Ng Lee-Ming, Peter Lee King-Huan (e.g. 'Indigenous Theology: Overcropped Land or Underdeveloped Field?', vol. XVII, no. 1, 1974) and Tang Shiu-Ming (e.g. 'China Under the Sign of Unity', vol. XXI, no. 1, 1978).

13. See also Raymond Fung, 'Industrial Mission and Evangelism', *International Review of Mission,* July 1975; 'A Spirituality, and Strategy for Mission', *Change,* no. 43, 1978. Ding Li-Kiu has also written regularly in *Change* (e.g. nos 37 and 41) esp. concerning social and political issues in Hong Kong.

14. Cf. Aloysius Chang, 'A Critical Review of Chinese Catholic Thinking', *Ching Feng,* vol. XXII, no. 3, 1979.

15. See for example Theological Education Fund Staff, *Ministry in Context,* and *Learning in Context,* London, Theological Education Fund 1972 and 1973.

16. Song's major work is found in *Christian Mission in Reconstruction,* Madras, CLS 1975, and *Third-Eye Theology,* New York, Orbis Books and Lutterworth Press 1979.

17. See *CTC Bulletin,* CCA Commission on Theological Concerns, November 1979. The *Taiwan Church News,* issued by the Presbyterian Church of Taiwan, is a unique source for such reflection.

18. The National People's Party, formed by Sun Yat-Sen 1911, and later led by Chiang Kai-Shek. The name is still used by the government of Taiwan.

19. Founded in 1965, and now the church including by far the largest proportion of Taiwanese, the main body of whom are either aboriginal or are descendants of those who settled in Taiwan prior to 1900. They comprise 85% of the church's total membership of 200,000.

20. The full text of this and other statements issued by the Presbyterian Church in Taiwan is given in *The Presbyterian Church in Taiwan under the Cross,* New York, Formosan Christians for Self-Determination 1978.

21. Upon publication, the Declaration was immediately seized by the

government. It became quickly known, however, both inside and outside Taiwan.

22. In earlier sections of this chapter (10), and especially pp. 217–18, the author has described what he terms 'the politics of God ... in construction and reconstruction'.

4. Philippines

1. See *An Asian Theology of Liberation: The Philippines*, Future of the Missionary Enterprise no. 5, Rome, IDOC Documentation Participation Project 1973, pp. 1–8, 12ff., and J. Underwood, F. B. Stumpf, J. Mensch, *The Philippines: American Corporations, Martial Law and Underdevelopment*, New York, IDOC 1974.

2. See Manaligod's later articles on Filipinization and a Theology of the Local Church, *Philippine Priests' Forum (PPF)*, 1970 (1), 1971 (3), 1972 (4). Cf. J. Schumacher, *Jose Burgos: Priest and Nationalist*, Ateneo 1972.

3. For Mapano see *Selected Sermons*, Manila, NCCP 1973; Rigos' second volume was *Christians and Revolution*, Manila, Cosmopolitan Church 1972; Nacpil's longest study is *Mission and Change*, Manila, EACC 1968. Volumes edited by Lagunzad include *The Shape of Theological Education and Role of Field Experience in the 70s*, 1971, and *A Search for a Liberating and Uniting Theological Education in the Philippines*, 1975, Manila, Interseminary Program of Education.

4. For example, Christians for Social Justice, Xi Rho, Philippines SCM, Laymen for Post Vatican II Reforms, and Philippine Priests Incorporated.

5. In literature: Lope K. Santos, Carlos Bulosan, Amado Hermandez and E. San Juan. In politics, F. Garcia, Claro Recto, Jose Ma Sison. In historical scholarship, Epifanio de los Santos, Teodore Agoncillo, Renato Constantino. In the area of Philippines philosophy and culture; Carman Nakpil, Leonardo Mercardo, Ramon Reyes, F. Landa Jocano, Jaime Bulatao, and Mary Hollensteiner.

6. de la Costa, 'International Dimensions of Our Jesuit Apostolate' in *Four Papers on Mission, Justice and Peace*, St Paul, Society of Jesus 1974, p. 3.

7. Gorospe, *The Morality of Demonstrations and Violence*, Manila Ateneo University 1970, p. 26. See also Gorospe and R. Deats (eds.), *The Filipino in the Seventies*, Manila, New Day Publishers 1973.

8. Arevalo, in *Philippine Studies*, vol. XX, no. 3, 1972, pp. 421f. Regarding 'the signs of the times', ibid., pp. 243ff.

9. Abesamis, *Salvation, Total and Historical*, Quezon City, JMC Press 1978, pp. 41, 43, 39. Compare Manalo Radel (pen-name for a Theological Group), 'The Theologian at Work, Philippines 1970s–80s: A Suggestion', *Philippine Studies*, vol. XIX, no. 3, 1971, pp. 445–55.

10. Figures given in reports of the Asian Development Bank, World Bank and the University of the Philippines, 1976–80; quoted in *Development Dossier*, July 1980, Australian Council for Overseas Aid; *Philippines 1980*, London, Philippines Research Group, 1980; *Background*

Information on the Philippines, Dossier of the National Secretariat for Social Action (NASSA) 1979; and in Joel Rocamora, 'Representations to the International Tribunal of Peoples', mimeographed, Antwerp, October 1980. See the studies by Robert Youngblood, 'Church Opposition to Martial Law', reprint from *Asian Survey*, 1978, and 'The Protestant Church in the Philippines New Society', *Bulletin of Concerned Asian Scholars*, vol. XII, no. 3, 1980.

11. See C. R. Avila, *Peasant Theology*, Bangkok, WSCF Asia 1976; *Pintig: Lifepulse in Cold Steel*, Hong Kong, Resource Centre for Philippine Concerns 1979.

12. Early articles by de la Torre appeared in the *PPF*, 1969–70; a small collection of 'Excerpts, Essays and Speeches' was issued by Christians for National Liberation, 1975 (mimeographed), and three papers were published by Kilusang Khi Rho Ng Filipinas Readings, 1972. 'Christian Participation in the Struggle for Liberation' appeared in Oh Jae-Shik and J. C. England (eds), *Theology in Action,* second edition, Tokyo, EACC 1973, and 'Five Years in Prison' in *IDOC Bulletin*, New Series, nos. 8, 9, 10, 1980.

13. F. F. Claver, *The Stones Cry Out*, New York, Orbis Books 1978, pp. 20–22. Apart from this collection of letters and addresses, Claver's writing has also appeared in, for example, *IDOC: An Asian Theology of Liberation*, op. cit.; *Church Alert*, no. 11, 1976; and *The Communicator*, vol. III, no. 20, 1975.

14. L. Oracion, *Jesus Christ Frees and Unites,* mimeographed 1975, pp. 6, 16. Oracion participated in the Symposium on Theology and Ideology reported in the book of that title (CCA 1980), and his latest article is 'Theological Dimensions of Our Ecumenical Task', *Tugon*, vol. 1, no. 1, 1979.

15. A previous section has outlined Mao's teaching on nationalism, quoting in particular Mao Tse Tung, 'On the New Stage', *Selected Works*, II, p. 209, and the *Constitution of the Communist Party of the Philippines*, 1969, preamble.

16. See Jaime Bulatao, *Split-Level Christianity*, Manila, Ateneo University 1966.

17. *'Gospel and Revolution* – Manifesto by 16 Bishops of the Third World', *New Blackfriars*, December 1967, pp. 140–48.

18. Movement for a Democratic Philippines.

19. New People's Army, a revolutionary guerrilla movement active throughout the Philippines.

20. Student movements politically rightist.

21. See Amado Guerrero, *Philippine Society and Revolution*, Manila Pulang Tala Publications 1970, p. 2.

22. 'The mind is mixed up, the knees are weak.'

23. 'My being a Christian always probes me to the depths, my heart trembles.'

24. The Metrocom is a metropolitan police force trained in surveillance and suppression of public dissent.

25. A handbook series published by Cachos Hermanos Inc., *Proclamation Nos. 1081/1104 and Related Documents* lists some Presidential

Decrees which are 'not for general circulation'; others which are 'not yet released'; still others of which 'no copy is available for circulation'. The publication has the approval of both the government Department of Public Information and the Mass Media Council (author's note).

26. The Wednesday Forum is a regular meeting of the Wednesday Fellowship, an ecumenical organization concerned for 'truth, justice and peace in the Philippines'.

5. Mainland South East Asia

1. See Thich Nhat Hanh, *Vietnam: The Lotus in the Sea of Fire*, SCM Press 1967, and H. Haas and Nguyen Bao Chong, *Vietnam: The Other Conflict*, Sheed & Ward 1971.

2. Pierre Gheddo, *The Cross and the Bo Tree*, New York, Sheed & Ward 1970, pp. 252ff.

3. Sam Isaacs, 'Why We Serve', in Ruth Cadwallader (ed.) *Signs of Christian Presence* I, Bangkok, EACC 1971. This also contains 'Manifesto for Christians in the Midst of Conflict.'

4. Tram Tam Tinh, 'Christian Mission in Vietnam' in *Vietnam: Beyond Aid and Development*, IDOC Dossier 18, 1976, p. 18.

5. Binh Nguyen Van, 'Pastoral Letter and the Independence Day Celebrations, 2nd September 1975', in *Being Christian in Vietnam Today*, Zurich, Second International Assembly for Healing the Wounds of War and for the Reconstruction of Vietnam, April 1978. (This includes a series of statements and dialogues of Roman Catholic leaders in Vietnam in 1975. Many mimeographed documents are also available from the Fraternité de Vietnam, Paris, including the letter of Ho-Thanh-Bien quoted below.)

6. For Koson Srisang see below. Samrit Wongsang's papers are issued by the Urban Industrial Mission Office, Church of Christ in Thailand, Bangkok.

7. Bunluen Mansap, 'Development from Within', in Yap Kim-Hao, *Report of an Ecumenical Consultation on Development: Priorities and Guidelines*, Singapore, CCA 1974, p. 40.

8. Both documents mimeographed, Bangkok 1976.

9. U Kyaw Than outlines these and later developments in 'Theologizing for Selfhood and Service', G. Anderson, *Asian Voices in Christian Theology*, pp. 58–62. Cf. F. R. von der Mehden, *Religion and Nationalism in Southeast Asia*, University of Wisconsin 1968, pp. 182–91.

10. See U Hla Bu, 'The Christian Encounter with Buddhism in Burma and the Search for New Foundations', in Kyaw Than (ed.), *Witnesses Together*, Rangoon, EACC 1962.

11. U Kyaw Than, 'Context in Mission' in *Conversations*, Fall 1974, p. 9. Along with other lay theologians mentioned above, Kyaw Than wrote for the *South East Asia Journal of Theology (SEAJT)* in the early 1960s, but much of his writing comes from his work (until 1973) as Associate General Secretary, later General Secretary, of the EACC. The EACC journal *Asia Focus* (formerly *Church and Society*) contains his regular articles and many EACC volumes have been either written or

edited by him. See for example, *Joint Labourers in Hope*, Bangkok, EACC 1973.

12. U Khin Muang Din, 'Some Problems and Possibilities for Burmese Christian Theology Today' in D. J. Ellwood, *What Asian Christians are Thinking*, Manila, New Day Press 1976, p. 103.

13. The exodus to the South of 800 priests and 600,000 faithful representing 72% of the clergy and 45% of the Christians of North Vietnam, following the defeat of France, 1954.

14. 'Christian Action in the Asian Struggle' in *Christian Action in the Asian Struggle*, Singapore, CCA 1973, pp. 1–10. See also M. M. Thomas, *Towards a Theology of Contemporary Ecumenism*, Madras, Christian Literature Society, and Geneva, WCC 1978, pp. 175–90 (author's note).

15. 'Christian Action in the Asian Struggle', p. 7.

16. *Third-Eye Theology*, New York, Orbis Books and London, Lutterworth 1979, p. 10.

17. E. P. Nacpil and D. J. Elwood (eds), *The Human and the Holy Asian Perspectives in Christian Theology*, Manila, New Day Publishers 1978, p. 155.

18. Report of a consultation on 'Patterns of Domination and People's Power in Asia', sponsored by CCA Committee on International Relations and Human Rights, August 1979. To be published by CCA.

19. Julio de Santa Ana (ed.), *Separation Without Hope?*, Geneva, CCPD/WCC 1978, p. 153.

20. All the quotations in this paragraph are taken from M. M. Thomas, *Christian Action in the Asian Struggle*, p. 2.

21. Saw U here quotes the Burmese Way to Socialism Party: 'Our Belief' and 'Our Pledge', as an illustration of the goal for a just society.

6. Indonesia

1. Roman Catholics first arrived in Indonesia in the thirteenth century, and received a separate administration in 1847. Cf. Digan in *Pro Mundi Vita*. For the Protestant background see F. L. Cooley, *Indonesia: Church and Society*, New York, Friendship Press 1968 and 'Focus on the Indonesian Church' in *Occasional Bulletin of Missionary Research*, October 1977, special issue.

2. Johannes Liemena, 'The Task of Restoring Fellowship in the Indonesian Church and Nation', *SEAJT*, vol. IX, no. 3, 1968. The points following were made in his address to the Assembly of the DGI, 1964.

3. Simatupang, *The Christian Task in the Revolution*, Jakarta, Badan Penerbit Kristen (BPK) 1967, p. 8.

4. Simatupang, 'The Confessing Church in Contemporary Asia', *SEAJT*, vol. VIII, no. 3, 1967, p. 63.

5. Latuihamallo, 'Missiology and Politics', *SEAJT*, vol. X, no. 2/3, 1969, p. 124. See also his 'State, Religion and Ideologies in Indonesia' in M. M. Thomas and M. Abel, *Religion, State and Ideologies in East Asia;* and for the full account of the theology emerging, A. C. Thomson, 'Faith and Politics: the Indonesian Contribution', *SEAJT*, vol. XI, no. 1, 1970.

6. 'Panca Sila', the five principles chosen by Soekarno and Hatta as

the basis of the modern Indonesian state: (1) Belief in God (2) Humanity (3) Nationalism (4) Democracy (5) Social justice.

7. Sidjabat, *Religious Tolerance and the Christian Faith*, Jakarta, BPK 1960.

8. Ukur, 'The Work-Dialogue Becomes Popular', *Berita Oikumene*, no. 6, 1972, p. 11. Quoted in K. A. Steenbrink, 'Christian Faith in an Indonesian Environment', *Exchange*, no. 5, 1973. For Dharmapatera, see his *Tolerance, Harmony and Development*, Jakarta, BPK 1971.

9. See J. W. Mastra, *The Impact of the Gospel and Balinese Culture*, ThM Thesis, University of Dubuque 1967. Christian periodicals like *Basis* and *Peninjau* often deal with similar issues, and English summaries appear in *Exchange*, Bulletin of Third World Christian Literature, Leiden.

10. Indonesians have the lowest per capita income in South East Asia ($100 in 1976) while 60% of national capital is held in Jakarta and 81% of the population live in the villages. One result is severe malnutrition in areas of central Java, and the death of 15% of all Indonesian children before the age of one year. See Parig Digan, op. cit., and cf. the British Indonesia Committee, *Repression and Exploitation in Indonesia*, Nottingham, Spokesman Books 1974.

11. Danuwinata, 'Religion's Tussle with the Problem of Development', *Prisma* 4, August 1975.

12. Hardowirjono, 'Service of the Faith in East Asia', *Teaching All Nations*, vol. XIV, no. 1, 1977. Protestant writers who have dealt with such themes, although in more muted vein, include Soritua Nababan (General Secretary of DGI), J. L. Abineno and Ikhromi (both sometime Rektors of the STT). The DGI monthly *Berita Oikumene*, and the many publications of the BPK, ably directed by Alfred Simandjuntak, frequently discuss the formation of an Indonesian theology.

13. The article is found in *SEAJT*, vol. XIV, no. 2, 1973. Yang affirms the church's role in criticism and in evaluation of the use of government power, in 'The Church in the Indonesian Revolution', in W. B. Sidjabat (ed.), *Christian Participation in Indonesian Nation Building*, Jakarta, BPK 1968, pp. 107f.

14. The last appears in *The Kingdom of God and the Way of Peace*, ed. the Mennonite Central Committee and the Mennonite World Conference, Lombard, Illinois 1978, pp. 47–60.

15. Those providing leadership in programme activities and in the theological reflection based on them include Johannes Rumambi (a former Member of Parliament), Herman Pooroe (of the DGI Staff) and Ed Lalisang (Director of the Cikembar Development Centre).

16. See 'The Incarnation as Subversion' in A. Kee (ed.) *The Scope of Political Theology*, SCM Press 1978; and the Bulletin *Refleksi* for 'Translating the Gospel of Liberation in the Community – A Theology of Kampong', no. 3, 1978; and 'Jesus the Villager', no. 4, 1979.

17. In T. K. Thomas (ed.), *Testimony Amid Asian Suffering*, Singapore, CCA 1977.

18. These have appeared in, for example, *IRM*, April 1979; *Asia Focus* 1979 (Women in Asia); and the *Far Eastern Economic Review*.

19. The Decree of the 32nd General Congregation of the Society of Jesus.

20. *Our Mission Today,* note 26.

21. Second Bishops' Institute for Social Action, of the Federation of Asian Bishops' Conference, Tokyo 1975.

22. Report of the Calcutta Session of the Catholic Bishops' Conference of India, 1974, quoted by A. Nambiaparambil in 'Dialogue in India', *Bulletin Secretariatus pro Non-Christianis,* vol. X/2, no. 30, p. 253, 1975 (author's note).

23. Message of the Pope to the United Nations on the occasion of the 25th Anniversary of the 'Universal Declaration of Human Rights'.

24. Menno Simon in *The Cross of Christ,* ed. H. Bender, Scottdale, Pennsylvania, Mennonite Publishing House 1964, p. 28.

25. The fetter of the 'law' refers to the current approach to the whole of Western theology which is considered imperative for the 'younger' churches (author's note).

26. Wijaja also refers to the assessment by Indonesian churches of their dominant pietistic theology, as described in S. A. E. Nababan (ed.), *Pergumulan Rangkap,* Jakarta, BKP 1971.

27. Raden Adjeng Kartini (1879–1903) who is regarded as an early spokeswoman for Indonesian nationalism. Her letters have been published under the title *Letters of a Javanese Princess,* ed. Hildred Geertz, New York, Norton 1964.

28. In *Newsletter,* no. 3, WSCF Women's Project, Geneva, May 1979.

29. Margaret Wold (ed.), *The Shalom Woman,* Minneapolis, Augsburg Publishing House 1975.

30. Katoppo follows this with sections on 'The Concept of God from the Feminist Perspective' especially in relation to Indonesian culture and experience.

7. Sri Lanka

1. Cf. F. Houtart, *Religion and Ideology in Sri Lanka,* Bangalore, TPI St Peter's Seminary 1974, esp. part III.

2. The journal *Social Justice,* which Pillai founded, continued until *Logos* replaced it as the journal of the Centre for Religion and Society.

3. D. T. Niles, *Upon the Earth,* Lutterworth Press 1962, p. 134. The John R. Mott Lectures 1959 appear in Lesslie Newbigin, W. A. Vissert' Hooft and D. T. Niles, *A Decisive Hour for Christian Mission,* SCM Press 1960, pp. 72ff. For the work of the Ashram see *Twenty-five Years of the Christa Seva Ashram,* issued by the Ashram Board, Manipay 1964. Bibliographical and biographical data for Niles are given in *Asia Focus,* vol. 4, 1970, special memorial issue.

4. de Silva's chapter 'Theological Construction in a Buddhist Context', appears in G. Anderson, *Asian Voices,* which also lists some of de Silva's (and Niles') writings. Ariaraja's booklet, *Dialogue,* has been issued (1980) by CCA Singapore. Pieris's articles have appeared in *Logos, Ceylon Churchman* and in *Dialogue.* See especially issues for July 1972, November 1973, and November-December 1975.

5. Privately printed articles by Fred de Silva and James Mather described the 'Jesus of Lanka' and a church which truly served the nation.

6. *Manifesto for a New Reformation*, Colombo, C. Wickremanayake and Y. Devananda on behalf of a People's Committee of the Church 1970.

7. C. S. Ponnutherai (ed.), *Being the People of God*, Diocese of Colombo 1968.

8. Kanagaratnam and K. Fernando are both regular contributors to *Ceylon Churchman* of which C. S. Fernando has been for some years editor. But many writings by each of these have appeared only in mimeographed form, cf. Neville Jayaweera's articles on Christian communication.

9. In 1969–70, 80.8% of the total population received less than Rs. 400 per month, while one tenth of the population received 22.6% of the nation's income. See Silan Kadirgamar 'A Brief Survey of the Political and Economic Situation in Sri Lanka' in *Sishya*, January 1977; Houtart, *Religion and Ideology in Sri Lanka*, pp. 310ff.

10. Abeysekera's paper appeared in *Dialogue* (old series) no. 7, 1965. See also his 'The Role of Structural Analysis and Theological Reflection' in *Logos*, vol. XIX, no. 3, 1980. The 1968 study guide, *Social Change in Ceylon*, is one of many booklets used by the CWF. See for example, *Meeting the Crisis*, 1974, and the periodical *Christian Worker*. Vijaya Vidyasagara of the CWF staff has also contributed to theological reflection in e.g. 'Christian Workers' Fellowship of Sri Lanka', mimeographed 1975.

11. Devananda, *If They Had Met*, Ibbagamuwa, Devasavana Aramaya 1968, and *Ventures in Dialogue and Development*, Hong Kong, WSCF Asia 1977. Amongst many documents which have been mimeographed are his 'New World Liturgy' (1973), and 'Socialist Parables' (1975).

12. Between 1973 and 1978, the share of total income received by the poorest 40% of Sri Lankans declined from 15.1 to 12.3% while that of the richest 10% increased from 30–39%. See C. L. Wickremasinghe, 'The Truth about the Strikes', CWF Pamphlet, October 1980.

13. Apart from regular articles in the *Ceylon Churchman*, Wickremasinghe's writing appears in *Satyodaya, Philippine Priests' Forum, The Guardian* (Madras) and the *Ceylon Daily News*. Amongst longer papers, 'Religion and the Ideology of Development' is in G. Gunatillike, *Religion and Development in Asian Societies*, Colombo, Marga 1973; and 'Living Faiths in Dialogue', *IRM*, October 1979.

14. Balasuriya's two volumes *Jesus Christ and Human Liberation* (1976) and *The Eucharist and Human Liberation* (1977) SCM Press and Orbis Books 1979, partially collect earlier writings. But many others appear in *Teaching All Nations, Concilium*, in *Logos* (which he edits), or as separate booklets. Partial listing in 'The Development of the Poor Through the Civilising of the Rich', Wellington, New Zealand, CORSO 1972.

15. Caspersz' writings can be found in *Satyodaya*, the monthly bulletin of his centre (see especially issues for April-June 1975 for his 'Marxism

and Religion', parts I-III), in *Dialogue, Impact, World Mission* and *New Blackfriars*.

16. Mark Schoof OP, *Breakthrough: The Beginnings of the New Catholic Theology*, Dublin 1970, p. 17.

17. For a lucid exposition of the Latin American breakthrough, cf. Jon Sobrino, 'El conocimiento teologico en la teologia europea y latino-americana', in *Liberacion y Cautiverio: Debates en Torno al Metodo de la Teologia en America Latina*, Mexico City 1975, pp. 177–207. For a neat summary of it cf. Alfred T. Henelly SJ, 'Theological Method: the Southern Exposure', *Theological Studies*, vol. 38, no. 4, December 1977, pp. 708–35 (author's note).

18. Cf. Aloysius Pieris SJ, 'Western Christianity and Eastern Religions: A Theological Reading of Historical Encounters', a paper read at the German Theology Professors' Seminar, Bossey, Switzerland, September 27–30 1978, p. 25.

19. Wickremasinghe has made a special study of both the radical and reformist movements he mentions. See 'Experimental and Institutional Ministries', *Ceylon Churchman*, October 1973; 'Sarvodaya and the Christian Approach to Development', *Colleagues in Development*, CCA, May 1978; and in Gunatillike *Religion and Development in Asian Societies*.

8. India

1. For outlines of the thought of Brahmobandahav, Sundar Singh and Apassamy see R. L. Boyd, *Indian Christian Theology*, Madras, CLS 1975, pp. 58–140.

2. M. M. Thomas, in G. Anderson, *Asian Voices*, p. 21.

3. George's books are *Gandhi's Challenge to Christianity*, Allen & Unwin 1939; *The Life and Teachings of Jesus Christ*, Madras, G. A. Natesan and Co. 1942; *The Story of the Bible*, Ahmedabad, Nevajivan Publishing House 1951. Selections from these writings are in T. K. Thomas, *The Witness of S. K. George*, Madras, CISRS-CLS 1970.

4. The 'Rethinking' group issued in 1938 the book *Rethinking Christianity in India*, Madras, A. N. Sudarisanam. Selections from the writings of Chakkarai and Chenchiah appear in P. T. Thomas, *The Theology of Chakkarai*, 1968, and D. A. Thangasamy, *The Theology of Chenchiah*, 1966, both Bangalore, CISRS. Other members of the group were Eddy Asirvatham, S. Jesudason, G. V. Job, A. N. Sudarisanan and D. M. Devasahayam, all laymen.

5. S. J. Samartha and Nalini Devanandan (eds), *Sermons and Bible Studies*, Bangalore, CISRS 1963, pp. 67f. Quoted in Boyd, op. cit., p. 190, who on pp. 186–205 outlines Devanandan's thought. See also P. Devanandan, *The Gospel and Renascent Hinduism*, SCM Press 1959, and *Preparation for Dialogue*, Bangalore, CISRS 1964.

6. P. Devanandan, *Christian Concern in Hinduism*, Bangalore, CISRS 1961, pp. 119–20.

7. More scholarly studies of indigenization later appear in e.g. the works of Raimundo Panikkar *(The Unknown Christ of Hinduism*, 1964)

and Mark Sundar Rao *(Concerning Indian Christianity,* 1973). Cf. Boyd. op. cit., pp. 214ff.

8. Led by D. S. Amalorpavadas, Samuel Rayan and Joseph Volken, respectively.

9. M. M. Thomas, *The Acknowledged Christ of the Indian Renaissance,* SCM Press 1970, pp. 284ff.

10. Other major volumes for our purpose are *Man and the Universe of Faiths,* 1975; and *The Secular Ideologies of India and the Secular Meaning of Christ,* 1976, both CISRS-CLS.

11. See for example T. K. Thomas (editor for both CISRS and CLS), 'The Christ Figure in Contemporary Secular Literature of India', *Religion and Society (RS),* vol. XIX, no. 3, 1972; S. L. Parmar (Reader in Economics at Allahabad University – d. 1978), *Lift Up Your Eyes,* CLS-ISPCK-Lucknow Publishing House 1972; D. A. Thangasamy (Principal of St John's College, Palayamkottai – d. 1974), *India and the Ecumenical Movement,* Madras, CLS 1973.

12. See M. Zachariah (ed.), *The Indian Church: Identity and Fulfilment,* 1971; *Beyond Identity: On to Participation,* 1973; *The Church: A People's Movement,* 1975, all Nagpur, National Christian Council of India.

13. See especially *Freedom and Authority,* CLS-ISPCK-LPH 1974. Amongst numerous articles (in *Ecumenical Review, RS,* et al.), see 'Hermeneutics in India Today – in the Light of the World Debate', *Indian Journal of Theology (IJT),* January 1979.

14. A collection of Mathew's writings has been made in J. R. Chandran, *The Secular Witness of E. V. Mathew,* Madras, CISRS-CLS 1972. See also *The Role of Law in a Revolutionary Age,* Bangalore, CISRS 1965.

15. J. Vaddakan, *A Priest's Encounter with Revolution,* CISRS-CLS 1974.

16. Other related centres are the Ecumenical Christian Centre, Whitefield, Calcutta Urban Service and St Mark's Cathedral, Bangalore. At the last, Paul Siromoni and Alex Devasandaram have written frequently on church and society issues.

17. See for example, the chapters by Abraham, Philip and Premasagar in Zachariah, 1975, op. cit.

18. Biswas' papers appear in the *IJT, NCCI Review, North Indian Churchman,* and *St Paul's Magazine.* His *Lord Let Me Share* was published by the Church Missionary Society in 1978.

19. See for example, 'Social Involvement for Mission in Theological Education', mimeographed 1975; 'Theological Guidelines for Christian Participation in Development', *RS,* vol. XVIII, no. 4, 1971.

20. M. J. Joseph has also written in *RS* and *IJT,* and *Prayers and Meditations* were published in Erlangen, Evangelical Lutheran Mission Verlag 1978. Chatterji's books include *Religious Values and Economic Development,* CISRS 1967; and *The Meaning of the Indian Experience: Emergency,* edited for CISRS 1978.

21. Rayan in *Jeevadhara,* no. 21, May-June 1974, p. 245. Rayan's

volume *The Holy Spirit* was issued by Orbis Books, New York 1978, and articles are found in *IJT, RS, IRM, Jeevadhara,* et al.

22. Kappen issues a regular newsletter '*Anawim*', and his *Jesus and Freedom* is also published by Orbis Books. For Paulose mar Paulose's lectures see *Church's Mission,* Bombay Urban Industrial League for Development, n.d.

23. Emilio Castro, *Amidst Revolution,* Belfast 1975, p. 61.

24. Samuel Amirtham, *Biblical Essays on Salvation, Preparatory Material for Bangkok,* p. 14.

25. Quoted by Castro, op. cit., p. 53.

26. Dickenson, *Poverty and Development,* Bangalore 1974, p. 208.

27. Charles Elliott, *The Development Debate,* SCM Press 1971, p. 79.

28. *Manifesto of the Communist Party,* Moscow 1966, pp. 64–5.

29. Castro, op. cit., p. 55.

30. *International Review of Mission,* vol. LXIII, no. 246, April 1973, pp. 164–65.

31. Castro, op. cit., p. 72.

Short Bibliography

For background reading, the following national and church histories for each country are recommended.

Korea

Han Woo-Kevn, *The History of Korea*, University of Hawaii 1971
McCormack, G. and Gittings, J. (eds), *Crisis in Korea,* Nottingham, Spokesman Books 1977
Palmer, S. J., *Korea and Christianity,* New York, Hollyn 1967

Japan

Story, Richard, *A History of Modern Japan,* London, Penguin Books 1969
Halliday, Jon, *A Political History of Japanese Capitalism,* New York, Pantheon Books 1975
Drummond, R. H., *A History of Christianity in Japan,* Grand Rapids, Eerdmans 1971

China

Hsu, C. Y., *The Rise of Modern China,* London, Oxford University Press 1975
Orr, Robert G., *Religion in China,* New York, Friendship Press 1980
Ng, Lee Ming, 'Christianity in China', in T. K. Thomas, *Christianity in Asia,* Singapore, Christian Conference of Asia 1979

Philippines

Constantino, R. and L. R., *The Philippines: The Continuing Past*, Manila, Foundation for Nationalist Studies 1978
Deats, Richard, *Christianity and Nationalism in the Philippines,* Southern Methodist University 1967
Gowing, Peter G., *Islands under the Cross,* Manila, National Council of Churches 1966

South East Asia

Fitzgerald, C. P., *A Concise History of South East Asia,* London, Penguin Books 1966

Pluvier, Jan, *South East Asia from Colonialism to Independence,* London, Oxford University Press 1974

Anderson, Gerald (ed.), *Christ and Crisis in South East Asia,* New York, Friendship Press 1969

Indonesia

Caldwell, M., *Indonesia,* London, Oxford University Press 1968

Holt, Claire (ed.), *Culture and Politics in Indonesia,* Ithaca, Cornell University 1972

Cooley, Frank, *Indonesia – Church and Society,* New York, Friendship Press 1968

Sri Lanka

Ludowyk, E. F. C., *The Modern History of Ceylon,* London, Weidenfeld and Nicolson 1966

Houtart, Francis, *Religion and Ideology in Sri Lanka,* Colombo, The Ecumenical Institute 1975

Wilson, D. K., *The Christian Church in Sri Lanka,* Colombo, The Ecumenical Institute 1975

India

Spear, Percival, *A History of India*, vol. 2, Penguin Books 1968

Srinivas, M. N., *Social Change in India*, Madras, Orient Longman 1972

Neill, Stephen, *The Story of the Christian Church in India and Pakistan*, Grand Rapids, Eerdmans 1970

Biographical Notes

Samuel Amirtham's doctoral work was in the area of Old Testament studies and he was, until 1978, Principal of the Tamilnadu Theological Seminary, Madurai. While there he pioneered new methods in theological education, community involvement and evangelism. He is now on the staff of the Program for Theological Education, Geneva.

Father Bao is Vietnamese and a monk of the contemplative order La Vierge des Pauvres. Prior to 1975 he lived in a poor district of Saigon, and earned his living through part-time work as a 'cyclopousse' driver. He now works for the Catholic newspaper *Gong Giao Va Dan Toc* in Ho Chi Minh City and continues the life of his small community which includes a number of young people.

Paul Caspersz is a member of the Society of Jesus and leads the Satyodaya commune and centre for Social Research and Encounter in Kandy, Sri Lanka. He is a trained economist and a founder member of the Co-ordinating Secretariat for Plantation Areas which with Satyodaya carries out a wide range of adult education and development programmes.

Francisco F. Claver SJ is a member of the Bontoc Igorot tribal group in the Philippines and by training an anthropologist. He has been Bishop in Malaybalay, Mindanao since 1969 and is also a member of the Vatican Commission for Non-Believers. He has lectured in Europe and in the USA and is one of the most outspoken critics of martial law in the Philippines.

Raymond Fung is a Baptist layman who from 1969 to 1979 directed the Christian Industrial Committee of the Hong Kong Christian Council. He is now Secretary for the Division of Mission in the Council and an active participant in the Commission for World Mission and Evangelism of the WCC.

Robert Hardowirjono SJ is Rector and Professor of Theology in the Institute for Philosophy and Theology, Yogyakarta, Indonesia. He has lectured widely in Asian countries and is a member of the General Secretariat of the Indonesian Conference of Bishops.

Henriette Marianne Katoppo has been active in the Indonesian Student Christian Movement and since graduating from the Sekolah Tinggi Theologia, Jakarta, has undertaken a number of ecumenical assignments. She is also a prize-winning novelist and practising journalist on the staff of the Obor agency, Jakarta.

Kim Chi-Ha was born in the Cholla-Do province of Korea and is a graduate of Seoul National University. He had worked amongst poor farmers in 1961–2 and in 1966, but tuberculosis (from which he still suffers) then interrupted his writing of poetry and of scripts for film and theatre. Since 1970 he has been regularly imprisoned for his writing, being released only in December 1980 after almost 6 years of solitary confinement.

Kim Chung-Choon studied theology in Japan, Canada and Scotland and has since 1961 taught Old Testament in Hankuk Theological Seminary and in Yonsei University, both of Seoul, Korea. He completed ten years as President of Hankuk in 1980. His account of his recovery from a near-fatal bout of tuberculosis, *Sickness unto Life* (1949), became a best-seller in Korea.

Kim Yong-Bok studied for his doctorate at Princeton Theological Seminary and from 1971 was on the staff of Sophia University, Tokyo. While there, he also worked in establishing a documentation agency for action groups in Asia and is now Co-director with Cho Syung-Huk of the Institute for Justice and Development, Seoul.

E. V. Mathew was a member of the Mar Thoma Church and a leader both in the YMCA and SCM. An eminent lawyer in Bangalore, he was from 1964 until his death in 1971 Editor of the Madras Guardian. At the Delhi Assembly of the WCC he was one of the main speakers and later a member of the International Secretariat of the Christian Peace Conference.

Levi Oracion's doctoral studies were completed at Chicago and until 1975 he was Dean of the School of Theology, Silliman University, Dumaguete. He is now Vice-President for Theological Education in Philippine Christian University, Manila, and a theological consultant for CCA Urban Rural Mission concerns. He is also a member of the Wednesday Fellowship of church and community leaders.

Aloysius Pieris SJ is director of Tulana, a Buddhist-Christian Centre for Research and Encounter, Kelaniya, Sri Lanka, and closely associated with the Ecumenical Institute for Study and Dialogue, Colombo. He is lecturer on Buddhism for the Gregorian University in Rome, and lectures on Asian Thought for the East Asia Pastoral Institute, Manila.

Samuel Rayan SJ directs the Lumen Institute, Delhi, and is Dean of the Faculty of Theology of the Vidyajyoti Institute, a Jesuit Seminary there. From 1968 he was for some years Catholic theologian on the Faith and Order Commission of the WCC.

Alan Saw U is a Burmese and by training an engineer. He is active in the leadership of Urban Rural Mission programmes of the Burma Christian Council, Rangoon. He is also part time lecturer in Ecumenics and Church and Society at the Burma Institute of Theology.

Song Choan-Seng did post-graduate studies in Edinburgh and New York and until 1970 was Principal of Tainan Theological Seminary Taiwan. In 1976–77 he was visiting professor at Princeton University and is currently Associate Director of the WCC's Faith and Order Commission.

Koson Srisang was director of the Student Christian Centre, Bangkok and later gained his doctorate from Chicago. After a period as lecturer in the Theological Seminary Chiangmai, he was elected General Secretary of the Church of Christ in Thailand 1976. He is now on the staff of the CCPD, Geneva.

Takao Toshikazu was ordained minister of the United Church of Christ (Kyodan) in Japan and taught until 1971 at Kanto Gaquin, University of Yokohama. He is the translator of Jürgen Moltmann's *Theology of Hope*, and Ernst Bloch's *Atheism in Christianity*. He now lectures at Hosei University, Tokyo.

Takenaka Masao was born in Peking and studied economics and theology at Kyoto. He received his PhD from Yale University and has been visiting professor at Union Seminary New York (1962–3) and at Yale (1973). He is Director of the Research Institute for Humanities and Social Science and Professor of Christian Ethics at Doshisha University, Kyoto, since 1958.

Ting Kuang-Hsun was ordained priest in the Sheng Kung Hui (Anglican Church) and was on the staff of the World Student Christian Federation prior to 1950. He then returned to China and was later Bishop of Chekiang Diocese and President of Nanking Theological Seminary. He is now Chairman of the newly formed China Christian Council and of the national Three-Self Patriotic Movement.

Edicio de la Torre SVD was born in Oriental Mindoro, the Philippines, and ordained priest in 1969. He was until 1972 Professor of Theology at the Divine Word Seminary, Tagaytay and also Chaplain to Chi Rho and the Federation of Free Farmers. One of the founders of Christians for National Liberation (1972), he was arrested in 1974 and released only in June 1980. He is now doing further study in Rome.

Tsutomu Shoji has studied at Waseda University, Tokyo Union Theological Seminary, and Union Theological Seminary New York. He has been a pastor in the Kyodan since 1967 and active in his church's Faith and Order, Human Rights and Korean concerns. Since 1978 he has been General Secretary of the National Christian Council in Japan, based in Tokyo.

C. Lakshman Wickremasinghe studied at Oxford University and from 1958–1972 was Chaplain at the University of Ceylon. He was then consecrated Bishop of the (Anglican) Diocese of Kuranegala. He is a member of the (world) Anglican Consultative Council but has declined many international engagements that would absent him from his ministry in Sri Lanka.

Albert Widjaja's studies have been in theology (Princeton) and government (Claremont Graduate School). He has lectured in economics at the University of Indonesia, Jakarta and been consultant to the Metropolitan Government of Jakarta. He was chairman of the Board of Institute Oikumene, Indonesia until 1980, when he was appointed Associate General Secretary to the Christian Conference of Asia, Singapore.

John C. England was formerly on the staff of the Christian Conference of Asia (1969–75) and visiting lecturer in the Chicago Cluster of Theological Schools (Fall 1976) and the Selly Oak Colleges, Birmingham (1975–77). He is now Research Fellow and Programme Co-ordinator at the Tao Fong Shan Ecumenical Centre, Hong Kong.

Related Orbis books . . .

Gerald H. Anderson, ed.
ASIAN VOICES IN CHRISTIAN THEOLOGY
"Anderson's book is one of the best resource books on the market that deals with the contemporary status of the Christian church in Asia."

Choice
321pp. Cloth $15.00
Paper $7.95

Walbert Buhlmann, O.F.M. Cap.
THE SEARCH FOR GOD
An Encounter with the
Peoples and Religions of Asia
"A journalistic introduction to the new phase of Christian mission and presence in the non-Western world, this work provides insight into the movement in Christian witness away from traditional missionary triumphalism to a new form of witness by presence and dialogue."

Theology Today
224pp. Paper $7.95

Paul Clasper
EASTERN PATHS AND
THE CHRISTIAN WAY
"To all whose communities are being more or less 'invaded' by far Easterners such as Taiwanese, Vietnamese, and Cambodians, and to all who are aware of the subtle, though gentle influence of Eastern cultures and religions, this book will be a godsend, both for its discretion and its brevity. This book tops the list of books that I shall recommend to a class I will be teaching in the Cults and World Religions." *Provident Book Finder*
144pp. Paper $5.95

Bishop Francisco F. Claver, S.J.
THE STONES WILL CRY OUT
Grassroots Pastorals
"Bishop Claver is the gadfly of the Philippine Catholic hierarchy who persistently buzzes in the ears of President Fernando Marcos and all his toadies. The bishop's book is a collection of fighting pastoral letters to his congregation after martial law closed the diocesan radio station and newspaper." *Occasional Bulletin of Missionary Research*
196pp. Paper $7.95

Eric O. Hanson
CATHOLIC POLITICS IN CHINA AND KOREA
Winner of the 1980 award for the best study on the Church and China from the Chicago Institute of Theology & Culture
"Much of the book's value lies in its careful compilation of source accounts, and its comparative treatment of Catholic situations in the People's Republic of China, Taiwan, South Korea and Vietnam. No one concerned with the political function of religion in East Asia today should miss this book."   *Religious Studies Review*
160pp. Paper $9.95

Everett Nichols Hunt, Jr.
PROTESTANT PIONEERS IN KOREA
Foreword by Martin E. Marty
"Considering the amazing strength and growth of the Christian church in Korea, this book is well worth studying. It is a very readable book furnishing valuable missionary history."   *Evangelical Missions Quarterly*
128pp. Paper $7.95

Sebastian Kappen
JESUS AND FREEDOM
"This book is to be welcomed as an expression of 'liberation theology' from the perspective of India, especially since previous Latin American efforts have not been in contact with the great world religions. Kappen is both eloquent and almost ruthlessly honest."   *Theological Studies*
186pp. Cloth $8.95
Paper $3.95

Marianne Katoppo
COMPASSIONATE AND FREE
An Asian Woman's Theology
"This volume is a unique contribution to the literature about women by women. She makes denunciations, but she also gives positive recommendations."   *Sisters Today*
96pp. Paper $4.95

Kosuke Koyama
50 MEDITATIONS
"This refreshing book of anecdotes and reflections is written by a leading Asian theologian who was at one time a Japanese Kyodan missionary to Thailand and is now on the faculty at Union Theological Seminary in New York City. The author has a gift for focusing on meaningful everyday experiences and discovering theological implications. He expresses his insights through concrete verbal images. The author's entertaining line drawings enliven the pages. It's a book as thought provoking as it is enjoyable."   *Response*
191pp. Paper $4.95

Jung Young Lee
THE THEOLOGY OF CHANGE
"An intriguing and thoughtful attempt to find ways of expressing the Christian Faith in eastern terms." *Inner Paths*
155pp. Paper $5.95

Emerito P. Nacpil & Douglas J. Elwood
THE HUMAN AND THE HOLY
Asian Perspectives in Christian Theology
(Selected by the Editors of *Occasional Bulletin of Missionary Research* as one of the Fifteen Outstanding Books for Mission Studies)
"There is great need today to evolve a new theology of the relation between God, Humanity, and Nature as the foundation for building up a just, participatory, and sustainable society in our technological age. This book struggles with this crucial ecumenical problem and perhaps points toward what Asian Christianity might eventually contribute to its solution."
Theology Today
384pp. paper $14.95

Geevarshese Mar Osthathios
THEOLOGY OF A CLASSLESS SOCIETY
"A book of importance for us in the West because it is an authentic and relevant voice of the Orthodox Church of South India, a helpful contribution to discussion on the trinitarian understanding of God, and a foundation of social ethics without secularism on trinitarian grounds." *Jurgen Moltmann*
160pp. Paper $8.95

Raimundo Panikkar
THE UNKNOWN CHRIST OF HINDUISM
"A most stimulating book, even for those who know little about Hinduism."
Clergy Review
208pp. Paper $7.95

James M. Phillips
FROM THE RISING OF THE SUN
Christians and Society in Contemporary Japan
"A very interesting and fact-filled assessment of the reactions of the Christian community in Japan to the Japanese defeat in 1945 and subsequent events, internal and external, through 1978. After a chapter on the historical context, subsequent chapters deal with politics, education, social work, outreach, the role of foreign missionaries, ecumenical movements, biblical studies, and theology. All sects and persuasions of Christianity are dealt with equally and impartially and the sources of information are impressive in range. Besides the extensive bibliographic notes to each chapter, a detailed bibliographic commentary lists very basic resources, both English and Japanese, for anyone wishing to pursue specific aspects of the subject." *Library Journal*
319pp. Paper $14.95

S. J. Samartha
COURAGE FOR DIALOGUE

The search for understanding among people of differing faiths is the theme of these eleven essays. As the title of this volume suggests, it is not only intellectual understanding that is required of those who encounter neighbors of other faiths; there is also a need for the courage to be free and open in such meetings. Here then is a challenge to Christians who live—as all of us increasingly do—in a world of religious pluralism. It is a call to overcome "the fear of losing one's identity, of being shaken in one's comfortable beliefs, of being confronted with and perhaps compelled to acknowledge the truth in another camp, of recognizing that the stranger at the gate might turn out to be a fellow pilgrim."

176pp. Paper $8.95

C. S. Song
THIRD-EYE THEOLOGY
Theology in Formation in Asian Settings

"C.S. Song has given us a theology of the primal impulse of the whole creation toward life, love, and peace in this unhappy world. Perhaps only an Asian theologian, post-Vietnam, could have directed us so forcefully to the blood and earthiness, the pain of childbirth and self-immolation, that challenges the neonlighted, cellophane-wrapped Christianity of the West and its imperialisms. Song calls us back to the guts of biblical religion—of all religions—to the God of a common, redeemed humanity and to politics and religion as one and inseparable."

Prof. Gayraud S. Wilmore, Colgate Rochester Divinity School
288pp. Paper $9.95

THE COMPASSIONATE GOD

"C.S. Song is among the most creative theologians writing today. He is one of the reasons why many today contend that the most important theological writings are coming from Third World theologians. *The Compassionate God* is an excellent theological text which invites Christians to look beyond the particularities of their Western culture to the cultures of other people. I recommend it highly."

Prof. James H. Cone, Union Theological Seminary, New York
304pp. Paper $12.95